WYNDHAM LEWIS
THE ARTIST

PORTRAIT OF T. S. ELIOT

WYNDHAM LEWIS
THE ARTIST

FROM 'BLAST' TO BURLINGTON HOUSE

By

Wyndham Lewis

LAIDLAW & LAIDLAW

First published 1939
LAIDLAW & LAIDLAW LTD.
32 Alfred Place, London W.C.1

CG109579-6

370178

750.4

Made in Great Britain
Printed by Sherratt & Hughes, at the St. Ann's Press
Timperley, Cheshire
Set in Caslon Old Face

Preface

It seemed to me better to make my " Introduction " a new pamphlet, instead of a mere historical *foreword*; a pamphlet in which I should survey all that has occurred to painting in England up-to-date—with reference especially to the controversies of the moment, and with an account of the desperate position in which the painter finds himself, and a hint as to the way out. *Nature*, it seems to me, must be the watchword. And if the English painter must have a *super* to help him along, let it be *super-nature* rather than *super-real*.

Although *Super-nature versus Super-real* has the status of an independent pamphlet, in that, and the shorter pamphlet that follows it (*The Skeleton in the Cupboard Speaks*) will be found all the material the reader requires by way of introduction to the Notes and essays which are here reprinted. I have outlined the principle upon which the illustrations in this book have been selected in the course of these preliminary polemics.

Contents

Illustrations

9

SUPER-NATURE
VERSUS SUPER-REAL

Super-nature versus Super-real

i

Here is a considerable body of criticism dealing with the visual arts, and it is imbued with one consistent purpose, since it is the work of a practitioner of an art, not of a detached and eclectic theorist. All of the Notes and essays collected in this book are therefore dogmatic. Further, they advertise a bias in favour of the new and the untried, in painting, sculpture, architecture, and design.

I will start this Introduction by defining the nature and the limits of that bias. These Notes and " vortices " set out from the conviction that it is not so good a thing, at the present day, to paint a picture in the manner of Tiepolo, or of Velasquez, or of Manet, as in some new or different manner, more appropriate to the beliefs and conditions obtaining in the twentieth century. Yet nowhere will you discover a disposition to assert that the work of Tiepolo, or of Velasquez, or of Manet is *inferior* to what would be done if the contemporary artist had a free hand and were encouraged to evolve a new style of painting.

Although dogmatic, therefore—as becomes an artist, who stands upon what he does; who argues back, as a matter of course, from what he himself chooses to do, with all his intellect and his sensuous nature thrown into

13

Wyndham Lewis the Artist

the scales of pro and contra, this school or that—these critical utterances are not what might be described as chronologically parochial. I am happy to be able to claim for them this immunity from intolerance. I have no fondness for the merely fashionable, or for absolutism that has not its roots in some creative necessity.

I was not a little flattered to encounter, in a book published the other day (*Modern Painting*, by Charles Marriot) a quotation from my *Blast* days, approving my clairvoyance at that period and "moderation". Painting, I had said, would after a time withdraw, would "flow back into more natural forms from the barriers of the Abstract." For even when most furiously engaged, blasting-tools in hand, upon that granite frontier of the universe of 'pure form', I never pretended that such purist exercises were for all men, or for any man for more than a certain period. That was, as it were, a conventional limit. A *direction* was imposed by going to the end of the road, where the form of the artist becomes indistinguishable from that of the geometrician. My designs were no more arbitrary or absolutist than that.

Of course, as to what "the beliefs and conditions obtaining" at this moment, or at any moment, *are*, no two men could be found to give the same answer. Some would say, even now, that Dr. Freud was the most typical "modern" man; some that Dr. Rosenberg (the Nazi ideologue) was he. Some would point to such a figure as we have in Father d'Arcy, say, asserting that nothing was so modern as the New Catholic.

14

Super-nature versus Super-real

But at least there are certain fundamental ways in which this age, or this century, differs from the age of Pericles, or of Louis XIV, or even of Napoleon III. In some form this difference should be taken count of— that is all one can perhaps reasonably affirm: though in 1914–25 I obviously went very much farther than that. I envisaged an absolute revolution in the principles that govern the visual arts, in response to a fundamentally altered world. And at that time—however fallaciously —it did seem as if the visual arts were about to enter upon a period of drastic revaluation.

Such a revaluation—such a revolution in values— would run counter to all nationalist thinking, especially nationalist thinking of the type with which we are familiar to-day. And, at a moment when even the most extreme internationalism is seen to be merging back into nationalism again, what has to be reckoned with more than anything else is this movement of return to what is anchored in the soil, and sunk deep in the past, and away from all that is merely contemporary or *abstract*. As it was what has been called "abstract art" that I, more than any other Englishman, was identified with, nationalism, and what it implies in the visual arts, must be my theme for a moment.

For my part I was not unalive to the limitations imposed upon artistic expression by climate, by national tradition, by the cultural environment of the individual artist. The "vorticist" manifestoes, which were com-

15

posed by me, demonstrated that. (*Cf.* "Bless England,"
etc., *Blast* No. 1.) Yet such thoroughgoing revolution
in the visual arts as I advocated could not recommend
itself, that is obvious, to the nationalist or the traditionalist.

The Machine Age has made nonsense of nationalism,
or so it appears to me, by destroying all the landmarks
upon which national sentiment nourishes itself. In
shearing off the pigtail of the Chinese—by restricting
the use of the turban, the tarboosh, and the topper—by
abolishing the national costumes of the European peasantry—by substituting bourgeois-capitalist architecture
for the organic architecture of the feudal state, or of the
small urban oligarchies—in a word, by standardizing
life throughout the world, the technique of industry has
imposed internationalism upon us, whether we desire it
or not.

All nationalism, of necessity, tends to be artificial and
unreal, with the nations themselves no longer psycho-
logically watertight, nor their distinguishing marks
intact. Even the most robust of it is tainted with the
gas-lit artifice and false sentiment of *Cavalcade*, and is
of the same family as the Lord Mayor's Coach and the
druidic togas of the Eisteddfod.

Politics have so great a bearing upon art—and
especially the politics of nationalism, upon the extremes
of artistic expression—that I must continue for a
moment to be politically controversial.

It is difficult to see why the extremes of artistic
expression, upon some ideal plane, should not be con-

tained within the frontiers of a nationalist consciousness. But in practice these two things appear to be to each other as oil is to water. Nationalism, perhaps because it is to-day self-conscious, is invariably antiquarian. And a steel-and-glass writing table cannot cohabit with an escritoire or a grandfather-clock.

But are we justified in ascribing a superior reality to what has for some decades been regarded as " the new "? May not the grandfather-clock and the escritoire live again, and enjoy a second term of existence? And in no country so much as in England is the " dead hand " the *real* hand, and more powerful than any hand of mere flesh and blood.

On the European continent, in the nationalist states, from Gibraltar to the frontiers of the Soviet, the " dead hand " has been galvanized into tremendous life: it wields a very up-to-date and startlingly real machinery. Can we deny *reality* to such an imposing manifestation? —It looks to us a little unreal—as if a gang of energetic ghosts had laid hold of a power-station, or manned a battleship. But is it our eyesight that is playing us tricks?

I do not think so. But because of political necessity a thing which is in itself, and in the larger perspective, unreal, may, for a stated time, acquire a reality of sorts. So much must be conceded. Even if persisted in—and no one can say how long certain modes of feeling prevailing in many countries to-day will be persisted in—it might supersede, with its arbitrary reality, what would seem the more natural time-order of the Real.

Upon the longevity of those modes of feeling it is

perhaps idle to speculate. The present violent return to the sentiment of nationhood—in opposition to the natural evolution (as it seems) towards a commonwealth of nations—may persist for so many years, and take such roots, as to deflect, or attract to itself, the main course of history. It appears to me improbable; but stranger things have happened. The *esprit-de-corps* of the Byzantine sporting factions (in the course of whose pitched battles thousands died) was a far stranger thing than even the campaign of the Chaco, where the irrational ferocity of national pride reached its climax of absurdity—seeing that both sides spoke the same tongue and were identical in racial origin.

The vorticist, cubist, and expressionist movements—to return to them—which aimed at a renewal of our artistic sensibility, and to provide it with a novel alphabet of shapes and colours with which to express itself, presupposed a new human ethos, which undoubtedly must have superseded, in some measure, modes of feeling of a merely national order.

That these movements have not succeeded is plain enough: for now let us come to to-day—the early months of the year 1939—and endeavour to arrive at some not too prejudiced idea of what is happening—of what is *the actual*, if it is not the *real*.

Super-nature versus Super-real

What has *already happened*—that can be said at once —is that modern art, of the highly experimental sort advocated in these essays and manifestos, is at an end. It is all over except for the shouting—of the rearguard, as they fly, but who, true to the best traditions of contemporary journalism, affect to be *advancing*, what while they hurry off the stricken field.

In the form of Expressionism all that smells of the "modern" in art has been booted out of Germany, and the door been bolted against it. In Italy its only manifestation was "Futurism", which lived but three years. It was buried in 1914. Giorgio Chirico has taken to chocolate-boxes—upon which a symbolical charger, more and more fatigued, languidly prances. (It was the Horse, actually, that killed Chirico, it is said.) He was the solitary important Italian.

As to Paris, there it is the *crépuscule*. The picture-market has collapsed (and the French book-market is down fifty per cent., as reported year ending 1938): all the graceful *petit maitres*, a great store of which France always possesses, have crept out of their holes, as the Catalan sun sets—in human blood, alas! As Barcelona falls, and the phalangist standard is unfurled there, we can all see that that is the end of a chapter—of painting, among other things. There will be no more Catalan painters, to act as hormones to the old Paris *cocotte*.

Under the shadow of Politics, the great movement in the arts celebrated in these pages, bankrupt or refugee, is expiring. "But *surrealism*—that is a very advanced movement, is it not?" you may demur. "That is still with us." Yes, but that is anti-movement. That is merely the road *back* (*via* " advanced " subject-matter) to the portals of Burlington House and Mr. Russell Flint. (The late Mr. Glyn Philpots, R.A., actually went half-way to meet it, hat in hand.)

No: surrealism is not the last of a *new* movement, but the whimsical and grimacing reinstatement of the old—and of the bad-old at that, the " academic ". This perhaps should be qualified; read *continental-academic* for academic. Most of it leads straight back to *The Islands of the Dead*—of which mausoleum Dr. Freud has become the curator, demonstrating upon the cadaver, in his dank magician's cave, the functioning of the libido.

Let me, however, give more definition to the word " modern ". Admittedly, it is a silly word. It fatally conjures up such clichés as " Miss Modern " or " a modern girl ". In religion it stands for dilution of dogma. Politically it signifies an understanding of the out-of-dateness of the Capitalist System, and a desire to expedite its demise. In its popular sense, " modern " is used to convey a liberal outlook in all things—not much more than that.

As applied to pictures, music, and books, a rupture of tradition is indicated; a tendency to do something *new* is expressed. New? Well, surprising, and, in England, " shocking ". But it is all a little vague, of course, because people think or feel vaguely about everything.

The Germans are relatively logical. Why *they* do not like pictures or books to be " modern " is for what at first sight appears a sound sociological reason—because

they identify all very modern movements in the arts with Karl Marx, and his theories of armed proletarian revolt against the Capitalist System.

But this has always seemed a little shallow to me; because, in the first place, the Germans themselves are just as much a threat to the Capitalist System as are the most orthodox Marxists—if indeed not rather more so; secondly, because nothing could be less proletarian than Picasso, who is the high-priest of "modernism" in painting; and, more generally, all these manifestations, whether in the visual arts or in literature, have had much more to do with scientific thought than with political thought (as far as the latter can be dissociated from the former).

We have learnt only this year, from the pen of Miss Gertrude Stein, that Picasso is a Jew. The Germans and others assert that all " modernism ", or extreme liberalism, is Jewish, and therefore an alien and inappropriate mode of expression for the European. But though Picasso is Jewish, James Joyce is—I was about to say, the *opposite*! Again, though the Dadas were for the most part Jewish, Auden is a Nordic Blond.

As to extremist painting, Cézanne, much more than Picasso, is at the bottom of that. He is the chief culprit in the pictorial revolution. And Cézanne was not a Jew, but a Provençal Frenchman—nor was " Vincent ", nor was Rodin (a great subverter in his day—and he was the forerunner of Mr. Epstein, not the other way round).

James Macneil Whistler is another famous artist who

did not conform to the *racial* theory of the origin of revolution—Whistler, who for many years was regarded, by the Anglo-Saxon part of the Germanic World, as a menace to all civilized society, because he painted those peculiarly gentle and beautiful pictures, the " Miss Alexander " in the Tate, and the " Portrait of Thomas Carlyle " in Glasgow.

Neither the Germans nor the Anglo-Saxons like the visual arts very much, and usually they drag in God and the Devil, in order to put their aversion upon an unassailable theological footing, insisting that they stand for God and the artist for Satan. I suspect that both really regard painting as " unclean " and a bit " dago ". And certainly painting does seem to be a dago art. It would appear to belong to those countries where the sun is strong. A visual art is clearly at a disadvantage in a London fog or a Scotch mist.

．　　．　　．　　．　　．

However, let us sum up. If it is the *crépuscule* in Paris, it is the night here. It would be idle for me to pretend that what you are about to read—the essays for which I have written this Introduction—represents a doctrine belonging to a movement that is alive. It is so palpably dead that it would be impossible, even if I wished to do so, to proceed very far with that deception.

On the other hand, while there is any art at all for us to talk about—and in the sequel I shall not disguise my belief that in a very few years there may be no art whatever to discuss—the influence of this movement that has failed will be considerable. Brief as was its reign, its works will stand there behind us to obstruct too abject a return to past successes. It is a snag in the path of those who would sneak back to Impressionism. Some of its vigour will remain, and inform the phases of the great withdrawal that is everywhere taking place, and at least prevent the retreat from degenerating into a rout.

I am quite certain therefore that these critical *obiter dicta* can be perused with advantage by any artist or theorist, whether he was ever drawn towards such disciplines himself or not.

I must say that all this panorama of defeat does not distress me over much. I survey this stricken field—strewn with cubes and cones, with fearsome masks with billiard balls for eyes, venomous futurist hat-pins, and bashed-in Catalan guitars—with considerable equanimity.

People flung themselves into those movements for different reasons. Some hurled themselves in as a dog does, when his master is about to move house, into the chaos of objects surrounding the packing-cases. Being no lover of impermanence and disorder, that was not my motive. The promise of an intenser discipline, and less impermanent equivalents for our personal experience, was what attracted me. The cortex, massive and sharply outlined, not the liquefaction within, I have always regarded as the proper province of the artist.

Then I was not an "extremist" because I was technically incapable of being anything else. I am a master in

23

the painting of tradition. And it suits me just as well to paint close to Nature, as to paint for the megalopolitan glass and concrete of a Brave New World. In Rome I paint as the Romans do. Luckily I am able to do it at least as well as the Romans.

ii

It is far better not to delude ourselves as to the position of the arts; of all the arts, though especially of the visual arts. The issue is much wider than the fate, merely, of a "new sensibility", and the discouragement or not of its exponents.

Much more it is a question of the imminent extinction of any sensibility whatever. The issue is not less considerable than that. It is a case of *Men Without Art* indeed (to make use of the expressive title of one of my books). In a generation or two our society may have arrived at that nadir, with all that such a condition entails.

It may be that then no adult art will remain. There will be the scribbling of children—abruptly terminated by the onset of puberty—over whose productions parents would bend moist-eyed. There would be, it is true, what remained of the primitive races. But the Esquimaux, Black Boys, and all other "primitives", are dying out: there would be no savages left to carve a totem-pole or embellish a canoe. So even they would not be there to help us to illustrate this lost sensibility: only the kiddies.

Adult art—the adult art of civilized man—may thus

become a memory of the unenlightened ages. National Galleries may close, and all the Raphaels and the Rembrandts be transferred to the ethnological sections of the Museums. These pictures in oils would be preserved as records of an extinct pre-logical activity.—In that case their value would diminish, or practically disappear: and that of course is the reason why the picture-dealer still stages exhibitions by *living* artists (in spite of the fact that no pictures by living artists any longer sell, except for figures so small as to make it uneconomic to accord them wall-space). I can imagine no other reason. The "Old Master" must be prevented from slipping over entirely into the class of things dead and done with, curiosities of historical value only.

This world without art—except for the scribbling of children—upon the imminence of which I have just been speculating, is no phantasy of mine. It is an extremely plausible solution of what we observe on all hands to-day. It is not in the same class as the prognostications of the man of science, foreshadowing a time when mankind will have shrunk to dwarf-stature, marrying at five years old and dying at ten. On the contrary, it is the only logical issue to much contemporary theorizing upon the functions of the arts.

If you will allow me I will suspend the course of my main statement for a moment to make good this assertion. And I will go to the books of my old friend Mr. Read for the evidence I require.

What is required, is it not, is evidence that the typical

theorist of "advanced" visual art points to the Child as the *perfect artist*—or something like that? And as obviously children are better at being children than adults are—however hard the latter may try—*in the end* the adults will give up the unequal contest.

Then, it is not unreasonable to assume, only the scribbling Child will remain. The little savage of ten or eleven will do his caveman stuff: he might even have his own religion and medicine men, once it was generally recognized that this savage and irrational phase through which man is compelled to pass possesses not only its appropriate æsthetic, but also its appropriate theological, oddities. The adult would look on: no "art" for him, nor any "religion" either. Even females aged nine or ten of this new organized savagery (of "tender years", as idiomatized by the Victorian) might weave quite delightful fabrics—typically geometric—which adult women would acquire and incorporate in their summer beach-fashions. Children might even be segregated, to make this infant-culture more effective. They might even attack their elders in their war-canoes—though the adult world, with a few well-placed machine-guns, would experience no difficulty in repelling them.

Mr. Herbert Read has an unenviable knack of providing, at a week's notice, almost any movement, or sub-movement, in the visual arts, with a neatly-cut party-suit—with which it can appear, appropriately

caparisoned, at the cocktail-party thrown by the capitalist who has made its birth possible, in celebration of
the happy event. No poet laureate, with his ode for
every court occasion, could enjoy a more unfailing inspiration than Mr. Read; prefaces and inaugural addresses
follow each other in bewildering succession, and with a
robust disregard for the slight inconsistencies attendant
upon such invariable readiness to oblige.

Under these circumstances, to correlate Mr. Read's
many utterances is not unlike attempting to establish a
common factor of eclectic inspiration in the rapid succession of "models" emanating from some ultra-
fashionable Parisian dressmaker. The *Read Model* for
January 1939 is probably quite different, superficially,
from that of October 1938, the last with which I am
acquainted.

Yet there is something that is essentially *Read*. This
man has a core to him, which is not unlike that to be
found at the centre of his young colleague, Mr. Day
Lewis, whom he resembles in his emotional make-up,
as in his obviously official destiny. And that central
impulse leads him to the sensational and sentimental
quarter of the philosophic compass. Naturally enough,
he finds in the Italian philosopher Vico the intellectual
authority that he requires.

Now for my quotation, which will be my sufficient
evidence, not for the prognostications I have ventured
upon above, but for my inclusion of Mr. Read in the
ranks of those who are actively promoting such a utopia
of the immature, and busy making the world safe for

Wyndham Lewis the Artist

the Child. It is from *Art Now*; from a subsection headed *Vico and the rise of the genetic concept of art.* It happens to be poetry about which Mr. Read is speaking. But of course these remarks apply to painting even more than to poetry, since for every adult we find doing an infantile poem, we find ten doing a child-art picture.

"Vico identifies poetry with the primitive phase in the history of man: poetry is the first form of history, it is the metaphysics of man whilst he is still living in a direct sensuous relation to his environment, before he has learned to form universals and to reflect. Imagination is clearly differentiated from intellect, and all forms of poetic activity are shown to depend on the imagination; in civilized epochs poetry can only be written by those who have the capacity to suspend the operation of the intellect, to put the mind in fetters and to return to the unreflecting mode of thought characteristic of the childhood of the race."

Mr. Read then proceeds to "throw out the prediction that we are going to hear a great deal more about Vico in the immediate future", and that, in short, "his theories are going to play a predominant part in the development of modern criticism."

"Art no longer conceived as a rational ideal . . . but conceived as a stage in the ideal history of mankind"— that is the conception of art which finds expression upon the walls of our present-day Nursery—a nursery of *rich* children, naturally; for the proletariat, though suitably childlike, do not possess nurseries.

If Mr. Read can "throw out a prediction", why

should not I throw out one too? In an essay in the *Criterion*, in 1924, entitled *The Apes of God*, I fore-shadowed a state of affairs which has now come to pass —so I have this advantage over Mr. Read, that a prediction of mine has already been confirmed by events.

My present prediction is this: that "modern criticism", as that is understood by Mr. Read, will continue to find arguments, month after month, and year after year, for the Nursery where our capitalist children play at being artists, but that before very long this "criticism" will only be read by themselves: that all "art-criticism" will first diminish in volume, and then entirely disappear from the Press (except for an annual outburst on the occasion of the R.A. exhibition); and that then the small private nurseries (or highbrow picture-galleries) will be shut up, and Herbert's occupation will be gone! I am sorry, for I like the beggar. But when prophet meets prophet, well, each has to "throw out" what is travailing within. And, say I, without fear of the issue, let the best augur win.

iii

These childish backwaters of Anglo-Saxon culture—which are in the main clumsy glosses upon the French, from which most that is non-academic in England derives —are not cheerful places to go sightseeing in, especially just now. London reflects not only the culture but the

29

disintegration of its continental original; upon a small amateur screen, but with a reasonable fidelity.

The forces of what in politics would be called "reaction" are everywhere in the ascendant, in England as much as elsewhere. The crescendo of the struggle for political power; the struggle for mere subsistence in a world of "want in the midst of plenty"; the universal decline in the intellectual standards of the capitalist class; the impoverishment of the middle class, the paralysis of the energies of the aristocrats, the peasantry, and the proletariat—all this has relegated the arts to a position of nonentity. "Intellectual" has become a term of contempt (as if the only worthy use of the intellect were in money-spinning or in the power-game of the politician): as much among us as in the "dictator" states is this the case.

All ruling factions are at one in a tacit—or stridently advertised—resolve to discourage irresponsible intellectual attainment, in the unmoneyed and the destitute-of-power. The Bourgeoisie—either *la haute Bourgeoisie* enthroned in the democratic states, or the little Bourgeoisie enthroned in the dictator-countries—are of one mind when it comes to the "uppishness" of what used to be termed, in the bad old days of Liberalism, *genius*. There are two things: there is Money, and there is Power. Outside of that there is nothing. And both Money and Power are recognized as possessing the right to exploit, without return, all that is creative, or to crush it when it suits their book.

In this section of my Introduction I confine myself

to the London scene, or, rather, continue my unveiling of that, begun in the last chapter. It is there that I propose to show the working out of those detestable principles. The backgrounds of that English scene are of course Europe, and its deadly schisms. What we see is in part made up of the political blight reaching us from the continent, in part the intellectual blight which is an inalienable feature of all Anglo-Saxon society, as much in the "capital of empire" as in any drab colonial hamlet. These intellectual shortcomings are not improved by the decay of taste and good sense in Europe.

.   .   .   .   .

The jealousy of the "lower animals" for the "higher animals" would be a standing difficulty for the staff of any Zoological Garden, if the animal world had ac-quired our habits of introspection and of speech. But as indications of how this principle operates—that of exalting the Big Battalions and banishing from the public view all that offends the monied or the power-inflated "Great", by reason of its insolent and uncomfortable intelligence—I will select two instances from among many: both express, in their different ways, the triumph of what Arnold called "the Philistine" in England.

(1). My first illustration is a homely one. It is the Honours List.—For what qualities is a man marked down for honour by the State? You do not have to examine the Honours List very closely to discover that,

31

in a majority of cases, it is for demonstrating his capacity as a money-spinner—for before you can distribute money, in a good cause or the reverse, you must first *make* it. In no case is it the *creative* faculty that is singled out for these coveted awards. You will find in these lists the names of people who purchase and exploit the inventions of others, not of the inventors: of people who publish books, not of those who write them: of the middleman who corners the distribution of milk, not of the farmer who has the care of the cows which produce it.

There is no artist I hope who is so fatuous and so lost to all self-respect as to desire the sword and knee-breeches of a modern "knight", and it might be represented as a subtle compliment, that such vulgarities are not even suggested to us. But I hardly think that that interpretation is correct; the less flattering one is the more likely, namely that it never crosses the mind of those concerned that there is anything except buying cheap and selling dear (whether it be soap, milk, oil, toilet-paper or tobacco) that deserves notice.

(2) My second illustration, is a matter of more specialist observation.—The other day I picked up an English newspaper and occupying half of its available space for the reviewing of books I was confronted with a large photograph of a portrait of Lord Castlereagh— or of Lord Aberdeen or Lord Melbourne, I forget which, but that is all one.

This "new biography" was "hailed", in the best flunkey-accent of inflated deference, in a two column puff. The author had no name that I can remember: *he* did not come into it of course. It was Lord Castlereagh —or Lord Aberdeen or Lord Melbourne—that did it. There is no hack who picks Charles II, or Lord John Russell, or Lord Randolph Churchill, or Lord Rosebery—there are plenty to choose from—and does a "life", who does not receive more space than Tolstoi would with *War and Peace* (which to-day would be lumped with six other "novels", and receive ten lines of comment; it might be "hailed" as a masterpiece, but so would the other five).

We all know what "great statesmen" really are like to-day: we hear them on the radio, we see a million close-ups of them. It is impossible for us to preserve our glittering illusions. But we have every reason to infer that dressed in a periwig and with lace ruffles they would be no different, except for an occasional man of parts like Pitt. Yet all dead politicians are "great", and many living ones too, to the flunkey who sits in the editorial chair. And such "great statesmen" as Lord Baldwin would in the editorial mind eclipse a hundred Gibbons or Faradays. This vulgarity is extremely symptomatic. And it grows in volume and intensity, the more tenuous the reality upon which it reposes becomes. Such things belong to that *sham-antique* system, in the clutch of whose "dead hand" we gasp for breath.

Alongside the above significant pieces of mass-observation, place another—concerned likewise with the editorial mind, and the policy of the great newspapers.

Reviews of books—reports of concerts and other musical news—still occupy considerable space in the Press. The Theatre is well reported too. That is because capital-interests of some magnitude are involved.—But the visual arts are in a different category. The art of the dead encroaches daily upon the space that was once devoted to the art of the living.

We have given up the living as hopeless—or rather the capitalist system seems to have said—"How could art coexist with *us*? There *can* be no good living artists, in such a time as *ours*! "

Reports of auctions (with prices fetched) of Old Masters: reports of charity exhibitions (with totals obtained for this or that fund): reports of shows by school children (as Educational news): of painting by post-office workers or candlestick makers (Labour item —or "human interest"): exhibitions of pictures or sculpture by members of the Royal Family or by titled persons ("Court and Society" of course)—all these take the place, more every day, of critical articles about picture-shows by professional artists.

I am not suggesting that a sorter at a post-office, or a Duchess, or an impoverished clubman, is incapable of painting a good picture. All I am asserting is that the *best* results are obtained by the career of a painter being open to everybody. And to-day it is not.

But *professional*—there is a word that to-day can hardly any longer be used. All the whole-time artists, or artists *de metier*, are in fact *rentiers*. Some are small rentiers, some very large rentiers: but all are rentiers.[1]

Practically all picture-exhibitions therefore are in the *amateur* category, as much as is the annual tennis tournament at Wimbledon. Furthermore, the number of works that sell in them (outside of purchases by friends or relatives) is negligible.

As to the Royal Academy, ninety per cent of the annual exhibits are by people of amateur status too—who do not live by their work: they are the work of retired sea-captains, wives of prosperous surgeons, society women, "stinks" masters at Public Schools, bird-fanciers, stock-brokers. It is a large yearly bazaar of well to do people, who meet and show each other "what they have done", with a sprinkling of "professionals" to make it look a real and serious affair.

For many years the Royal Academy has been as extinct economically as it is artistically. Last year the total of sales was reported in the Press after it had been open some weeks: the number of exhibitors among whom this total was distributed, also was mentioned. At the time I worked it out, basing my arithmetic upon these data: if you had a picture accepted, it seemed you stood a one-sixteenth chance of selling it, for a sum averaging £37. Once a year you had a one-sixteenth chance of making £37! Supposing you were a "professional" artist, and this exhibition was the great

[1] There are, outside official or state-subsidized artists, a dozen genuine artists *de metier* in England at this moment perhaps: John, Spencer, Nash, Bone, to name four.

annual event for you, that would not be a very rosy prospect, to say the least of it. You would not stand even a one-sixteenth chance of paying your studio rent. Studio rents in London start at about £150 per annum; though a good studio at that rent is not easy to find, most studios being occupied by musicians, bridge-clubs, dancing academies—scarcely ever by artists: since, as I have just pointed out, there are practically no professional painters left, and the amateur paints his picture in the drawing-room or tool-shed.

But if all this is true of the big official picture parade in Piccadilly, it is also true of the little affairs outside, in the highbrow backwaters of the West-end. And just how *little* these affairs are the public would be astonished to learn: little not only in the talent displayed—for except for two or three big "professionals" of talent (big *mercenaries*, as we might call them, like Chirico, Picasso, Dali, or Max Ernst) called in, at a *solde*, to lend weight to the enterprise, the rest are obviously very small fry—but *little* as to the amount of good honest cash that is expended by some excitable little backer, who soon gets tired of even that modest munificence.

When one reflects what is squandered upon some dud theatrical venture, which closes down after ten days run, the outlay involved in launching a painting "movement" is seen to be negligible. Three or four brand-new "movements" a year could be floated for what it costs to finance one fairly ambitious West-end theatrical flop.

For map out the sort of budget this entails: you are a capitalist (male or female) and are contemplating a "movement" in the painting line, suppose. The "cast" is insignificant. There are the two or three big names, of the foreign *mercenaries*. A one-man show of the recent works of one of these is a nice thing to have. But it is an extravagance—you can dispense with it. You do not need to retain the two or three big "pros". You merely borrow a few canvases from a Paris dealer. That, I suppose, entails no more than the transport costs.

Distance diminishes the horror that the little ones feel for the big ones: and you would probably hate so much your local "strong men" that you would sooner have no "movement" at all than call upon *them* to assist. But there is Mr. Paul Nash—he is a really good local man. And he a good "mixer". You would get him in to bulk out the thin amateur broth.

When you have received the canvases of the big stiffs, sent over from the Paris headquarters, you mix them well in with the local junk, and you start off with a bang: with a sizable "mixed" show. The local half-dozen movementeers (all except Mr. Nash, who is a "pro") have some money—they are not destitute, some may be rich; they are *friends*. Now and then you purchase the smallest of their pictures you can find. You may get off with the purchase of three or four—say fifty pounds the lot. What else is there, outside the rental and fitments, light and heat? Two or three women (one half-time) and a boy-of-all-work at fifteen bob a week. Stationery expenses next: a box of red tabs to stick on canvases "sold". Prospectuses, posters, an inch advert. now and then in a big Daily. A few inexpensive frames (modern pictures are *cheap to frame*, thank God).

It is not necessary to work this out to the last drawing-pin. You can see that for nine or twelve months it does not involve a great outlay. You *sell* nothing of course, except one or two canvases of the big "pros": for no one's fool enough to buy anything else, and scarcely any one ever visits the gallery, except for the opening cock-tail-party. But there is really no more economical way of amusing yourself; and for a month or two it must be good fun.—The last few months must drag.

But let us go into the question of the Painting Pro a little more deeply yet. I feel convinced that in that rapidly disappearing figure is to be found the key to any serious inquiry as to the prospects of English painting in the future.

The "Gentlemen and Players" business would not be so bad if *gentleness* were not synonymous with *cash*, and if money were not the criterion of *fitness to paint*. If none but members of the family of the Reigning House, or of the territorial nobility, were allowed to paint, or draw, or sculpt, that would simplify matters. Everyone would be able to grasp the issue—everyone would be indignant. The depressed "pro" could compose a letter of protest to the newspapers, with certain chances of redress.

But *money* and its privileges are so much more ticklish things to cope with than "Norman blood". There, you are treading upon consecrated ground. And just as it is natural that the fair offspring of a commission agent, or a pawnbroker, with a nice overhand service and a flair for attractive tennis-panties, should be protected against the unfair competition of the "pro" (some brawny minx in an ill-cut canvas skirt) so it is exceedingly difficult to make people understand why the son of a railway porter or of a miner, should have the same facilities for painting a picture (*surely* an occupation more appropriate to the son of a prosperous cotton-spinner or chain-store executive) as his betters. In an Anglo-Saxon country it is uphill work explaining. Napoleon did not call us a nation of shopkeepers for nothing.

Things have gone so far that this discussion is perhaps academic. When the *Apes of God* was written, yes; there was still time for the public to act. But with a war twice the size of the last one hanging over our heads, I doubt if a pulse can be stirred, upon such an issue as an *art*. But one never knows.

.   .   .   .   .

English "pros" in painting are exceedingly scarce, as I have said. (I am not counting pavement-artists.) They are almost as rare as the hansom-cab, or the Mauritius penny-red '47.

A certain number of men technically of amateur status are in fact "pros"—that is to say they enjoy the privileges of the "amateur", and dispute his miserable pickings with the "pro". But in England it is a pitiable thing to be a pure "pro", in painting as much as in cricket or tennis. I did not *start* as a "pro". I went to the Eton of art-schools, the Slade. I had a good "allowance", as it was called in the pre-war, which enabled me afterwards to continue my studies in Holland, France, Germany and Spain. I began in the amateur class, or I should not be as well off even as I am, now that I have dropped into the pro-letariat.

No one in Great Britain, starting from scratch, stands the proverbial Chinaman's chance.—"What porridge had John Keats?" But you know what happened to *him*—"snuffed out by an article", telling him to get out of the poetry-racket and go back to his job behind the counter of the chemist's shop.

Ninety-seven per cent of picture-painting in England to-day (by painters who have no means) is an affair of charity. It is a not very munificent reward for social services. The *picture* never comes into it. People may even forget, when they have "bought" it, to hang it up on the wall—especially as they probably dislike it.

If I may be forgiven such an extreme lapse into the vulgar and the personal, I should say that I am one of the half-dozen painters in England whose pictures are bought not because the people who purchase them like *me*, but because they have a fancy for the picture.

That is not so conceited as it sounds, for it might be better for me if they liked me a little more and my pictures a little less. People are prepared to pay more for a disarming personality than they are for a rather alarming picture. I do not blame them at all. They have come to look upon pictures as a fly does upon a fly-paper—nasty sticky things where you are lucky if you get away with the loss of a couple of tenners—not nice things that you are lucky to possess for so little as a thousand odd, as in Whistler's day.

My main handicap as a "pro" in England has been that I am in the heavyweight class. That has been my main difficulty. Being a great big heavyweight stresses the *professionalism*, you see. It makes it much more uncomfortable for the "pro" concerned. Even now I am always afraid that I shall be accused of *bullying* whenever I paint a canvas over 30″ x 20″. And indeed at the time of one of my exhibitions I *was* denounced as a bully, because, it was said, I was not being "fair" to the flyweight who was holding an exhibition in the next room.

Heavyweight is not my word. In an interesting article the other day Mr. Newton very sensibly suggested this classification of painters, into heavyweights, featherweights, and so on. He adjured people not to expect from the heavyweight what was only to be had from the flyweight—I beg your pardon, it was the other way

41

round, but only because it was one of the more thought-ful of our critics. And ah how often I have wished that some such principle could inform the responses of the public—who of course in England look upon a heavy-weight as in some way not quite nice—just as heavy-hitting by a professional cricketer is really scarcely "cricket"—and for whom *all* power is slightly obscene.

Though I am able to be personal about myself, no one may be explicit about other people (unless they are too poor to hit back). I should otherwise be able to supply you with statistics showing that what I have been saying is in the main an understatement. Things are *worse* than I have said—more silly than I have said; more so than it would be possible to convey in words. I have been white-washing things, for fear of depressing you too much.

There are painters, with "European reputations", who depend for their livelihood upon the bounty and goodwill of one or two *richissime* collectors, who like what those big "pros" do for some semi-pornographic, or pathologic, reason—nothing, at all events, to do with *la belle peinture*. They like having frescoes of half-dissected male torsos in their bathrooms, perhaps: or a pictorial *frisson* or two upon the walls of the room in which they eat. It is much the same story as that of Lawrence, for instance, who never had more than a modest sale for his books until he wrote *Lady Chat-terley's Lover*.

·   ·   ·   ·   ·

Super-nature versus Super-real

Such, at all events, is the state of affairs in our great profession—where the private collector has practically disappeared (only the freak collector is left, or the rich and jealous amateur) and state-patronage is not yet born —except for such an institution as the Chantry Bequest, which is the preserve of the Royal Academy.

A student when he leaves the Royal College of Art —the largest art-school in England, or I daresay in the world—has not one chance in ten thousand, if that, of becoming a painter. He becomes either (1) an art master, or (2) a commercial-artist—entering a sort of factory, where he works at a small salary, and becomes a slave to the requirements of the advertiser. Anyone who does not do that is a *rentier*. Such are the plain facts of the case: and an extremist "art-critic" like Mr. Herbert Read is acquiring an agreeable reputation by writing about something that does not exist, except for a handful of monied dilettantes, amusing themselves by being childish in public.

iv

I will have seemed to have been saying, to some readers, perhaps, that the art of painting is at an end, that those who write about that art as "critics" are amusing themselves at the public expense, and that hence this book of mine is a cynical evolution in the void, performed by an out-of-work abstractist, designed apparently to annoy a handful of wealthy nobodies, and to fill up an idle hour.

43

Things are not quite so bad as that. Nor did I intend to convey that impression—though I see that I may have done so, in glancing over what I have just written. This impression I will endeavour to dispel.

It used to be said of Austria—before its absorption by Germany—that things were *always desperate* there, but *never serious*. It is the same with us, in the painting-racket. The art of painting is bankrupt but beautiful; moribund but high-spirited: artists, though they paint less and less, as the price of gas and electricity goes up, and the price of frozen meat climbs, run into debt to a society that hates pictures, and they settle their debts with images everyone agrees are worthless. Pictures are like dud cheques, but dud cheques that have attained a kind of disreputable currency of their own. Drawn for a thousand pounds, they change hands at one or two per cent of their ostensible value.

Austria, however, could provide us with a yet more striking parallel. For what could be more like the present status of the Fine Arts than the great capital city of the Hapsburg Empire, Vienna, become the metropolis of a German province of seven million people; all the splendid palaces, theatres, museums, hotels still there, but nothing now but a head without a body? How strikingly that recalls the present condition of the Fine Arts—the visual arts, in a world that has ceased to use its eyes, and so the "visual" ceases to concern it.

No, I never said that painting had quite ended—though I agree that I said that it might. Unless something is done to preserve it, and to keep alive the few

Super-nature versus Super-real

artists who are able to do it—life may flicker out. Our grandchildren may lisp: "What *were* artists mama? Why aren't there any now?"

I did say, certainly, that it could not survive as a mere sport of the rich, like tennis or like ski-ing, nor can it. I said that since it is no longer possible to proceed to any far-reaching experimental reforms except in a hole and corner way, it would be better frankly to go back to the natural function of painting, and, in a word, *imitate*.

Imitation is its Aristotelean definition. Hogarth's *Shrimp Girl*, or Goyal's *Maja Desnuda*, are quite respectable acts of creation. By way of imitation, they create. They are good enough things to do. So get in the Shrimp Girl, say I, or disrobe the lovely "maja", and proceed to create by way of imitation.

If I favour this return to nature, it is because I am a painter, not a critic, impresario, or politician. I do not repine at finding myself amongst such relatively orthodox images. And I am persuaded that that is the road to take—the only road open to the painter to-day—if painting is to be salvaged. It has been scuttled by the clowns of "super-realism"—which was a sort of revenge of the second-rate. In order to come back, it must become popular.

The painter has a long score to settle with those journalist parasites who have exploited his *métier* for their own anti-artist ends.

To paint a shrimp girl as Hogarth did is at the least good painting. What is *bad* is to pretend; is to make-

45

believe that you are creating new forms when you are only dishing up old ones, but disguising them in surface novelties. These novelties are not even formal or technical novelties, but *frissons* imported from the clinic of the psychologist.

The *surréel* is work done for a few dozen people at the outside. The smaller the theatre becomes, the more fuggy and subjective the work.

What has been really deadly for painting has been what was first " Dada ", and then all that irresponsible journalism of the " super-real " that came out of Dada. As painting slumped, that fungus waxed and flourished.

I am ready to believe that such things take in Mr. Read. (One of the few illusions I have left is a belief in the sincerity of Mr. Read). But all that *bad* advertisement—it was so obviously the kind of advertisement that painting did not want—that was the *coup de grâce*, to any but the possessor of a substantial pocketbook.

Dispassionately considered, things must have worked out that way, seeing that the public, especially here in England, are distrustful of art in any case. These exhibitions where the public paid its bob or its five francs to go and sneer or laugh was the point at which the goose that lays the golden eggs finally stopped doing so.

Potatoes, their earthen buttocks rouged, their " eyes " pencilled with mascara, joined to each other with umbilical cords of crimsoned flex: a bisected topper, with a fringe of pubic hair gushing upon its inner rim, standing upon a sawed-off water-main: a few large pebbles under a glass clock-case; these never very funny mock-exhibits were the undoing of the artist. No pictures *could* sell after a year or two of that, at least nothing off the beaten track.

This was the excuse that the British public, at all events, had been waiting for—to take *nothing* seriously, of all this " modern stuff ". It compromised for ever all serious invention—except for a few best-sellers like Braque.

Such freak exhibitions may be excellent nihilist politics—or they may be excellent fun for some small capitalist who is prepared to rent a gallery. They might even have a freakish educational value, for a class of children. But, as things were, they made it impossible for anyone thereafter to dispose of a picture that was not blamelessly orthodox. The unorthodox became associated fatally in the public mind with the clownish. It was felt that the " modern artist " had admitted that what he did was a practical joke. For everyone mistook this for the work of artists: there was no one to tell the public that it was only a " rag " organized by a band of political journalists.

I am anxious to make my position quite clear. The super-real was not an outbreak of high spirits. (Mr. Breton has announced in fact that *suicide* is the logical outcome of his theories, though it is a pity that his suicide did not *precede* these self-exhibitions, rather than the other way round): nor was it anything really to do with painting, and no good painters participated, until Dali stepped into the breach.

A dozen people, Paris " intellectuals ", who earned a

47

comfortable living as civil servants in ministries, or in advertising offices (which is what the "Dadaists" were) spent their spare time in concocting politico-æsthetic manifestos and promoting exhibitions of "more-than-real objects".

For twenty years or more before this the patience of the public had been sorely tried. It did not know that a new age had made its appearance—it thought, as it always does, that it was still living in the age of the French Impressionists. Van Gogh had been more than it could stomach; and Picasso had strained its credulity to the breaking point.—Then had come the War: a gigantic pause, when it got something it really *did* understand—shrapnel and poison gas. And, as I have indicated at the beginning of this essay, that wrote *finis* to any hope—for I daresay a century—of attending to the art-needs of the new-born epoch. Such dreams had definitely to be laid aside.

It was *then* that Dada got busy. The raree-shows labelled "super-real" (in which the public were solemnly shown a lot of uproariously assorted junk) the final effort of Dada, was like an answer to their prayer to be quit of all this "modern" nonsense. As if the poor public had not enough to worry about as it was!

They had at last become convinced that all along—and by *everybody*, who had ever "cubed" or "vorticised"—they were having their legs pulled. Here was the proof at last. The result was that people stopped buying pictures altogether, or bothering about "art" at all.

SPARTAN PORTRAIT

Super-nature versus Super-real

As things peter out on the continent, they come over here on tour: that is the rule. And during the last few years this intellectual circus has moved to London. In Mr. Read it has had an ideal spokesman. Without wishing to say anything unkind, Mr. Read is such a *solemn-looking* fellow that he was ideally suited, even physically, to preside at this macabre harlequinade. The public only had to look at the sad and earnest mien of the lugubrious promoter, to appreciate still more the pictorial jokes so decorously chaperoned by him.

It might be supposed that the "academic" artist would have benefited by this final break between the public and the "advanced" school of painting. That has not however been the case.

The Royal Academy, as I have said, or rather its small professional personnel, only just keeps its head above water. There can be no change in that, and the reason is obvious, to anyone at all acquainted with the market for those utterly discredited commercial wares.

The provincial galleries are plastered with Royal Academy pictures, acquired during the last seventy years, upon which millions of pounds were expended. When these pictures come into a sale-room, or pictures by the same hand, they are knocked down for less than the price of the frame.

If you were a hard-headed city elder what would your attitude be to the purchase of fresh oil paintings? When the curator of the municipal gallery approached you and suggested the purchase of a picture from the walls of Burlington House, you would gaze round the walls at the array of proved duds that you and your predecessors had acquired. You would undoubtedly shake your head. Why throw good money after bad?—If, on the other hand, the curator was an ambitious man, and had the temerity to suggest the purchase of an "ultramodern" canvas, you would burst out laughing.

What often happens in the latter case, however, is that the reaction of the city worthy is not so jovial, we are told. Instead of giving way to uncontrollable laughter, he squints suspiciously at the young and ambitious curator, and gives it as his opinion, at the next committee meeting he attends, that they have a "bolshie" in their midst. Should the tactless young curator persist in his solicitations, in favour of the new and untried, he is liable to lose his job. Should he have a wife and family, this may be a very serious matter for him. As a result, few modern pictures—of an "extremist", or even semi-extremist, variety—are bought for provincial museums.

One great provincial city is reputed to have a sum, which has attained the proportions of thirteen thousand pounds, lying idle. It represents bequest funds for the purchase of contemporary English pictures. For some years it has been untouched. The city elders just cannot make up their minds what to buy. Wherever they look, they see nothing but pictures that, by all sale-room precedent, are not worth the canvas they are painted on. The years pass, and the sceptical burghers refuse to allow the money to be squandered upon productions experience has taught them to be worthless.

When yearly the local magnate comes to peruse the notices which appear in the great London newspapers of the Royal Academy Exhibition, there is not much comfort there. That pillar of respectability, *The Times*, whose politeness would have in any case to be heavily discounted, is not even *polite*.

But that is the provinces: in London things are different, you might surmise. The answer there can be short and to the point. There is one gallery in London that buys and exhibits contemporary pictures, namely the Tate Gallery. And the Tate has five hundred pounds annually to spend for the purchase of pictures and sculpture. That for an Empire on which the sun never sets is not a great deal. Tens of thousands of pounds can be spent upon an " old master ". But, all told, there is five hundred pounds allocated annually for the support of the art of the living—for pictures, sculpture, and design.

I have said enough, I think, to explain the causes of the rot, which cannot be altogether accounted for by the impoverishment of our society, the suspension of all normal political progress, and the uncertain outlook caused by crisis and by artificial want. That accounts for the absence of that *surplus* of vigour and well-being which would make artistic initiative possible all along the line (we cannot help to build a new world, or anything of that sort, in conditions of such impermanence).

51

But it does not account for the complete severance of all relations between public and artist, and the extinction of all interest in the visual arts, even among educated men and women.

There is only one solution that I can see. I have indicated it already. The more influential artists (the R.A.'s do not count—I do not mean them) must repudiate the journalist, and the self-advertising clown, and return, even noisily, to nature, if so inclined, to romantic nature, without looking back—at once. Otherwise a handful of artists—we are only a handful—will remain in penniless impotence, while—with deep sincerity—Mr. Read and others write book after book about what is being done in this wonderful new world that is not there.

It would be a much less exciting world for the theorist; and there would be much less advertisement to be got out of it for the various eccentric parasites who batten upon the past prestige of the visual arts. But it would be better for us who want to paint pictures.

As it is, the situation is replete with absurdity. It is like a quite empty luxury hotel, occupied by a skeleton staff, in which an elaborate Menu was most ingeniously drawn up every evening (by a professor of cooking) for guests that were not there. A cocktail party in the lounge every now and then would scarcely justify its continued existence.—That such a fantastic establishment should be liquidated without delay is obvious.

Super-nature versus Super-real

England is a country with a fine tradition of its own in painting. We are better painters than the Germans, for instance: we have a lighter touch. And as one would expect, a number of men and women of talent, born under the Union Jack, are living to-day, and are as able and ready to paint a good picture as they are to wield a bayonet (or deftly insert a swab) should Britain require it of them.

A few of these able-bodied painters of marked talent succeed in painting pictures somehow or other—do not ask me how. And once whoever-it-is manages to get a picture painted, by hook or by crook, there are always plenty of dealers willing to hang it up on their walls, since, as I have remarked, it helps to sell their Old Masters and French Impressionists for large sums of money.

If you visit the Galleries, as of course you should, you will be able to verify this statement. These contemporary pictures (as you will see, if you will repress all antiquarian snobbery) are just as well worth buying, some of them, as the pictures of the dead. Lack of talent is not our difficulty.

Such painting as there is—such as is able, by means of subsidies or charities, to lift its head above the level of the deadly flood that has submerged most intelligent activities—displays one of three main tendencies, which I will briefly describe.

53

Wyndham Lewis the Artist

First, there is what is left of the old revolutionary art of " abstract ", or semi-abstract, experiment. A sculptor, Mr. Moore, is the most notable of these stalwarts. His latest Arp-like families of stones with big holes in them are excellent.

There are two painters (pros) Mr. Sutherland and Mr. Nicholson. The former starts with a romantic Scottish mountain landscape, which he ingeniously transforms into something like a still-life of Braque. When you consider the great difference between a mountain and a mandolin this is, in itself, no mean feat.

The second and third classes of artist are of a *back-to-nature* sort. And the two wings of the *back-to-nature* front converge upon the small island of abstractists (of say three pros, and three half-pros). The left wing is labelled *surrealist*. Let me deal with that first. It is not unmanageably large, and not so difficult to handle.

Super-realism (or surrealism) has crossed the Channel at last, thank God. It is in effect a sly return to old forms of painting, and not the most desirable at that. That is why I have put it under the heading back-to-nature. It can be described as sly, because it slips back to the plane of the *trompe l'oeil* clothed in a highly sensational subject-matter. The subconscious is ransacked to provide the super-realist with an alibi to paint like a Pompier.

What is meant by *subject-matter* (if you happen to require this information) is as follows. Supposing that Frith had painted pictures of crowds of nude men and

54

women, in a green light, with gold-hunters instead of eyes, and serpents instead of hair; with strips of flesh hanging loose here and there, exposing the muscles and blood-vessels; the *painting* would have been in all respects the same—neither better nor worse than his *Derby Day*—but the subject, being so extremely different, and so very sensational, it would have looked quite a different picture. Only painters would not have been taken in.

Superrealism is like that. Meissonier and Böcklin are the avowed masters of Dali: and Magritte (the next-best-known painter of that school) follows Dali very closely, with less skill however, or regard for workmanship.

The English professional representatives of that school are two in number—I said it was not an overpopulated school: Mr. Paul Nash and Mr. Armstrong.

Both are adherents of two years standing, one having come to it out of Cotman ("abstracted" into a tube-poster), the other out of the temples of the Pharaohs. These two painters have not the power of their Catalan master, whom they follow very closely, but both are excellent artists.

That two swallows do not make a summer it is unnecessary to stress. But they have a very active mouthpiece in Mr. Read: and if anybody could make a summer out of a couple of swallows—or bricks without straw—that man is Mr. Read.

Now I come to the third category, and it includes all the other good painters in England, from Mr. Matthew Smith (a half-pro, I believe) to Mr. Pitchforth (an art-master, I am informed). This is the class of my predilection; I have explained why.

Here (in however frenchified a form, as often occurs) we are back with nature again. As it is the little touch of nature that will make artist and public kin once more, it is that that I support. There are probably a dozen good pros (or half-pros) doing this. A hundred pure amateurs (or as good as) really make things look as if the art of painting were in full swing, once you reach these naturalist levels.

I need not go through these dozen painters, one by one: and among them are one or two who belong to that tiny band of artists, to be counted upon the fingers of one hand almost, whose pictures are bought not as a favour, or out of charity, or for old-school-tie motives, but because people who are complete strangers to the artists who do them like them and desire to acquire them. Mr. Stanley Spencer, a naturalist with a strongly Flemish fancy, is one of these.

Although I do not need to dwell upon the work of these painters individually, I should like to make a few general remarks. There appear to me to be two prerequisites to the rescue of painting from its present tragic eclipse. The first is the unconditional surrender, in face of *force-majeure*, of the minuscule colony of "abstractists": also the discovery of some effective deterrent, to prevent Mr. Read from falling in love with a new "movement" every six months, and entirely to no purpose (except to satisfy the vanity of half a dozen people out of forty million) and so disturbing the extremely jumpy, convalescent, British public—which has to be nursed back to health with every possible precaution.

That is the first thing—and you may object that it is unheroic and un-British. But those I am sure are the only terms upon which painting can be started up again, as anything but a sport of the rich, or decoy-duck for the sale of Old Masters. Faced with the alternative of *no painting* or the *Shrimp Girl* of Hogarth (to use her again) there is no painter who would not plump for the latter. And there are some who would be glad to-day if they had never left her, to run after geometrical will-o'-the-wisps.

The second prerequisite is something *positive* in the manner of this "return-to-nature". It must not have the look of a jaded return to an exhausted goldmine. It must have the air of a new gold-rush, or nothing. I will however explain myself.

Compare, if you like, the problem in question to an analogous one in politics. When a politician has to "ginger up the Democracies", the difficulty he encounters is the absence of a rallying-cry. He is at a disadvantage compared with the professional agitator, of either Left or Right. "Democracy", with which we are all so familiar, has no kick left as a watchword, or not enough to inflame the imagination to the requisite degree.

As an artist, I should be sorry to regard this as more than a superficial parallel. Nevertheless, our palate has been demoralised with strong sauces: and "nature" *tout court* is a little wanting in publicity-value.

If the painter is to return to nature, he should perhaps pause to reflect before taking his plunge, how diabolically interesting nature *is*. He should acquire an understanding of how unnecessary it is to strip off a man's skin, or to give him three eyes, or arms, instead of two, to make him an object of amazing interest. Even, it is a poverty of imagination that prompts anybody to require that of the artist.

Having thoroughly prepared himself by this moment of rapt contemplation, he can then precipitate himself upon this mystery we call " nature " (as if it were quite *natural* that " nature " should be what she is) with some prospects of taking the public with him.

All I would say of what has happened so far in the return-to-nature movement of some painters, is that they have not gone *directly* enough, and so have missed an opportunity. When I said I advocated a return to nature, I meant *really* to nature—not to Degas, to Tissot, to Delacroix, or to Meissonier. That is a very different thing, and not so likely to awaken the interest of an intelligent public.

That anyone with nature there *should* want to go back to Degas might require explaining, even. The *Cavalcade* spirit that has possessed itself of England is however the sufficient answer. To go back to a former *mode* of life and its expression, rather than to life itself, is typical of this exhausted time. Even nature has to be approached historically, and at second-hand.

Super-nature versus Super-real

vi

That I never deserted the concrete for the abstract—that I not only continued my interrogation of nature, but based my geometries upon that—I have already pointed out. And for the plates to accompany the text of this book I have gone to work in which I am seen deep in the imitation of nature, rather than exploring those independent abstractions that suggest themselves, as a result of any observation of nature that is at all profound.

To-day I am a *super-naturalist*—so I might call myself : and I wished the reader of these *Notes and Vortices* to see what could be done by burying Euclid deep in the living flesh—that of Mr. Eliot or of Mr. Pound—rather than, at this time of day, displaying the astral geometries of those gentlemen. I am, as an examination of the plates will reveal, never unconscious of those underlying conceptual truths that are inherent in all appearances. But I leave them now where I find them, instead of isolating them in conceptual arabesques.

Much modernist painting unquestionably is the work of inferior artists, who were unable to do the " straight " stuff, and disguised their limitations in a pretentious technical mumbo-jumbo. Of course *all* painters who ever experimented have been accused by their academic opponents of belonging to that class.

One always has to ask oneself, in looking at a picture in which imitation is abandoned, and elaborate distortions, for whatever reason, are indulged in, whether the painter in question is merely being evasive and mysterious because he would cut a poor figure if he challenged nature more openly—setting his forms and colours against hers, so that they could be readily checked by any trained eye. In a subtler way, even with a persistent *landscapist*, it is legitimate to enquire what sort of a job he would make of it if he matched himself against one of the great figure painters—a Bellini, or even a Cézanne. This is a relevant question, I think, even in the presence of such landscapes as those of Turner, or of Claude. The appropriate answer would tell you something about Turner, or about Claude, that you would otherwise have missed. In the last analysis, who would paint a tree when he could paint a man?

I hope, however, that by my selection of the pictures in this book, I shall have proved that these charges brought against the revolutionary artist are not always well-founded.

I have used the expression "super-naturalist", and like all such expressions, it has as much or as little meaning as you like to put into it. People are fond of tags. If I was looking for one for myself, that would be as good as any.

The super-realist (or *surrealist*) is, as I have pointed out, a naturalist pure and simple. He will copy an object in a slovenly or photographic fashion: it is essential to him that the object should be as *real* as possible, in the sense of a camera-study in a newspaper. And the stupider and more matter-of-fact the pictorial statement the better.

Super-nature versus Super-real

It is of the first importance to him, even, that nature should not be altered, or "interpreted", in any way. That is of course why Meissonier or Frith are regarded as better models by the super-realist than Velasquez or Rénoir. There would be much too much beastly *art* about an object as seen by either of the latter. It is not "nature seen through a temperament", but *nature* plain and unvarnished that is required. *For it is not an aesthetic emotion but a real emotion—like that experienced in the presence of a street-accident—that is required.*

Such, at least, is the *surrealist* ideal. Matter-of-fact nature—really, the photograph. Even real watches are stuck on to the pictures by Dali, lest his painted version of them should not be *real* enough. All the interest is in the queerness of the reality chosen; or in the odd juxtapositions of objects, or wholesale suppression of same. It is a psychological, rather than a pictorial, interest that is at work.

The *super-naturalist* would be aiming—in my case is aiming—at the opposite to the *super-realist*. The emphasis would be upon *nature*, not upon *the real*. With the super-naturalist it is from within nature that the change is effected, not from without. The "real", in the photographic sense, would never make its appearance at all. Art, as he understands it, involves a banishing of that kind of reality. The spectator is offered sensations, as if on the switchback at a fair, among the scenes of nature, by the super-realist. The sensations provided for him by the super-naturalist would be of a quite different order. Nature would be *predigested* for him. He would not be required to participate in any way in the real. Super-nature is not super-real. It is nature transformed by all her latent geometries into something outside "the real"—outside the temporal order—altogether.

Most artists are agreed that Salvator Dali is an admirable painter. With that judgment I am in accord. But if I were asked what I thought about super-realists, or *surrealists*, in general, I should be inclined to say that super-realism, as a method, served to disguise dullness, and bad painting, as much as ever Cubism did.

That should not be the case: for the naturalism which is the basis of super-realism ought to betray at once the dullard hiding his dullness or the incompetent concealing his lack of skill. But for my part I have found it quite possible to be momentarily deceived. That was not perhaps so much a lack of acuteness on my part, as a readiness to pass a pleasurable moment at this pictorial Maskelyne and Devants.

I have often found in going into a gallery, where there were surrealist pictures, that I have greatly enjoyed some jumbled scene, invented according to a surrealist receipt, with its witty incongruities and pictorial euphuisms. But once I have got used to it—as used to it as I am to Piccadilly Circus, which takes about five minutes—and the novelty has worn off, I am then left face to face with something that I find tawdry and second-rate. I feel a little humiliated that I should have been taken in. How easy I am to please—I say to myself—if all you have to do is to place an ill-painted iron-bedstead on top of an ill-painted alpine peak, amid obvious snow-white snow, to secure my approval!

Another experience of mine that is perhaps worth recording is that when some painter whose work I have not greatly enjoyed, but found a little crude and hard, suddenly goes "super-realist", I find I like him better. The more confused, the more haywire he becomes, the more able am I to enjoy what he does. On such occasions as these it is my habit to ask myself whether what I see is *really* better, or if it only seems so to me.

It is plausible to suppose that, released from the hard necessity of impressing the onlooker by his mastery of natural form, a not very first-rate painter should actually produce something of more intrinsic significance. Then, just as the onlooker likes novelty, so does the artist. The combined stimulation (1) of not having to worry about *facts*, and of (2) being amused by the topsy-turvydom indulged in, may result in a picture intrinsically better than otherwise he could do.

But, of course, just as the onlooker very rapidly grows used to some ingenious incongruity, and experiences a deception when able to examine soberly the stuff of which this trick-effect was made, so the painter himself cannot be amused for long over what was at first a pleasurable surprise.

He knows, far better than we do, the value, taken in isolation, of these ill-assorted objects. They are, after all, the same old units of the same old stock-in-trade, painted—in detail—in the same old way. He understands the advantage obtained by the jettisoning of

63

logic, of sequence, of àpropos. He cannot take in *himself* for long. Consequently we can discount very largely, I think, the stimulation administered to the artist by the mere jumbling, reversing, and telescoping of the eternal world of sense.

It is quite a different matter where, by the methods of elimination, or of simplification, the objects of nature are themselves transformed into something like themselves, yet differing, in reality, as much as chalk from cheese. This was the great achievement of the art of the Orient, especially the Chinese. And the movement of which Vorticism was a part was, as understood by me, a first step towards a reform in the European vision. It was a discipline preliminary to a complete abandonment of the naturalism we inherit from the Greeks.

That discipline *I* have undergone. The *Notes and Vortices* you are about to read are a record of that experience. The few examples of the *super-natural* (I regret that it has not been possible to include many more) which you will find reproduced in this book, will help to demonstrate the purpose of those disciplines.

THE SKELETON IN THE
CUPBOARD SPEAKS

E

The Skeleton in the
Cupboard Speaks

A.

" He blasts best who blasts last " refuted.

THESE *Notes and Vortices* are reprinted from *Blast*
(No. I.) and *Blast* (No. II.), which appeared in 1914
and 1915 respectively; and from *The Tyro* (No. II.)
which appeared in 1924.

The readers of a book in great part so technical as this
will be artists, or people concerned with the fine arts; so I
do not have to go into the circumstances that gave rise to
Blast; though why such a storm broke when it did in
Great Britain (rather than ten, fifteen, or twenty years
later which is the more usual procedure) I will make
plain.

The following pamphlets, articles, and manifestos
were written, of course, in defence of the experiments in
painting in which the " vorticist group " were engaged.
The " vorticist group " were a band of young painters led
by myself, and established in 1914, to make England a
land safe for a pictorial hero to live in. It did not succeed
—as was sufficiently indicated in *Super-nature versus
Super-real.* England continues to be a place highly unsafe
for a pictorial hero to live in.

You have only to reflect what an immense weight of
opposition is, in Great Britain, at once mobilized against

any innovation, to see how necessary such a defensive verbal barrage must be.

Almost, I have become a professional writer in the process of defending my paintings. Mr. Shaw's " Prefaces " tell the same story; Whistler's admirable pamphleteering was a phenomenon of the same kind.

" Vorticism " was, in 1914, decidedly over the odds. Nothing had prepared the British public for such unadulterated extremism: Mr. Fry with " Post Impressionism ", had taken its breath away a few years earlier, and left it—not disagreeably—gasping: but " Vorticism " was beyond a joke. It was in the nature of a foul blow, and a deep note of indignation was sounded, among the usual cat-calls, in the daily and weekly press.

Inevitably the painter indulging in such practices was obliged to spend at least half his time scribbling manifestos, or otherwise supplying explanations for every line he drew, or brush-stroke he delivered. This wasted a great deal of valuable time.

The " vorticists " enjoyed a life of a year or two, no more. They were snuffed out by the Great War. Some were wiped out by it in every sense.

The War came a few months after the publication of *Blast No.* I. I, who had been the principal exponent of " vorticism," attempted to keep the vorticist flag flying for a short while, then became a soldier: Gaudier Brzeska was killed in action within 6 months of the outbreak of war—that was a very great loss to the art of sculpture; Hulme, the philosopher-journalist of " abstraction " in 1914, was killed in action in 1917, only a few hundred yards away from my own gun—his battery was within sight of ours, a few hundred yards to the right, in the soggy coastal plain behind Nieuport in Flanders. The sergeant of my gun was killed and most of my gun-crew made casualties, during the same prolonged bombardment, which was the German answer to our preparations to attack.

Among these Notes you will find the following passage: "if out of the campaign in Flanders any material, like the spears in Uccello's *Battle* in the National Gallery, force themselves upon the artist's imagination, he will use it. The huge German siege guns, for instance, are a stimulus to vision of power." Great guns are just as magnificent as are unwieldy spears of armoured cavaliers. The guns were at all events my choice. I was not associated myself with a more imposing object than a six-inch howitzer; but I made what I could out of that. (My picture of a battery in action is in the Ottawa war-museum). Gaudier carved out of the butt of a German rifle a vorticist image.—We all of us went over into the War, and lost our "Vortex" in it. When we came back into art out of life—desperate life—again, we had no appetite for art-politics. At least I had not.

I had tried the "group" game, in the art-racket: I had found it more trouble than it was worth. And in *The Caliph's Design*, which comes after these *Notes and Vortices*, it was not as part of a rather bogus battalion, but as *a single spy*, that I was speaking.

69

Wyndham Lewis the Artist

It is always said that London follows the Continent, and especially Paris, after an interval of a decade or two. The " Nineties " movement in England, for instance, was the Seventies in Paris, reproduced upon our miniature island stage, in a romantic and self-conscious form. Verlaine was an Oscar Wilde—was advertising that particular vice—even went to jail, and recorded the fact in tragic verse—long before late-victorian England was electrified by the Queensberry trial, or before the *Ballad of Reading Gaol* saw the light, and touched with romance the English Prison System.

Really all that happened in England in 1914 (the pictorial disturbance of which *Blast* was the organ and rallying point) ought not to have happened then. It ought, by all the rules, to have happened about 1920 or 1930. And of course, it *is* really happening now—in due course and at its appointed time—just as if 1914 had never been at all. The great *massif* of the War barring off 1914 from 1918, makes this much easier, of course.

For a thing to have happened in England *at the same time* as in France was unheard of. And some of the participants in those irregular events felt that they were being a little hustled. At the time, I think I may add, several of my artist-companions—although, being young, eager enough to be up and doing—were a shade resentful. They were not entirely unconscious of the fact that they were being asked to do a thing *twenty years before it was supposed to be done.* Even, they were relentlessly invited to do a *new* thing—not merely imitate Picasso and the other chief exponents of Cézanne revolution: invited to attempt something *untried*, if you please—instead of, after a suitable decade or two, proceeding to an effortless mimicry in retrospect.

All this complicated matters a little bit for me (for I was the prime mover: I was the person—I say it without any vain-glory—who was solely responsible). Certainly since that time it has resulted in my assuming a little the position of a skeleton in the cupboard—a cupboard that, needless to say, had to remain *locked*.

I have, however, been extremely accommodating, I will say that for myself. Up there in my cupboard, I have kept remarkably quiet: I have been content to forget, and have never objected to other people conveniently forgetting, that there once upon a time was a big pink *Blast* that coloured the London sky: and now that I am beginning to throw myself about a little bit, I do so in as correct a way as my confined position allows.

That I had to expect a certain amount of odium to attach to me because of this tactless speeding-up of the British Workman was obvious: this or that painter persuaded by me to ignore the regulation British time-lag, would have much preferred to wait until 1924 or 1934 to do what I persuaded him to undertake in 1914. But how much more tiresome was it not for my old friend Mr. Read the critic, who would far rather have had nothing happen in 1914, so that when, by 1930 or thereabouts "abstraction" was ripe for discovery upon these shores, he could have weighed in without all these echoes of premature bombardment in his rear. "Abstraction" *should* not have been practiced here—and above all, been *written about*—fifteen years before its time. Ignore it as you might, this fact has been a skeleton at Mr. Read's little feast of reason.

Again, had I merely painted, instead of engaging in a verbal "blast"—or had I been in Paris, instead of returning to London to do it, it would not have mattered: that is of course the point. But to choose London to do it in was not quite playing the game. Certain Gentlemen were doomed thereby to anticlimax. The British time-table had been brutally dislocated. The comfortable belief that *He blasts best who blasts last* had been fatally undermined.

Now that Mr. Paul Nash is at last sowing his wild oats, I feel that I may break my long silence. I feel that we *must* be approaching the end of that particular chapter in the history of modern art. It was the spectacle of Mr. Nash as a matter of fact that gave me confidence to speak my mind once more, and as it were officially close this epoch.

As far as Mr. Read is concerned, there my mind is quite at ease. Once he learns from Paris that there is no young painter left who would be seen dead within a mile of a cube, a holed-stone by Arp, or a demented foetus

The Skeleton in the Cupboard Speaks

from the cabinet of Dr. Freud,* Mr. Read will not allow
the grass to grow under his feet, of that I am quite sure.
I am perfectly easy in my mind about *him*. He will evolve
from one day to the next a gentle salvationist technique
to deal with a rather thin and frivolous Chardin, or a
rather puerile shadow of Le Nain.

I have a sort of qualm about Mr. Moore. He is an
artist whose work I relish. He is a genuine hard case—a
sufferer from that famous British time-lag. He ought to
pack up, and come out of the land of plastic shorthand
(a certainly delightful shorthand but to which only a
dozen people are privy) and make his peace with Nature.
The odds are too great: the Brave New World was a
mirage—a snare and a delusion. He could steal back and
make a hole in a flat stone from time to time, or rig up a
little buttoned rock with trelliswork of taught twine.—
It is my hope that he will be so alarmed at the spectacle
of Mr. Paul Nash sowing his wild oats that he will pull
out one of these days in a sudden panic.

Well, I am sorry it was necessary to go back to the
super-real and all that, and to the last rose of the
" abstract " summer, and launch a second minor polemic
before getting down to the text of my reprinted articles.
But what I wanted to say was that even where remarkable
talent is displayed, or minor variations introduced to
freshen up the old stew, there is nothing being done in
1939 in England that was not done by us—Gaudier, Mr.

* A dealer who had gone prospecting in Paris the other day informed
me that in a large collection of " the under-forties " he could not find a single
non-naturalist picture.

73

Wadsworth, and myself—in 1914. That is a fact there is no getting round, I am sorry to say. We see every month or so things announced as " new " that we have all seen before, many times over: which is merely silly. Considering all the circumstances of the time, these stale " sensations," staged for an audience that is not there, is in the nature of an obstruction on the line. It holds back the reunion of the Public and the Artist, which is so greatly to be desired, and is so long overdue.

I regret that it is my melancholy task to announce the end of all that, and that it has devolved upon me, of all men, officially to close this bankrupt exhibition, of what are now nothing but freaks—repudiated by the Zeitgeist, let down by the very force that instigated their creation. But there it is.—And is Nature, then, so contemptible? The answer is thundered at us from the roof of the Sistine Chapel: or whispered to us by the feathery pale perfection of the trees in Corot's landscapes.

The Skeleton in the
Cupboard Speaks

B.
Explanatory Notes regarding Notes and Vortices.

THAT a new effort, both critical and creative, will be demanded of everybody engaged in the back-to-nature movement, is obvious. Nature, you will see me saying in the course of these Notes, of the year 1914, is a convalescent home, a retreat, for those deficient in vigour or intellect. And indeed that is the case, if nature is allowed to do all the work; or if some formula is embraced which enables the artist to pass off photography as creation.

"Nature is just as sterile a tyrant as Tradition," you will hear me say. And so it is. Naturalism can be just as dead as academicism. That is why *super-nature*, as a tag, might serve to remind the new naturalist that nature alone is not enough.

The problem of the artist does not change, and time is only a factor in his problem. The very severe and extreme disciplines that such a movement as Vorticism imposed did not alter the fundamental questions that had to be asked and answered. And the sort of thing discussed in these *Notes and Vortices*, or in *The Caliph's Design*—for instance (1) the non-identity of life and art; (2) the certain "deadness" and lack of inventive imagination that is inclined to dog the French School; (3) the place

75

of literary imagination in pictorial art; (4) the rôle of subject-matter in the art of the painter; (5) how far nationality must influence the painter; (6) what is the value and meaning of "originality"; (7) whether the Machine Age is incompatible with the visual arts—all these and many more considerations belong to the permanent material of critical investigation. I propose to run over, in advance, all the pieces reprinted here, selecting such passages as I find suggestive for discussion. The reader, if he prefers to do so, may proceed immediately to the text, returning to this commentary afterwards.

It must be remembered, to begin with, that the author of these *Notes and Vortices* is a dual personality. He is (1) a Revolutionary; and (2) a Traditionalist. He is those two things in that order, and not in equal parts. His traditionalism is impregnated with the spirit of his revolutionary alter ego. And so it comes about that *his* mother-nature is a super-natural nature. He cannot paint a dead nature (a *nature-morte*) if he tries: for that would be merely a *pattern*—which is not worth while, as he sees it.

The way in which Vorticism was supposed to differ from all other "isms" will transpire once you come to the vorticist text. I say was "supposed to," for it had only just been born when it met its untimely end in 1914; and it had scarcely had time to give effect, in canvas after canvas, and carving after carving, to its principles. It was a program, rather than an accomplished fact; but in such works as had begun to spring forth fully armed from the iron brains of a handful of adherents, it showed itself more resolute in its exclusion of the past than the Paris School, less concerned with the glittering jazzed-up spectacle of the megalopolis than the Italians, and much more distinct from architecture than the Dutch (such as Mondrian).

The fundamental injunction, in all the explanatory matter you will be reading, is *to invent*. That was, of course, the pure revolutionary impulse—for only the revolutionary says *invent*. There must be no echo at all of a former age, or of a former manner. Even *all* manner must be dispensed with if it suggest an earlier manner. No manner at all would be better than "the grand manner": though there was every reason, it was implied, to go out and seek the formidable, and the grand, in the new subjects made available by the more inhuman Context of the contemporary world.

The Cubists come under fire because they imitated nature—taking the things upon their breakfast tables as a basis for their designs, rather than inventing forms they could not see: however distorted this "photography" might be, these "nature mortes" were still treated as *photography* by the vorticist. If, on the other hand, the cubists departed from what was under their eyes, they went back to the academic foundations of their vision, and reproduced (in however paradoxical a form) an El Greco, a Buonarotti.

The extreme revolutionary position then was taken up prematurely, in Great Britain, in 1914. Everything must be *new*, in the Vortex, from top to bottom. Mr. Wyndham Lewis, the vorticist of 1914-15, was a "sea-green incorruptible." That is the first thing he understood. He thought the time had come to shatter the visible world to bits, and build it nearer to the heart's desire: and he really was persuaded that this *absolute* transformation was imminent. He was, in fact, a little like the Christians of the First Century who believed firmly that the end of the world was at hand.

What in fact happened was, as we know, the " Great War." At first this happy vorticist did not in the least understand what was occurring. The War looked to him like an episode at first—rather proving his contentions than otherwise. He did not fully recognize the significance of that disaster until he found himself in the mud of Passchendaele, and dimly discerned that he was present at a great military defeat, and that the community to which he belonged would never be the same again: and that all *surplus* vigour was being bled away and stamped out.

"Vorticism " accepted the machine-world: that is the point to stress. It sought out machine-forms. The pictures of the Vorticists were a sort of *machines*. This, of course, serves to define Vorticism as the opposite of an "escapist " doctrine. It was cheerfully and dogmatically external.

The philosophy of "escape" from the sordid and mechanical—which he describes as an "an inevitable tendency of the modern spirit"—Mr. Herbert Read has stated as follows:

"The more mechanical the world becomes (not only the visible world, but the actual process of living) the

The Skeleton in the Cupboard Speaks

less spiritual satisfaction there is to be found in the appearances of this world. The inner world of the imagination becomes more and more significant, as if to compensate for the brutality and flatness of everyday life."

In the case of Vorticism—and this is what I wish to stress—the " inner world of the imagination " was not an asylum from the brutality of mechanical life. On the contrary it identified itself with that brutality, in a stoical embrace, though of course without propagandist fuss.

It did not sentimentalize machines, as did the Italians, (the pictorial fascists who preceded the political fascists): it took them as a matter of course: just as we take trees, hills, rivers, coal deposits, oil-wells, rubber-trees, as a matter of course. It was a stoic creed: it was not an *uplift*.

Also Vorticism, unlike its contemporary rivals, was visual, not functional. That is to say, it did not identify the artist with the machine. The artist *observed* the machine, from the outside. But he did not observe the machine *impressionistically*: he did not attempt to represent it in violent movement. For to represent a machine in violent movement is to arrive at a blur, or a kaleidoscope. And a blur was as abhorrent to a vorticist as a vacuum is to nature.

A machine in violent motion ceases to look like a machine. It looks, perhaps, like a rose, or like a sponge. For in violent enough displacement the hardest thing takes on the appearance of the softest. A statue cut out of basalt would become more fluid than flesh, if whirled round sufficiently swiftly. So the very spirit of the machine is lost—the hard, the cold, the mechanical and the static. And it was those attributes for which Vorticism had a particular partiality. You will find, in the course of these notes and essays, the engravings of Mantegna mentioned more than once. In Mantegna you get a mechanical ideal expressed with great beauty and with consummate power. That is why vorticist literature (which is of course mainly my handiwork) returns so often to the name of the great Renaissance engraver.

I do not need you to tell me that all these distinctions between one school and another—schools that now are defunct—may seem otiose. I have enough experience of teaching to understand that. Vorticists, constructivists, futurists, cubists—all are much of a muchness to the outside observer, or even to the artist who is out of sympathy with such heresies.

I have said that Vorticism was " cheerfully and dogmatically external." The external world did not appear to Vorticist No. I. at least, as too horrible to contemplate.

To return to that great authority on all things "abstract," Mr. Herbert Read's explanation of modern "abstractness," of "geometric art," is that it was and is an *escape*, as I have just remarked.

" Is (our outer world of to-day) not rather a world

THE INFERNO

The Skeleton in the Cupboard Speaks

from which the sensitive soul, be he painter or poet, will
flee to some spiritual refuge, some sense of stability? And
is he not likely, in that tendency, to desert the perceptual
basis of the empirical art of the immediately preceding
epoch, in favour of a fixed conceptual basis? "

To *conceptual* form, in place of *perceptual* form,
Vorticism did certainly adhere. But it was not a clinging
to a lifebelt, or to a spar, or something satisfactory and
solid, in the midst of a raging perceptual flux: or not
more than *all* attachment to the conceptual is part of
the technique of living, which involves imposing laws
upon the perceptual chaos.

I am not sneering at Mr. Read's expression "sensitive soul" if I say that the vorticist made rather a point
of being tough, so that he might be in harmony with his
material. As you will see when you arrive at *The
Caliph's Design*, that "sensitivity" that was such a striking feature of the æsthete known as "the Bloomsbury"
was greatly deplored at the headquarters of the Great
London Vortex; indeed it was incessantly ridiculed by
Vorticist No. I.—even after he ceased to be a "vorticist" and became the solitary "enemy."

Now this was not entirely a "tough guy" attitude,
either. It was *deliberately* tonic. There were no school-
boy heroics, of the emotional Hemingway order about
it. It was just the sternness and severity of mind that is
appropriate to the man who does the stuff (in contrast to
the amateur who stands rapt in front of it once it is done
and stuck up to be looked at); especially when that stuff
is a harsh, reverberative, and indeed rather terrible

material. It was the actor's attitude to his tragic *décors* and property stilettos: it was, yes, *professional.*

Mr. Herbert Read will have it that this century proved so much more repulsive and horrible than the last that in its first decade and a half, artists "flew" to "abstraction," away from the sensuous, as if to a *steel*, rather than an ivory, tower. That would not be my way of putting it. The Renaissance in Italy, the age of Vasari, was turbulent, harsh, and to a "sensitive soul" would have seemed highly disagreeable. But its artists did not "fly" to geometric expression. And China was a welter of war and famine, when its artists were placidly pot-making and screen-painting, more naturalist, or super-naturalist, every day.

It is not my intention to paraphrase beforehand, or to "pot," the essays that are here reprinted. I will merely advertize, in advance, a few of the points upon which the central argument turns. In the first piece you come to (this text is chronologically arranged) "Life is the important thing," the "pure painter" snob is exposed, and shown to be a person still under the spell of the French Impressionist, rather than one belonging to the contemporary world. I contrast the pictorial creativity of Daumier with the academic camera that was

The Skeleton in the Cupboard Speaks

Dégas. I say of him; "Daumier combined in his art great pictorial gifts with great literary gifts: no doubt he was an impure painter, according to contemporary British standards. But it was great literature always, along with great art."

Again, in "relativism and Picasso's latest work," you will perhaps note, as you read these strictures brought against the string-zinc-and-threeply phase, how apposite they still are to-day—how little we progress, because of our famous time-lag.

When we come to *Blast* (No. II), in "Art subject to laws of life" there is a very valuable analysis of the hook-up of Cubism and Impressionism. "If we could see with larger eyes we should no doubt be satisfied . . . Finite and godlike lines are not for us, but, rather, a powerful but remote suggestion of finality." This passage is *against* the practice of adding weight to things that have no weight, or the conversion of the objects upon a tea-table into a Grand Canyon. So why choose them, if that is the effect you desire? Rather go to the towering Canyon itself : or if you cannot do that, evolve it out of your fancy. Such is my argument.

By the way, "Art subject to Laws of Life" contains a fair measure of tub-thumping, and I have felt it better, where that is going on, to retain the display-capitals. As to these methods of the mob-orator, they really had to be used: 1914 was not 1939—if you were a "movement" you were expected to shout. One was surrounded —one was hemmed-in—by mob-orators. To lift his voice, in 1914, was as essential to a *chef de bande*, as it was in 1915 to a drill-sergeant. I made a marvellous "bombardier," a year or so later. I had had a good deal of practice!

Section C (sub-sections 38–41) I will quote intact; it defines once and for all what a Royal Academy *should* be—namely a sort of *Cubist* Academy.

"The artist, in certain cases, is less scandalized at the comprehensible than is the Public. And the artist could 'represent,' or imitate, where the bad artist should be forced to 'abstract.'

"I am not quite sure, sometimes, whether it should not be the Royal Academy where the severity of the 'abstract' reigns, and whether we, who are outside the Academy, should not be conspicuous for our 'life' and 'poetry'—always within the limits of plastic propriety. Life, literature, and poetry should be the prerogative of the alive.

"To paint a recognizable human being should be the rarest privelege, bestowed as a sort of 'Freedom of Art?'"

I might have gone farther (as I at all events will go now) and have said that the limited, the immature, majority-person should be *compelled to paint primitive*; that "child-art," in other words, had its uses. There is nothing strange in many grown-up people continuing to paint as if they were fifteen years old. They have never progressed intellectually beyond the standards of that age; therefore when they paint they should not worry to do anything too grown-up—too mature, or too "professional."

The Skeleton in the Cupboard Speaks

And in this connection I come to Mr. Fry, who was all for the amateur, all for the eternal Child, and who wished to make of the painting-world of London a tight little right little world, safe for the amateur to live in. But I do not wish to say very much about Mr. Fry, in this place. He makes his appearance inevitably in the course of these essays. Although I cannot eliminate him, I do not wish to go into all that now. Mr. Fry is a sort of pink herring, merely (æsthetically, I mean, of course). Do not let us draw the great apostle of British amateurism across our trail in the present context.

In the section of "Art subject to Laws of Life" headed C. you will find what is described as "the most important feature of this new synthesis I propose," and indeed I think, quite apart from "vorticism," that the analysis of non-representation (or non-imitation, if that word is preferred) may claim your present attention. The questions raised—and answered *à la vorticiste*—are of permanent importance for the artist.

Of the *Blast* (No. II) material, I have placed first the long statement entitled "Art subject to Laws of Life:" after it the Editorial and the miscellaneous art-notes which this second (and final) number of *Blast* contained.

The Editorial, and some of the subsequent articles, deal with the problems of art and war. All are redolent of the illusion of the editor, namely that this was just a war like another, only bigger. No one in England (except apparently Lord Kitchener) realized the magnitude of the event.

"Modern caricature and Impressionism" is further testimony of how slowly changes are effected in England. "Why," I ask in 1914, "does not some enterprising newspaper-proprietor gather all this scattered (English) talent and wit together, and start an important Comic Paper, to supersede Punch?" I still ask that question in 1939. *Oh, Press Barons, where is your Vortex?*

"The Art of the Great Race" contains some of the most characteristic vorticist doctrine. The vorticists are described as "Primitives of a future equilibrium." And you have a few lines farther on a forecast of the political revolutions that have swept the world since that time. Thus "The only person who objects to uniformity and order (*One art—One Life*) is the man who knows that under those conditions his 'individuality' would not survive. Every real individuality and excellence would welcome conditions where there would be hierarchy of power and vitality. The Best would then be Free. Under no other conditions is any true freedom at all possible."

The Skeleton in the Cupboard Speaks

I now come to *The Caliph's Design* and then, last of all, to the *Tyro* material. In both cases I was no longer a "vorticist": I had not severed my connection with what was left of the other vorticists: I merely did not, after the War, wish to go on with that particular game, and the "great London Vortex" consequently fell to pieces. Yet *The Caliph's Design*, written just after the War, was another *Blast*, and it continued the criticism of *Blast* (No. I) and *Blast* (No. II). The review called *The Tyro* (two numbers of which appeared) might be regarded as *Blasts* number four and five. The year of *The Tyro* was 1924. I was already coming back to nature, though in much that I did then, and do to-day, nature does not occupy the whole of the picture. But in 1924 dogmatic "abstraction" had disappeared, in my critical utterances, as it had in my pictures, its splendid disciplines having served their turn. My "Tyros" were about upon the same plane of naturalism as Rouault's moralistic dolls. I was already back in the naturalist fold—though I have still a mark on me that I do not seek to hide; and I still worked from the skeleton outwards.

The Caliph's Design was, I believe, one of the main sources of inspiration for the very modernist architect in Great Britain. So I did not shout, "Architects, where is your Vortex!" quite in vain. Yet as you read "The first great modern building that arose in this city would soon carry everything before it," you perforce will think to yourself that this revolutionary optimism has hardly been justified by events.

We have seen a number of "modern buildings" go

up in London, here and there. You have to look for
them: they are few and far between. To-day they are
regarded rather as white elephants (far, far too *white* to
start with) or as "follies" of some person too up-and-
coming to be altogether "sound." If flats, they are not
popular. If buildings in the country, they are violently
objected to by the owners of week-end thatched cottages
or bungalows in the neighbourhood, on the ground that
they are un-English and spoil the peace and rustic beauty
of the scene.

Apart from its preoccupation with architecture, there
is much else of more specific interest to painters in *The
Caliph's Design*. But in the *Notes and Vortices* there is
a section entitled "The Improvement of Life" which
might be read in conjunction with the later pamphlet:
it is there that I have stated most clearly the relation of
the art of the architect to that of the painter.

This is summed up in an imaginary question,
addressed to a naturalist painter.

"One of the most obvious questions that might have
been put to any naturalist painter of the last century, or
for that matter to Rembrandt or Pieter de Hooch, was
this:

"'Is there no difference, or if so, what difference,
between a bad piece of architecture or a good piece represented in a painting: or rather, would it be a greater type
of art that had for representative content objects in themselves finer?'"

The question is still extremely relevant to-day, and
must be at all times, because of all the other questions, of

first moment to the painter, to which it gives rise.—If one of the "back-to-Impressionism" painters now engaged in illustrating London scenes—since London was where he lived, so that is what he *must* paint—put up his easel in Kensington Gardens and painted the Albert Memorial—a great London landmark—would he be guilty of a crime not only against Beauty, but against ordinary decency and commonsense, or would he not?

Everyone is agreed that the Albert Memorial is a visual scandal of the first order. It combines ugliness and silliness in the highest degree. Is it then permissible to use it as the subject-matter for a picture? We cannot help *seeing* it. But need we *paint* it?

In one degree or another, however, that objection would apply to most things in London at the present time. Once the negative principle was accepted, the painter of London scenes would have to cut out *typical* London altogether—except for the very poor and miserable quarters (Islington, Limehouse or Crouch End). Those he would be allowed to paint because of their unadulterated horror; because they aroused sensations of pity and terror, and so came within the tragic canon. Their very evil would exempt them, lifting them upon a different plane to the silly face of our "residential" districts, or the offensive ineptitude of our public monuments.

These, at all events, are the sort of secondary questions that haunt the text of *The Caliph's Design*, which is primarily a fight-talk for backward architects, at the beginning of the post-war.

Wyndham Lewis the Artist

The *Essay on the Objective of Art in Our Time* is unfortunately unfinished. There was no *Tyro* No. III. But as it stands it has some completeness. It investigates rather fully the relation of art to games.—It insists upon the *contingent* nature of art. Like the whole of Life, art is no more than a game played by children. But *all* life, likewise, is a game. And among all the games of which human life is composed—the political game, the business game, the sex-game, the game of science—art is as important as any. It is for this reason, of course, that the "amateurism" attacked in my pamphlet *Super-nature versus Super-real*—and which would degrade the visual arts to the status of a merely physical exercise, like tennis or cricket—should be combated.

But I need say no more about what you are shortly to read: enough in the way of a "guide," has been, I think, already provided. In conclusion I would like, at the risk of appearing a little *nationalist*, to deprecate the artistic ascendancy of Paris in the Anglo-Saxon world. If English painters—and American, too—are to go back to nature, to English nature and American nature, they need bother very little about Paris.

Paris has its function; but it is that of an art-school, nothing more. A *finishing school*, let us call it. I myself am Paris-finished. Rowlandson, the most English of artists, was Paris-trained. Indeed Rowlandson could not have been so superbly English if he had not learnt how to do it in Paris: but he could not have done it at all if he had not forgotten all Frenchiness, and kept his eyes fixed upon the English scene.

The Skeleton in the Cupboard Speaks

All that the French have to teach us is *technical* matters. In receiving at their hands a technical instruction, we should at all times be careful not to absorb along with that a spirit that is not our affair. The Anglo-Saxons cannot dispense with the *technical* instruction, unfortunately; they are defective, like the Germans, in visual sensibility, in any case. They are much better poets than they are painters; and France is the handiest country in which to correct native shortcomings. But the French School has its shortcomings too, of another order.

Paris is a much more delightful city to live in than any in the Germanic or Scandinavian countries: and the political enervation of the Spaniards, their national poverty, made Paris the intellectual metropolis for them as well. What has been called the "Cézannean revolution" was conducted by immigrant Catalans, Braque being the only outstanding Frenchman in that upheaval.

The limitations of the French genius should not be less carefully noted and weighed than that sensitive accomplishment that has made of Paris the Mecca of the painter. It is not in order to belittle Paris painting, which is fine and sure, if it is shallow too often, that I am writing this, but to reassure all those timid provincials, whether British or American, who suffer from an inferiority-complex regarding "the latest" from the rue de la Boétie. What is best in Paris is Spanish, Belgian, or Russian: and *nothing* except technical dexterity and a sensitive approach to the visual world is to be found there that cannot be found elsewhere.

The French School, on the whole, has been at all times, surprisingly *unheroic*. I am the last person to wish to deal in nationalist claptrap: but how can one avoid the conclusion that Chardin, say, is the typical Frenchman, Michelangelo the typical Italian? I have an active distaste for such unsatisfactory counters as " French " and " Italian." But if I open a book of photographs illustrating the art of Italy, and then one illustrating the art of France, compare them I must—just as I am obliged to compare a very tall man standing by the side of one of modest stature.

When I think of Italy, in connection with the art of painting, I think of the terrific images of superhuman power associated with the names of the great Italian masters. But French painting conjures up nothing of that sort—there are no Leonardos, Giottos, Signorellis there. The impression one brought away from the " Chef-d'oeuvres de l'art français " at the Paris Exhibition was of a patient and exquisite observation of nature; sometimes more urbane than the Dutch, but quite as remote from the heroical as were the latter.

To " cultivate one's garden " is a very fine thing to do —if you do it with such consummate grace as the French. But there *are* such things as the Circumnavigation of the Globe, the ascent of Everest, the discovery of the North Pole, stratosphere flights, hunger-strikes " unto death," the investigation of disease, with all its labours and dangers. And the Sistine Ceiling is in that latter category; in the *heroic*.

The Skeleton in the Cupboard Speaks

Heaven forfend that I should be thought to assert that such adventures are *better* than the modest effort entailed in planting a gooseberry bush, or pushing the mowing-machine over the lawn. No: I am a good enough democrat to recognize that "small" and "big" are terms it is better not to use, where that can be avoided. Yet, unimportant as scale is from a certain standpoint, how can we disregard it in considering—let alone *assessing*—artistic achievement? The Sistine Ceiling is in a *different* category, at least, to what is most typical of the French School, just as the scenery of the Himalayas is *different* from (not better than) Box Hill.

In the light of their artistic output the Italians appear to us as a nation of heavyweights (to revert to Mr. Newton's classification): the French as a nation of lightweights. The British are in the "cruiser" class: but, ideologically, inclined to aspire to the Flyweight title.

It is quite ridiculous talking about nationality in the arts—it would be like introducing the sex-war into art criticism. But there is reason to suppose that Cézanne was in fact Cezanni. Must we say—*Hence his severity?* attributing to his Italian origin that rather sombre power, which used Impressionism to make a quite new and more imposing revolution—with the aid of a superbly gifted Catalan Jew?

All this is, however, going much farther than is necessary. To stick to this century, the *école de Paris* has not been a French School at all. About what is truly and typically French in painting there is a smallness, a neatness, a prettiness—something like the delightful, airy, tinkle of a French music-hall air. This is not a thing to be shunned: but also it need not be an object of obsequious imitation.—A good deal of the criticism you are about to encounter, and some that you have already met with in the course of these preliminaries, is related to the above merely geographical facts. I have demonstrated that to the economic interpretation of art I am by no means blind. Now I have shown that I am alive, as well, to the geographic factor.

NOTES AND VORTICES

I

NOTES AND VORTICES
I

"*Life is the important thing*"

I N the revolt against Formula, revolutionaries in art
sell themselves to Nature. Without nature's aid the
"coup" could not be attempted. They become quite
satisfied slaves of nature, as their fathers were of
Formula. Nature is just as sterile a tyrant as tradition,
but they do not see it. This is what happened with the
Impressionists.

Many people regard "nature" as synonymous with
freshness, richness, constant renewal, the vital principle.
"Nature" and naturalist art is synonymous they think
with "life." This idea, paraded in various forms, re-
minds one of a remark that is commonly heard—pro-
voked by the natural aversion aroused in the Plain Man
by any puzzling innovation in the arts: "You artists are
so indirect, so *intellectual*. You worry your heads about
all sorts of unimportant things, while life is there all the
time."

If you inquire of these people what they mean by
LIFE (for there are as many lives as there are people
in the world), it becomes evident that no profounder
view of life was in their mind than can be included in
the good dinner, good sleep, plenty of dough, "bit of
skirt" category.

G
97

Wyndham Lewis the Artist

"After all, *life* is the important thing!" In that trite affirmation is expressed the typical cowardly attitude of those who have failed, and are discouraged and unstrung before the problems of the Spirit; who fall back on their stomachs and the meaner satisfactions of the senses.

Nature will give you, then, grass enough for cow or sheep, any fleshly conquest you can compass. One thing she is unable to give; namely, what is peculiar to men. Such stranger stuff men must get out of themselves.

Consider for a moment however that widely-held notion, that "nature," as the majority mean it, is synonymous with Life; with inexhaustible freshness of material. It is not so at all. Nature is no more inexhaustible, fresh, welling up with invention, and so on, than is life to the average man of forty. He has his little round of habitual distractions, he is "in a groove." So is nature.

It is true, Life *is* there all the time. But a man cannot get at it except through himself. For him too, even— apart from his daily fodder—he has to draw out of himself any of that richness and fineness that is something more than and different from the provender and the contentment of the ruminant. Imagination is what *he* has. That does not belong to nature.

For the suicide, with the pistol in his mouth, "Life is there," as well, with its variety and its possibilities. But a dissertation to that effect would not influence him; on the contrary it would make him press the trigger.

For those men who look to her for support, nature does not care at all. "Life" is a hospital for the weak

Notes and Vortices: I

and incompetent. "Life" is a retreat of the defeated. It is very salubrious—the cooking is good—amusements are provided. Even a brothel is attached to the premises. A psycho-analyst is in constant attendance.

Nature is a blessed retreat, in art, for those artists whose imagination is mean and feeble, whose vocational urge is unrobust. When they find themselves in front of infinite nature with their little paint-box, they squint up their eyes at her professionally, they coo with lazy contentment as they settle down to paint her. She does their thinking and seeing for them. Of course, when they commence painting technical difficulties crop up: they sweat a bit, anxiety settles down on them. But then they regard themselves as martyrs to their calling. They are lusty workmen—that is the idea—grappling with the difficulties of their craft.

No wonder, all things considered, that painting has been discredited! Life IS the important thing, indeed, if much painting from Life that we see is the alternative. Who would not rather walk ten miles across country and use his eyes, nose, and muscles, than possess ten thousand Impressionist oil-paintings of that country-side? For as to "impressions," one impression is as good as another.

There is only one thing better than "life"—than using your eyes, nose, ears, and muscles: and that is something very abstruse and splendid, in no way directly dependent upon Life. It is no *equivalent* for Life, but *another* Life, as *necessary* to existence as is the former. This *necessity* is what the indolent and vulgar journalist mind denies it. All the accusations of "cold intellect-uality" centre round misconception of this fact.

Before terminating my bombardment of this useful phrase—of unctuous "Life"—I would forestall a confusion. I have been speaking so far of the Impressionist sensibility, and one of the arguments commonly used in defence of that sensibility, to disparage the products of a new effort in art. Daumier, whose work was saturated with reference to life, has been, for instance, used to support the imitation of Nature, on grounds of a common naturalism. But Daumier would have been no more capable of squatting down and imitating the forms of life day after day than he would have been able to copy one of his own turbulent crowds.

It was life that *moved much too quickly for anything, but the imagination* for which he lived. He combined in his art great pictorial gifts with great literary gifts: no doubt he was an impure painter, according to contemporary British standards. But it was great literature, always, along with great art. And as far as "life" is concerned, the Impressionists produced nothing that was in any sense a progress from the masterpieces of this great realist, though much that was a decadence. Take Degas: compare his washer-woman with those of Daumier. Many reproductions of Degas paintings it would be impossible, quite literally, to distinguish from photographs. You could not say whether the original of many of his racecourse scenes, or his portraits, were old photographs, or oil-paintings: and his pastels only less so because of the accident of the medium—the relative purity of their palette, and consequent habituation of the public to brighter colours, was the only useful innovation of the Impressionists. Their analytic study of light led into the Pointilliste cul-de-sac—when it was found that although *light* can be decomposed, oil-paint is unfortunately not light.

Futurism, Magic and Life

THE Futurist theoretician should have been a Professor of Hoffman Romance, and attempt the manufacture of a living being. Art, to-day, merges in Life again everywhere.

The first Futurist was Leonardo and, incidentally, an airman among Quattro Cento angels. His *Mona Lisa* eloped from the Louvre like any woman. She is back again now, smiling, with complacent reticence, as before her escapade. No one can say when she will be off once more, she possesses such great vitality. Her olive pigment is electric: so much more so than the carnivorous Belgian bumpkins by Rubens to be found in a neighbouring room, who, besides, are so big that they could not slip about in the same subtle fashion if they wanted to.

Rubens IMITATED Life: he borrowed the colour of its crude blood, he traced the sprawling and surging of its animal hulks. Leonardo MADE NEW BEINGS, delicate and severe, with as ambitious an intention as any ingenious medieval Empiric. He multiplied in himself, too, Life's possibilities. He was not content to exist as an individual artist alone, any more than he was content with art alone.—Life won him with gifts and talents.

Notes and Vortices: I

2. In Northern Europe (Germany, Scandinavia, and Russia) for the last half century, the intellectual world has developed savagely in one direction—namely, in that of *Life*.

His war-talk, his sententious elevation and much besides, the present day Italian picked up from Nietzche the German. Strindberg, with his hysterical and puissant autobiographies, his life-long tragic coquetry with Magic, extensive probing of female flesh and spirit, is the great Scandinavian figure best representing this tendency. Bergson, the philosopher of Impressionism, stands for this new prescience in France.—The north of Europe has infected the south. Everywhere now LIFE is said instead of ART.

3. By "life" is not meant in this connection good dinner, sleep, and copulation. There is rather only room for one ONE Life, in existence, and Art has to behave itself and struggle. Also Art has a selfish trick of cutting the connections. The Wild Body and the Primitive Brain have found a new outside art of their own.—The Artist pleasure-man is too naturalistic for this age of religion.

"The theatre is immoral, because a place where people go to enjoy other people's sufferings and tears" (to d'Alembert). The soft stormy flood of Rousseauism, the sentimental ghoul-like gloating of Dickens over the death of little Nell, the beastly and ridiculous spirit of Keat's lines:

> " If your mistress some RICH anger show,
> Imprison her soft hand and let her rave,
> While you feast long," etc.

disgusted in 1870 or thereabouts people whose heads were, with an honest Brummagem twist, straightly screwed into their bodies. The good artists, as well, at that time, repudiated the self-indulgent, privileged, priggish and cowardly rôle of " artist," and joined themselves to the Birmingham screws. About 1900 England emerged from Lupanars and Satanics, the Bourgeoisie having thoughtfully put Wilde in prison, and Swinburne being retired definitely to Putney.—This brings you down to the famous period where we are at present gathered, in which Humanity's problem is " to live with the minimum of pleasure possible for bare existence."

4. Killing somebody must be the greatest pleasure in existence: either like killing yourself without being interfered with by the instinct of self-preservation—or exterminating the instinct of self-preservation itself perhaps! But if you begin depositing your little titivations of pleasure in Humanity's Savings Bank, you want something for your trouble.—We all have a penetrative right over each other, to the tune of titivations lost, if not of heart blood.

· 5. Not many people have made up their minds yet as to the ultimate benefit or the reverse of this state of affairs. Some people enjoy best by proxy, some by masturbation; others prefer to do things themselves, or in the direct regular partnership of existence.—You are fiercely secretive and shy, you dislike interference: or you are the reverse. It takes all sorts to make a world. Most fine artists cannot keep themselves out of wood and iron, or printed sheets. They leave too much of themselves in their furniture. The street they live in takes too much out of them. They cannot look at a lamp-post without losing to it a fragment of themselves. As to *people*, they are pillaged by them.

For their universality a course of egotistic hardening, if anything, is required.

Buddha found that his disciples, good average disciples, required a severe discipline of *expansion*. He made them practice every day torpedoing East and West, to inhabit other organisms, and become wise and gentle. But the artist favours solitude, conditions where silence and purity are possible, as most men favour gregariousness, where they may shine, and in other people find their fulfilment.

6. It is all a matter of most delicate adjustment, between voracity of Art and digestive capacity of Life.

The finest Art is not pure Abstraction, nor is it unorganized life. Dreams come in the same category as the easy abstractions and sentimentalities of Belgian art, which they resemble.—Great Artists with their pictures and books provide Nursing Homes for the future, where hypnotic treatment is the principal stunt. To dream is the same thing as to lie: anybody but an invalid or a blackguard feels the discomfort and repugnance of something *malpropre* about it.

There is much fug in the Past—due, no doubt, to the commonplace fact that most of the ordinary Ancients neglected their persons. Realism is the cleanliness of the intellect. Actuality or "fashionableness" is the desire to be spick and span, and be a man remade and burnished half an hour gone—or that very minute.

Surprise is the brilliant and prodigious firefly, that lives only twenty minutes: the excitement of seeing him burn through his existence like a wax-vesta makes you marvel at the slow-living world. The most perishable colours in painting (such as Veronese green, Prussian Blue, Alizarin Crimson) are the most brilliant. This is as it should be. We should hate other ages: and we do not want to fetch £40,000, as if we were a horse.

7. The approximation of Art to Nature, which has been a feature of the Art of the last hundred years, and of which Impressionism was the supreme expression, tends to undermine all intellectual effort. The Artist, like Narcissus, gazing down into the mirror in the water, gets his nose nearer and nearer the surface of Life. He

will get it nipped off if he is not careful, by some Pecksniffian fish sunning its lean belly near the surface—or other lurker beneath his image, who has been feeding upon its radiance.

Reality is in the artist; the image, only, and not the reality, is to be found in life. The artist should approach life so near as is necessary for a good view, no more. The question of focus depends upon the power of his eyes, or the quality of his vision.

8. The statue of the futurist will move—it will oscillate, it will nod its head. Then it will live a little. But any idiot can do better than that with his good wife, round the corner. Nature is definitely ahead of us in contrivances of that sort. Where is the use in competing, not on our own ground but on hers? It is the problem of the *trompe l'oeil* over again.

We must remain children; less scientific than a Boy Scout, but less naïve than Flaubert *jeune*!—Nature is grown up.—*WE* could not make an Elephant.

9. With the present revolution in the pictorial and graphic arts, the figure of the Artist becomes still more blurred and uncertain. What is it the artist has and no other man; obvious pleasure, as an element, shrinking daily, or rather approximating with pleasure as it exists

in every other form of invention? Picasso has recently (in his *collages*) proved himself too amateurish a carpenter. Boot-making and joinering also occur to one, as crafts in which the artist might be proved incompetent. He is at the best only a sham engineer. Or the artist will cease to be a workman at all, perhaps, and take his place with the Composer and the Architect?

Up till now the artist has been his own interpreter, accidents of a definite medium playing a decisive part in what he did. To-day there are a host of first rate interpreters. The few men with the invention and the brains should have these at their disposal: but unfortunately they all want to be "composers" too, and their skill enables them to do very passable imitations.

Perhaps things are better as they are, however; for if you think of those stormy Jewish faces met in the corridors of the tube, Beethovenesque and femininely ferocious, upon the concert bills, or "our great Shakespearean actors," you feel that Beethoven and Shakespeare are for the student, and not for the Bechstein Hall or for the modern theatre.

At any period an artist should have been able to remain in his studio, not painting pictures, but imagining form; and provided he could transmit the substance and logic of his inventions to another man, should, without putting brush to canvas, have been recognized as the best artist of his day.

Note on some German Woodcuts at the Twenty-One Gallery

AT this miniature sculpture, the Woodcut, Germans have always excelled. It is like the one-string fiddle of the African. This art is African, in that it is sturdy, cutting through every time to the monotonous wall of space, and intense yet hale: permeated by Eternity—an atmosphere in which only the black core of life rises and is silhouetted.

The black, nervous fluid of existence in flood, forms into hard, stagnant masses in this luminous white body. Or it is like a vivid sea pierced by rocks, on to the surface of which boned shapes rise and bask blackly.

The Woodcut deals with man and objects subject to him, upon royal white, cut out in black sadness. White and Black are two elements. Their possible proportions and relations to each other are fixed.—All the subtleties of the Universe are driven into these two pens—one of which is black, the other white—with their otherwise confusing multiplicity.

It is African black. It is not black, invaded by colour, as with some modern artists in black ink, whose work is never simple enough for this blackness. But unvarying, vivid, harsh black of Africa.

109

Wyndham Lewis the Artist

The quality of the woodcut is rough and brutal: surgery of the senses, cutting and not scratching: extraordinarily limited and exasperating. It is one of the greatest tests of fineness in the arts. Where the Germans are best—disciplined, blunt, thick and brutal, with a black simple skeleton of organic emotion—they best qualify for this branch of the painter's craft.

All the things gathered here do not come within these definitions. Melzer is sculpture, too, but by suggestion, not in fact. The principle of his work is an infatuation for bronzes.

Peckstein has for nearest parallel the drawings and lithographs of Henri Matisse. Marc, Bolz, Kandinsky, Helbig, and Morgner would make a very solid show in one direction. Bolz's " Maskenfest " is a Kermesse of black strips and atoms of life. His other design, like a playing-card, is a nerve or woman, and attendant fascinated atoms, crushed or starred. Morgner drifts into soft Arctic snow patches. Marc merges once more in leaves and sun-spotting the protective markings of animals, or in this process makes a forest into tigers.

Some woodcuts by Mr. E. Wadsworth, though not part of the German show, are to be seen in the Gallery. One, of a port, is particularly fine, with its white excitement, and compression of clean metallic shapes in the well of the Harbour, as though in a broken cannon-mouth.

Customs House Officer and Artist

In France no Artist is as good as the little official who is an artist in his spare time. Rousseau the Douanier, the best of these, is better than Dérain, the best whole-time French artist. Not until French Art reaches the fresher strata of the People does it find a vigorous enough bed to flourish. There is too much cultivation, and only the Man of the People escapes the softening and intellectualizing.

There is one exception to this, namely the *crétin* or imbecile. Cézanne was *a Moron*, as Rousseau was *a Douanier*. Nature's defence for Cézanne against the deadly intelligence of his country was to make him a sort of idiot.—The limitations in such an arrangement are obvious.

2. In England it is quite the opposite. The Customs House Officer, the Policeman, the Gamekeeper, is dull.

The People (witness dearth of folk-song, ornament, dance, art of any sort, till you get to the Scottish Border or the Marches of Wales) is incapable of Art.

The Artist in England has the advantages and gifts

possessed by the Policeman or " Douanier " in France. And his position is very similar.

William Blake was our arch-subman artist. Had Blake, instead of passing his time with Renaissance bogys and athletes, painted his wife and himself naked in their conservatory (as, in a more realistic tradition, he quite conceivably might have done), the result would have been very similar to Rousseau's portraits. The English Artist (unlike the Frenchman of the people) has no artistic tradition in his blood, or so little that it is not worth bothering about. His freshness and genius is apt to be obscured, therefore (as in the case of Blake, THE English Artist—whom Michelangelo almost, but not quite flattened out) by a borrowed French or Italian outfit.

3. It is almost as dangerous in England to be a Moran, as it is in France to be intelligent.

Cézanne in England would have had to be a very intelligent fellow. (You can't be too intelligent here! It is the only place in Europe where that is the case, except perhaps Germany.)

Blake in France would have been a Douanier, a Policeman or a lavatory-attendant. It is finer to be an artist than to be a policeman or a lavatory-attendant.

SEATED FIGURE

Feng Shui and
Contemporary Form

T HAT a mountain, river or person may not "suit"
—the air of the mountain, the character of the person—
and so influences lives adversely, most men see. But that
a hill or a man can be definitely disastrous, and by
merely existing be as unlucky as hemlock is poisonous,
shame or stupidity prevents most from admitting.

A certain position of the eyes, their fires crossing;
black (as a sort of red) as sinister; white the mourning
colour of China; white flowers, in the West, signifying
death—white, the radium among colours, and the colour
that comes from farthest off: 13, a terrible number.
Such are much more important discoveries than gravitation.

The law of gravitation took its place in our common
science following the fall of an apple upon somebody's
head, which accident induced reflection.

The number 13 struck people down again and again
like a ghost, until they ceased hunting for something
human, but invisible, and discovered a Number betray-
ing its tragic nature and destiny.

Some Numbers are like great suns, round which the
whole of Humanity must turn. But people have a

H   113

special personal ordinal which for them in particular is an object of service and respect.

2. Telegraph poles were the gloomiest of all Western innovations for China: their height disturbed definitely the delicate equilibrium of lives. They were consequently resisted with bitterness. Any text-book on China becomes really eloquently scornful when it arrives at the ascendancy of the Geomancers. Geomancy is the art by which the favourable influence of the shape of trees, weight of neighbouring water and its colour, height of surrounding houses, is determined.

"No Chinese street is built to form a line of uniform height" (H. A. Giles), the houses are of unequal height to fit the destinies of the inhabitants.

I do not suppose that good Geomancers are more frequent than good artists. But their functions and intellectual equipment should be very alike.

3. Sensitiveness to volume, to the life and passion of lines, the meaning of water, the hurried conversation of the sky, or the silence of same; impossible propinquity of endless clay which nothing will counterbalance—a mountain that is a genius (good or evil) or a simple bore—such things make the artist; and the volume, quality, or luminosity of a star at birth as understood by

the astrologer, is also a clairvoyance within the painter's gift.

In a painting certain forms *must* be *so*; in the same meticulous, profound fashion that your pen or a book must lie upon your table at a certain angle, your clothes at night be arranged in a personal symmetry, certain birds be avoided, a set of railings tapped with your hand as you pass, without missing one.

Personal tricks and ceremonies of this description are casual examples of the same senses' activity, which select and arrange the impressions they receive, in order to compose a picture.

Relativism and Picasso's latest work

(Small structures made out of cardboard, wood, zinc, glass, string, etc., tacked, sewn, or stuck together, is what Picasso has most recently exhibited.)

Picasso has become a miniature naturalistic sculptor of the vast *natures-mortes* of modern life. He has come out of the canvas and has commenced to build up his shadows against reality.

Reality is the Waterloo, Will o' the wisp, or siren of artistic genius. "The real" is to the artist what "truth" is to the philosopher. The "real thing" is always Nothing. REALITY is the nearest conscious and safe place to "reality." Once an artist gets caught in that machinery, he is soon cut in half—literally so.

2. The moment an image steps out from the convention of the canvas into life, its destiny is different. The statue has been, for the most part, a stone-man. An athletic and compact statue survives. (African-Egyptian Art, where faces are flattened, limbs carved in the mass of the body for physical safety as well as for sacredness.)

You can believe that a little patch of paint two inches high upon a piece of canvas is a mountain. It is difficult to do so with a two-inch clay or stone model of one.

These little models of Picasso's reproduce the surface and texture of objects. So directly so, that, should a portion of human form occur, he would hardly be content until he could include in his work a segment of human flesh, hairs and all.

But it is essentially *NATURES-MORTES*; the enamel of a kettle, wallpaper, a canary's cage, a handle of a mandoline or mouthpiece of a telephone.

These wayward little objects have a splendid air, starting up in pure creation, with their invariable and lofty detachment from any utilitarian end or purpose. But they do not seem to possess the necessary physical stamina to survive. You feel that the glue will come unstuck and that you would only have to blow with your mouth to shatter them.

They imitate like children the large, unconscious, serious machines and contrivances of modern life. So near them do they come, that they appear even a sort of new little parasite bred upon machinery. Finally, they lack the one purpose, or even necessity, of a work of art: namely Life.

. 3. In the experiments of modern art we come face to face with the question of the *raison d'être* of Art more acutely than often before. The answer, too, comes more clearly and unexpectedly. Most of Picasso's latest work (on canvas as well) is a sort of machinery. Yet these machines are not dynamic. They neither propel, nor make, any known thing: they are machines without a purpose. If you conceive them as carried out on a grand scale, as some elaborate work of engineering, the paradox becomes more striking. These machines would, in that case, before the perplexed and enraged questions of men, have only one answer and justification. If they could suggest or convince that they were MACHINES OF LIFE, a sort of *living* plastic geometry, then their existence would be justified.

4. To say WHY any particular man is alive is a difficult business, and we cannot obviously ask more of a picture than of a man. A picture either IS or it IS NOT.

A work of art could not start from such a purpose or function as the manufacture of pen-nibs or nails. These mysterious machines of modern art are what they are in order *to be alive*. Many of Picasso's works answer this requirement. But many, notably the latest small sculpture he has shown, attach themselves too coldly to *other* machines of daily use and inferior significance. Or, he practically *MAKES* little nature-mortes, a kettle, plate, and piece of wall-paper, for example: he no longer so much interprets, as definitely *makes*, nature (and *dead* nature at that).

A kettle is never as fine as a man.—This is a challenge issued to all kettles.

The New Egos

A SOPHISTICATED savage, in a desert city, surrounded by very simple objects and a restricted number of beings, reduces his Great Art down to the simple black human bullet. His sculpture is monotonous. The one compact human form is his pictorial tom-tom.

We have nothing whatever to do with this individual and his bullet. Our eyes sweep life horizontally. Were they in the top of our head, and full of blank light, our art would be different, and more like that of the savage.

The African we have referred to cannot allow his personality to venture forth or amplify itself, for it would dissolve in the vagueness of space. It has to be swaddled up in a bullet-like lump. But we are not so constricted; Space has no terrors for us. Also the modern town-dweller of our civilization sees everywhere fraternal moulds for his spirit, the interstices of a human world.

Also he sees multitude; means of life offer themselves in infinite variety. It is a packed scene that he controls.

With him impersonality becomes a disease, or is apt to.

Parallel with this, upon the social plane, his egotism takes a different form.

Society is sufficiently organized for his ego to walk abroad. Life is no more secure in reality, or his egotism less acute, but the frontiers interpenetrate, individual demarcations are confused, interests are dispersed.

2. According to the most approved contemporary methods in boxing, two men burrow into each other, and after an infinitude of little intimate jabs, one collapses. In the old style, two distinct, heroical figures were confronted, and one ninepin tried to knock the other ninepin over at arm's length.

All of us to-day (possibly with a coldness reminiscent of the insect-world) are in each other's vitals—we over-lap, intersect, and are Siamese in our remarkable inter-locking.

Promiscuity is normal; such separating things as love, hatred, friendship are superseded by a more realistic and logical passion. The human form still runs, like a wave, through the texture or body of existence, and therefore of art. But just as the old form of egotism is no longer suited for such conditions as now obtain, so the isolated human figure of ancient Art is an anachronism.

The actual human body becomes of less importance every day. It now, literally, *exists* much less. Love, hatred, etc., imply conventional limitations. All clean, clear-cut emotions depend upon the effect of strangeness, the factor of surprise and of detachment.

Dehumanization is the chief diagnostic of the modern world of the Machine Age. One feels the immanence of some *reality* more probably than any former human beings can have felt it. This superseding of specific passions and easily determinable emotions by such uniform, more instinctively logical Passion of Life (of different temperatures, but similar in kind) is, then, the phenomenon to which we must relate the most fundamental tendencies in present art, and by which we must gauge its temper.

Orchestra of Media

Painting, with the Venetians, was like pianoforte playing as compared to the extended complicated orchestra aspired to by the Artist to-day. Sculpture of the single figure, on the one hand, and painting as a dignified accomplished game, on the other, is breaking up and caving in.

The medium (of oil-paint) is modifiable, like an instrument. Few to-day have forsaken it for the more varied instruments, or orchestra of media, but have contented themselves with violating it. The reflection back on the present, however, of this imminent extension—or, at least the preparation for this taking-in of other media —has for effect a breaking up of the values of beauty, of *de la belle peinture*, in contemporary painting. The surfaces of cheap manufactured goods—woods, steel, glass, and so forth, already appreciated for themselves, and their possibilities realized, have finished the days of fine paint.

Even if painting remain intact—as I hope it will— it will be much more supple and extended, containing all the elements of discord and of "ugliness" consequent upon the attack against traditional harmonies. The possibilities of colour—the exploitation of its discords, odious combinations of pigment, have been little exploited. A painter like Matisse has been invariably harmonious, with a scale of colour pleasantly Chinese.

Some other painters have been much more original and bitter. But there are fields of discord still untouched.

The Exploitation of Vulgarity

WHENEVER an ugly or uncomely person appeared upon the horizon of their daily promenade, Ingres' careful wife would raise her shawl, as a protective screen, and the master would be spared a sight that would have offended him. To-day it would be the other way round. The master's attention would be drawn to anything particularly hideous or banal, as a thing not to be missed.

Stupidity has always been exquisite and ugliness fine. Aristophanes loved a fool as much as any man his shapely sweetheart. Perhaps his weakness for fools dulled his appreciation of the Sages. In a perfectly "wholesome," classically-minded society, no doubt Humour would be almost absent, and discords would be scrupulously shunned, or exist only as a sacred disease with which an occasional man was blighted.

In our time we none of us desire things made entirely of gold (gold mixed with flint or glass, diamond with paste, perhaps) any more than a monotonous paradise of complete social security would be palatable. But the condition of our enjoyment of vulgarity, discord, cheapness, or noise, is an unimpaired and keen disgust with it. It depends, that is, upon sufficient health, not to relinquish our consciousness of what is desirable and beneficial.

Notes and Vortices: I

Rare and cheap—fine and poor: these contrasts are the male and female. They are the principle of creation to-day. It is found in the poetry of Mr. Pound or Mr. Eliot as much as in the paintings of the modern school.

This pessimism is the triumphant note in modern art. We affirm our robustness by embracing what is "bad taste—the beastly dross of life." A man could make just as fine an art in discords, and with nothing but "ugly" trivial and terrible materials, as any classic artist did with only the "beautiful" and the pleasant. But it would have to be a very tragic and pure creative instinct that achieved this.

Life to-day is giddily frank, and the fool is everywhere serene and blatant. Human insanity has never flowered so colossally, or at least the stupid has never before had it quite so much its own way. Our material of discord is to an unparalleled extent forcible and virulent. Pleasantness, too, has an edge or a softness of unusual strength.

Our society is very unstable. It might, at any moment, take a turn for the better, and become less vulgar and stupid. The great artist must be prepared for that eventuality. But he must not so dangerously identify himself with vulgarity as Picasso, for instance, inclines to identify himself with the contemporary phases of Nature.

There are possibilities for the great artist in the picture postcard. The ice is thin. And there is as well the perpetual peril of virtuosity.

The Improvement of Life

THE passion of his function to order and to transmute, is exasperated in the artist of to-day, by vacuity and frivolous complication, just as was the case with the initiators of Romanticism who sponsored "wild nature."

One of the most obvious questions that might have been put to any naturalist painter of the last century, or for that matter to Rembrandt or Pieter de Hooch, was this:

"Is there no difference, or if so, what difference, between a bad piece of architecture or a good piece represented in a painting: or rather, would it be a greater type of art that had for representative content objects in themselves finer?"

This kind of argument, of course, refers only to the representative painter. Rembrandt might have replied that there is no fine man or poor man; that vulgarity is as good as nobleness; that in his paintings all things were on an equal footing. But in taking Rembrandt the point may be confused by sentimentality about a great artist, about touching old beggar-men, or those "soul-paintings" of rugged crones. Similarly a sentimental issue might be raised regarding Newness, brand-newness, just as much as about age, ruins, dilapidation and dry-rot.

The interior of an A.B.C. shop we are all agreed is

126

not as fine as the interior of some building conceived by a great architect. Yet it would probably inspire a painter to-day better than the more perfect building. With its trivial ornamentation, its mirrors, cheap marble tables, insignificant spacing, it nevertheless suggests a thousand possibilities of witty treatment for the painter. Where is the advantage, then, for the painter to-day —for Rembrandt or for a Pieter de Hooch—in having a better standard of taste in architecture, in having finer dresses, and so forth?

2. If it were not that the host of cheap artisans compete in earning with the true artist immeasurably more than in a " great period " of art, and so economically things are made impossibly difficult for him, the present would be an ideal time for creative genius. Adverse climatic conditions — drastic Russian winters for example—account for work of great profundity and beauty. England, which stands for anti-Art, for mediocrity and brainlessness, among the nations of Europe, should be the most likely place for great Art to spring up. England theoretically should be ideal. It is just as unkind and inimical to art as the Arctic zone is to life.

This—where we live—is the Siberia of the mind. If you grant that, you will at once perceive the source and reason of my optimism.

Our Vortex

OUR vortex is not afraid of the Past: it has forgotten its existence.

To our vortex the Future appears just as sentimental as the Past. The Future, like the Past, is distant and therefore sentimental. The mere element " Past " must be retained to sponge up and absorb our melancholy.

Everything absent, remote—requiring projection upon the mind's dim screen, from its feeble lantern—is sentimental. The Present can be intensely sentimental—especially if you exclude the mere element " Past."

Our vortex does not deal in reactive action only, nor does it identify the Present with numbing displays of vitality. The new vortex plunges to the heart of the Present.

The chemistry of the Present is different to that of the Past. With this different chemistry we produce a New Living Abstraction.

The Rembrandt Vortex swamped the Netherlands with a flood of dreaming. The Turner Vortex rushed at Europe with a tidal-wave of light. We wish the Past and Future with us: the Past to mop up our melancholy, the Future to absorb our troublesome optimism.

With our Vortex the Present is the only active thing —Life is the Past and the Future. The Present is Art.

Notes and Vortices: I

Our Vortex insists upon water-tight compartments.

There is no Present. There is Past and Future: then there is Art.

Any moment not weakly relaxed, or, on the other hand, bloated in an optimist Nirvana, is Art. " Just life " —the *soi-disant* " reality "—is a fourth quantity, made up of the Past, the Future, and of Art.

This impure Present our Vortex despises and ignores. For our Vortex is uncompromising: we must have the Past and the Future—straight life that is—to discharge ourselves into, and to keep us undefiled for non-life, that is for Art.

The Past and Future are the prostitutes Nature has obligingly provided. Art is periodic escapes from this brothel. And the artists put as much vitality and delight into this saintliness, this jail-breaking, as most men do their escapes *into* similar places, out of the bourgeois pales of respectable existence.

The Vorticist is at his maximum of energy when stillest.

The Vorticist is not the slave of Commotion: he does not suck up to life. He lets life know its place in a Vorticist Universe!

In a Vorticist Universe we do not get excited at what

we have invented. If we did it would look as though it had been a fluke. It is not a fluke.

There is one Truth, ourselves, and everything is permitted. But we are not Templars: we are proud, for the most part handsome. We are predatory. What we hunt is *machines*. They are our favourite game. We invent them and then hunt them down.

Our Vortex is proud of its polished sides. It will not so much as hear of anything but its disastrous polished dance.

NOTES AND VORTICES

II

Art Subject to Laws of Life

THE painters have cut away and cut away warily, till they have trapped some essential. European painting to-day is like the laboratory of an anatomist: things stand up stark and denuded everywhere as the result of endless visionary examination.

But Life, more life than ever before, is the objective; some romancing of elixirs, as the rawest student will: and all professing some branch of energy. When they say LIFE, they do at least mean something complete, that can only be meant by dissociating vitality from beef and social vivacity, from good dinners and everyday acts of propagation.

Painting has been given back its imaginative horizons, without renouncing the scientific work of the Impressionists: without, also returning, beyond that, to a perpetual pastiching of old forms of art, which in a hundred ways we are unable to assimilate.

The fundamental qualities are the same, naturally, in the great art of every time. All that an artist has to learn of the art of another age is that fundamental excellence. But if he is a fine artist he contains this fundamental force and excellence, and therefore has no need to potter about museums; especially as life supplies the rest, and is short.

Wyndham Lewis the Artist

There have grown up three distinct groups of artists in Europe. The most important, in the sense that it contains the most important artist, and has influenced more men of talent than any other, is the Cubist group. Pablo Picasso, a Spaniard living in Paris, is chiefly responsible for this movement. Definitely inspired by this group, but, with their Italian energy and initiative, carried off to a quite different, more pugnacious and effervescent, point of the compass, is the Futurist group, having in Balla, Severini and Boccioni (given in order of merit, as I think) three important artists.

The third group is that formed by the EXPRES-SIONIST movement. Kandinsky is its principal exponent. We will consider these three groups critically; insisting on those aspects in which they do not finally satisfy the needs of modern painting, which were responsible for their appearance.

The IMPRESSIONISTS carried naturalism to its most photographic extreme, in theory. The ROMAN-TICS, their predecessors, would have no Jupiters and Ariadnes, and substituted Don Juan and Gretchen. The IMPRESSIONISTS, in their turn, hustled away all the Corsairs, Regency rakes and teutonic maidens, and installed their mistresses and landladies on the front of the stage. They had not, at first, much time to think of anything else, this heroic act monopolizing all their energies.

In painting, the IMPRESSIONISTS wished in

everything to be TRUTHFUL. It was the age of
scientific truth. Colour out of the earth had to imitate
the light. The pigment for its own sake and on its own
merits as colour, was of no importance. It was only
important in so far as it could reproduce the blendings
of the prism. Then there was a sort of five-mile limit
beyond which a REALIST must not move. He must
paint what is under his nose—"composition" or arrangement, that is, as understood by them—anything but
scientific unmodified transcriptions are an academicism.
Roughly speaking, your washing-stand or sideboard
must be painted, with due attention to complementaries,
and in form it must be Nature's empiric proportions and
exactly Nature's usually insignificant arrangements. If
the line becomes unruly and independent, it must be
suppressed. If the colour insidiously suggests that it
would be happier near some other colour, it must be
listened to ONLY if it belongs to a body that can, while
still appearing "natural," be shifted nearer the objects
dyed in the colour desired by its own tint. But this
would be a physical feat, very often, requiring unexampled ingenuity. Things were usually left as they
were, therefore, or hustled into careless "arrangement."
Dégas, by violent perspectives (the theatre seen from its
poulailler) or Cézanne by distortion and "bad drawing,"
escaped from æsthetic legislation. So this pedantry,
with its scornful and snobbish ukases, may be seen establishing its academies.

An analysis of Impressionism may appear unnecessary. It is not, for the following reason: one of the most

important features of the painting of the CUBISTS', and in Pablo Picasso's practice, is a tenet they have taken over wholesale and unmodified from the IMPRES-SIONISTS. Picasso, throughout the whole of his "Cubist" period has taken for starting-point in his creations, however abstract, his studio-table with two apples and a mandoline, the portrait of a poet of his acquaintance, or what not. His starting-point is identical with that of Cézanne or of Manet.

At the beginning of his "Cubist" period Picasso was momentarily diverted into a Gauguinism à la Dèrain. But after that the portraits of men with mandolines and apples and guitars succeeded each other with regularity.

As regards this aspect of Picasso's later painting, how-ever, it must be always remembered that he was first known as a painter of purely stylistic and scholarly pic-tures. They were softish El Greco or attenuated Daumier, and were "composed" with a corresponding logic and rhythm. Picasso consequently, at the outset of his Cubism, was in the same position as the Impressionists, and felt the need to react violently against the languors and conventions of his earlier period.

There was, again, the practical influence of the French. As to the rest of his Cubist colleagues, they are converted Impressionists in the main and are inclined to *cube* over their first effort, merely, instead of making a fresh start. Others, not ex-Impressionists, suffer from a form of conscience similar to his.

To describe CUBISM, then, it is useful to lead off with its least picturesque attribute, namely, that of naturalism. As to content and the character of its force-arrangements, it is essentially the same as Impressionism, largely dosed in many cases with a Michelangelizing of the everyday figure or scene. (Metzinger's "Femme à la Tasse," etc.) For the great licence Cubism affords tempts the artist to slip back into facile and sententious formulas, and escape invention.

The other link of CUBISM with IMPRESSION-ISM is the especially scientific character of its experiments. Matisse, with his decoration, preceded the Cubists in reaction against scientific naturalism. But CUBISM, as well, though in a sense nearer the Impressionists than Matisse, rejects the accentless, invertebrate order of Nature seen *en petit*. Any portion of Nature we can observe is an unorganized and microscopic jumble, too profuse and too arbitrarily distributed to be significant.

If we could see with larger eyes we should no doubt be satisfied. But to make any of these minute individual areas, or individuals, too proudly compact or monumental, is probably an equal stupidity. Finite and god-like lines are not for us, but, rather, a powerful but remote suggestion of finality; or a momentary organization of a dark insect swarming, like the passing of a cloud's shadow or the path of a wind.

The moment the Plastic is impoverished for the Idea, we get out of direct contact with these intuitive waves of power, that only play on the rich surfaces where life is crowded and abundant.

We must constantly strive to ENRICH abstraction till it is almost plain life, or rather to get deeply enough immersed in material life to experience the shaping power amongst its vibrations, and to accentuate and perpetuate these.

So CUBISM pulled Nature about with her cubes, and organized upon a natural posed model, rather than attempting to catch her every movement, and fix something fluent and secret. The word CUBISM at once, for me, conjures up a series of very solid, heavy and usually gloomy Natures Mortes—several bitter and sententious apples (but VERY GOOD WEIGHT) a usually pyramidal composition of the various aspects of a Poet or a man with a mandoline, Egyptian in static solemnity, a woman nursing disconsolately a very heavy and thoughtful head, and several bare, obviously tremendously heavy objects crowded near her on a clumsy board —a cup and saucer and probably apples.

I admire some of these paintings extremely. Only we must recognize that what produced them was an admirable enterprise and will to experiment; if we are to carry forward this burst of great initiative, we must not abate in our interrogation.

The FUTURISTS, briefly, took over the plastic and real, rather than the scientific, parts of the practice of the Cubists. Only they rejected the POSED MODEL, the imitative and static side of CUBISM, and substituted the hurly-burly and exuberance of actual life. They have not brought a force of invention and taste equal to the best of the Paris group to bear on their modification of the Cubist formulas. Their work is very much prejudiced by Marinetti's propaganda, which is always too tyrannically literary, and insists on certain points that are not essential to their painting and is in itself rather stupid. His " Automobilism " is simply an Impressionist pedantry. His War-ravings is the term of a local and limited pugnacity, romantic and rhetorical. He is a useful figure as a corrective of very genuine character. But the artist is NOT a useful figure. In fact the moment he becomes USEFUL and active he ceases to be an artist. We most of us nowadays are forced to be much more useful than we ought to be. But our painting at least should be saved the odour of the communistic platform or of the clinic either.

None of the Futurists have got, or attempted, the grandness that CUBISM almost postulated. Their doctrine, even, of maximum fluidity and interpenetration precluded this. Again, they constituted themselves POPULAR ARTISTS. They are too observant, impressionist and scientific; they are too democratic and subjugated by indiscriminate objects, such as Marinetti's moustache. And they are too banally logical in their exclusions.

The EXPRESSIONISTS finally, and most particularly Kandinsky, are ethereal, lyrical and cloud-like—their fluidity that of the psychic-picture, whereas the Futurist's is that of nineteenth-century science. Kandinksy is the only *purely* abstract painter in Europe. But he is so careful to be passive and medium-like, and is committed, by his theory, to avoid almost all powerful and definite forms, that he is, at the best, wandering and slack. You cannot make a form more than it is by the best intentions in the world. In many of his abstract canvases there are lines and planes that form the figure of a man. But these accidents are often rather dull and insignificant regarded as pieces of representation. You cannot avoid the conclusion that he would have done better to ACKNOWLEDGE that he had (by accident) reproduced a form in Nature, and have taken more trouble with it FOR ITS OWN SAKE AS A FRANKLY REPRESENTATIVE ITEM.—A dull scribble of a *bonhomme* is always that and nothing else.

In the first show held by the FUTURISTS in London, in the same way, from their jumble of real and half-real objects, a perfectly intelligible head or part of a figure would suddenly stick up. And this head or part of a figure, where isolated and making a picture by itself, you noticed was of an extreme conventionality. It discredited the more abstract stuff around it, for those not capable of discriminating where abstractions are concerned.

In addition to these three principal tendencies, in contemporary painting, there are several individuals and newer groups who are quite distinctive. Picabia, in France, reducing things to empty but very clean and precise mathematical blocks, coldly and wittily tinted like a milliner's shop-front, stands apart from the rest.

This reducing of things to bare and arid, not grandiose, but rather small and efficient, blocks of matter is on a par with a tendency in the work of several excellent painters in England, following the general Continental movement. Only in their case it is sculpturesque groups of lay figures, rather than more supple and chic mannequins. The Human Figure is, in the first place, exclusively chosen for treatment. Secondly, this is reduced to a series of matches, four for the legs and arms, one thick one for the trunk, and a pair of grappling irons added for the hands. Six or Seven of these figures are then rhythmically built up into a centralized, easily organized, human pattern. However abstracted by dividing up into a mosaic, this bare and heroic statement is the starting point. The traditionalism inculcated at the Slade School is largely responsible for this victory.

Less interesting than either Picabia or the English tendency I have just described, is the Orphiste movement. Delaunay is the most conspicuous Orphiste. Matisse-like colour, rather symbolist forms, all on a large scale, make up these paintings.

These reviews of other and similar movements to the Vorticist, appear disparaging. But in the first place this inspection was undertaken, as I made clear at the start, to show the ways in which we DIFFER, and the tendencies we would CORRECT, and not as an appreciation of the other groups brought under review, which would be quite another matter. They are definitely an analysis then, not an appraisement. Everything is analysed. Nothing is *right*, or there would be nothing further to do. We are inventors.

Vorticism is opposed above to the various groups in continental painting. I will recapitulate these points of disagreement. In so doing I can best explain the aims of Vorticism to-day.

A.

1. The Cubist, especially Picasso, founds his invention upon the posed model, or the posed Nature-Morte, using these models almost to the same extent as the Impressionist.

This practice Vorticism repudiates as an absurdity and sign of relaxed initiative.

2. HOWEVER MUSICAL OR VEGETARIAN A MAN MAY BE, HIS LIFE IS NOT SPENT EXCLUSIVELY AMONGST APPLES AND MANDOLINES. Therefore there is something requiring explanation when he foregathers, in his paintings, exclusively with these two objects.

3. We pretend that the explanation of this curious phenomenon is merely the system of still-life painting that prevailed amongst the French imitators of nature of the last century, and that was re-adopted by Picasso in violent reaction against his El Greco Athletes, æsthetic Mumpers, and Maeterlinck-like Poor-Folk.

4. We assert that the extreme languor, sentimentalism and lack of vitality in Picasso's early stylistic work was pathologic, a *tare* existing in his make-up as

positive as phthisis or anæmia, and that therefore his reaction, and the character of this reaction, should be discounted as a healthy influence in modern painting, which it is not.

5. We further assert that the whole of the art based, from this angle, upon Picasso's unique personality is suspect.

6. The placid empty planes of Picasso's later "natures-mortes" the *bric-à-brac* of bits of wallpaper, pieces of cloth, etc., tastefully arranged, wonderfully tastefully arranged, is a dead and unfruitful tendency.

7. These *tours - de - force* of taste, and DEAD ARRANGEMENTS BY THE TASTEFUL HAND WITHOUT, not instinctive organizations by the living will within, are too inactive and uninventive, and the same objections can be made to them as to the Matisse decorativeness.

8. The most abject and anæmic—the most *amateurish* —manifestation of this Matisse "decorativeness," or Picasso deadness and bland arrangement, could no doubt be found (if that were necessary or served any useful purpose) in Mr. Fry's curtain and pincushion factory in Fitzroy Square.

9. The whole of the modern movement, then, is, we maintain, under a cloud.

10. That cloud is the exquisite and accomplished, but discouraged, sentimental and inactive, personality of Picasso.

11. We must disinculpate ourselves of Picasso at once.

Wyndham Lewis the Artist

B.

1. We applaud the vivacity and high-spirits of the Italian Futurists.

2. They have a merit similar to Strauss's Waltzes, or Rag-Time; the best modern Popular Art, that is.

3. Sometimes they sink below the *Blue Danube*, and *My Home in Dixie*. Sometimes (notably in Balla's paintings) they get into a higher line of invention, say that of Daumier.

4. The chief criticism that can be made as regards them is that which can be levelled at Kandinsky: that they are too much theorists and propagandists; and that to the great plastic qualities that the best cubist pictures possess they never attain.

5. Their teaching, which should be quite useful for the public, they allow also to be a tyrant to themselves.

6. They are too mechanically reactive, too impressionistic, and just as they do not master and keep in their places their ideas, so they do not sufficiently dominate the contents of their pictures.

7. Futurism is too much the art of Prisoners.

8. Prison-art has often been very good, but the art of the Free Man is better.

9. The Present DOES influence the finest artist: there is no OUGHT about it, except for the bad artists, who should justify their existence by obedience.

10. Futurism, and identification with the crowd, is a strident hypocrisy.

BOOK-COVER

11. The Futurist is a hypocrite, who first takes himself in by the impact of his own voice: upon his stilts he is easy to shoot down.

12. To produce the best pictures or books it is possible to make, a man requires all the peace and continuity of work that can be obtained in this troubled world, and nothing short of this will serve. So he cannot at the same time be a big game hunter, a man-about-town, or a political agitator. Byron owed three-fourths of his success to his life and personality. But life and personality fade out of work like fugitive colours in painting.

13. The effervescent, Action-Man, of the Futurist imagination, would never be a first-rate artist.

14. Furthermore, the lyrical shouts about the God-Automobile, and so forth, are a cul-de-sac, surely. *The automobile would smile if it could.* Such savage worship is on a par with Voodooism or with Gauguin-Romance.

15. But there is no reason why an artist should not be active *as an artist*: every reason, rather, why he should.

16. Our point is this: the artist *cannot* have to the full the excellent and efficient qualities we admire in men of action, unless he *eschews* action and sticks hard to thought.

17. The Futurist propaganda, in its pedantry, would tend to destroy initiative and to halt development.

18. The leisure of an ancient Prince, the practical dignity required by an aristocratic function; a Guardsman stamping before he salutes his officer, the grace and

strength of animals, are all things very seldom experienced to-day, but which it might be desirable to revive.

19. Should we not revive them at once?

20. In any case, the "Monico" of Severini, night-clubs, automobiles, etc., are for the rich. May not the Rich gradually become less savage, even in England, and may not amplitude, "Kultur," and ceremony be their lot and ambition to-morrow? Perhaps it would be well to make clear to them that the only condition of their remaining rich will be if they make this effort.

21. A democratic state of mind is cowardice or muddle-headedness. This is not to deny that in certain periods the underdogs are far preferable, individually, to their masters.

22. The People are in the same position as the Automobile. They would smile sometimes, if they could.

23. But they cannot.

24. We go on calling them God.

C.

1. In dealing with Kandinsky's doctrine, and tabulating differences, you come to the most important feature of this new synthesis proposed by us.

2. I indicated in my notes some pages back the nature of my objection to the particular theoretic abstraction of Kandinsky.

3. In what is one painting representative and another non-representative?

4. If a man is not representing people, is he not representing clouds? If he is not representing clouds, is he not representing masses of bottles? If he is not representing masses of bottles, is he not representing houses and masonry? Or is he not representing in his most seemingly abstract paintings, mixtures of these, or of something else? Always REPRESENTING, at all events.

5. Now, if he is representing masses of bottles in one " abstract " picture, and masonry in another, the masses-of-bottles picture would, by ordinary human standards, be less interesting or important than the picture made up of masonry, because houses are more interesting, or rather dignified, things, for most of us, than bottles.

6. But, from the plastic and not-human point of view this deciding factor as to interest would not hold.

7. And it is no doubt wholesome, so long as the " too great humanity " of humanity lasts, for critics to insist on this detached, not-human factor, and judge works of art according to it.

8. But this again is a human and reactive reason, and for an artist who has passed the test of seriousness in weeding sentiment out of his work, and has left it hard, clean and plastic, this consideration, proper, perhaps, to the critic, need be no part of his programme.

9. For the integrity of this movement, it is necessary to face all the objections of those who would hustle us off the severe platform upon which we have taken our stand.

10. But we must not provide reasonings for the

compromisers and exploiters thrown up by any serious movement. On this dangerous ground we cannot be too precise.

11. Before proceeding, I would consider one point especially.

12. Kandinsky, docile to the intuitive fluctuations of his soul, and anxious to render his hand and mind elastic and receptive, follows this unreal entity into its cloud-world out of the material and solid universe.

13. He allows the Bach-like will that resides in each good artist to be made war on by the slovenly and wandering Spirit.

14. He allows the rigid chambers of his Brain to become a mystic house haunted by an automatic and puerile spook, that leaves a delicate trail like a snail.

15. It is just as useless to employ this sort of Dead, as it is to have too many dealings with the Illustrious Professional Dead, known as Old Masters.

16. The Blavatskyish soul is another spook which needs laying, if it gets a vogue, just as does Michelangelo. (Michelangelo is probably the worst spook in Europe, and haunts English art without respite.)

17. I return to the question of representation.

18. If it is impossible, then, to avoid representation in one form or another:

19. If, as objects, the objects in your most abstract picture always have their twins in the material world— they are always either a mass of bottles, clouds, or the square shapes of masonry, for instance:

20. Is it, under these circumstances, a fault or a weak-

ness if your shapes and objects correspond with a poetry or a sentiment, that in itself is not plastic, but sentimental?

21. I would draw your attention to two things in this connection.

22. Picasso, in his L'HOMME A LA CLARINETTE (1912)—there are more striking examples, but I have not the titles—is giving you the portrait of a man.

23. But the character of the forms (that is the now famous Cubist formula) is that of masonry. Plastically, to all intents and purposes this is a house: the colour, as well, helping to this effect.

24. The supple, soft and vital elements, which distinguish animals and men, and which in the essential rendering of a man or an animal would have to be present, even if not insisted upon, are here transformed into the stolid masonry of a common building.

25. The whole Cubist formula, in fact, in its pure state, is a plastic formula for stone or for brick-built houses.

26. It may be objected that all the grandest and most majestic art in the world, however (Egyptian, Central African, American) has rather divested man of his vital plastic qualities and changed him into a more durable, imposing and in every way harder machine; and that is true.

27. This dehumanizing has corresponded happily with the unhuman character, the plastic, architectural quality, of art itself.

28. A rigidity and simplification to a more tense and angular entity (as in the case of Mantegna) has not prejudiced their high place, or the admiration due to, several great artists.

29. It is natural for us to represent a man as we would wish him to be; artists have always represented men as more beautiful, more symmetrically muscular, with more commanding countenances than they usually, in nature, possess.

30. And in our time it is natural that an artist should wish to endow his "bonhomme," when he makes one in the grip of an heroic emotion, with something of the fatality, grandeur and efficiency of a machine.

31. When you watch an electric crane, swinging up with extraordinary grace and ease a huge weight, your instinct to admire this power is, subconsciously, pro-human. It is a pity that there are not men so strong that they can lift a house up, and fling it across a river! That is the feeling you register.

32. In any heroic, that is, energetic representations of men to-day, this reflection of the immense power of machines will be reflected.

33. But, in the first place, Picasso's structures are not ENERGETIC ones, in the sense that they are very static dwelling houses. *A machine is in a greater or less degree, a living thing. Its lines and masses imply force and action, whereas those of a dwelling do not.*

34. This deadness in Picasso, is partly due to the naturalistic method, of "cubing" on a posed model, which I have referred to before, instead of taking the

life of the man or animal inside your work, and building with this life fluid, as it were.

35. We may say, this being so, that in Picasso's portrait the forms are those of masonry, and, properly, should only be used for such. They are inappropriate in the construction of a man, where, however rigid the form may be, there should be at least the suggestions of life and displacement that you get in a machine. If the method of work or temperament of the artist went towards vitality rather than a calculated deadness, this would not be the case.

36. A second point to underline is the disparity between the spectator's and the artist's capacity for impersonal vision, which must play a part in these considerations.

37. A Vorticist, lately, painted a picture in which a crowd of squarish shapes, at once suggesting windows, occurred. A sympathiser with the movement asked him, horror-struck, " are not those windows? " " Why not? " the Vorticist replied. " A window is for you actually A WINDOW: for me it is a space, bounded by a square or oblong frame, by four bands or four lines, merely."

38. The artist, in certain cases, is less scandalized at the comprehensible than is the Public.

39. And the fine artist could " represent," or imitate, where the bad artist should be forced to " abstract."

40. I am not quite sure, sometimes, whether it should not be the Royal Academy where the severity of the abstract reigns, and whether we, who are outside the Academy, should not be conspicuous for our " life " and

" poetry "—always within the limits of plastic propriety. Life, literature, and poetry should be the prerogative of the alive.

41. To paint a recognizable human being should be the rarest privilege, bestowed as a sort of " Freedom of Art."

D.

1. The human and sentimental side of things, then, is so important that it is only a question of how much, if at all, this cripples or perverts the inhuman plastic nature of painting. If this could be detected we should know where we were. For my part I would put the maximum amount of poetry into painting that the plastic vessel would stand without softening and deteriorating: the poetry, that is to say, that is inherent in matter.

2. There is an immense amount of poetry, and also of plastic qualities as fine as Rembrandt's, in Vincent Van Gogh. But they remain side by side, and are not assimilated perfectly to each other.

3. On the other hand, Kandinsky's spiritualist values and musical analogies seem to be undesirable, even if feasible: just as, although concurring in the existence of the supernatural, you may regard it as redundant where the pragmatical or " life " values are concerned. The art of painting, further, is for a living man, and it is the art most intimately attached to life.

4. My soul has gone to live in my eyes, and like a

bold young lady it lolls in those sunny windows. Colours
and forms can therefore have no DIRECT effect on it.
That, I consider, is why I am a painter, and not anything else so much as that.

5. The eyes are animals, and bask in an absurd contentment everywhere.

6. They will never forget that red is the colour of
blood, though it may besides that have a special property
of exasperation (for we know that it was once used to
induce dementia in *louche* asylum).

7. They have a great deal of the coldness of the cat,
its supposed falsity and certain passion.

8. But they like heat and the colour yellow, because
it warms them: the chemicals in the atmosphere that are
good for the gloss of their fur move them deeply; and
the " psyche " sentimentalizes them just so much as it
may without causing their hair to drop out.

9. This being so, the moonlight and moon-rack of
ultra-pure art or anything else too pure *se serait trompé
de guichet* if it sought to move *me*.

10. But I have no reason to believe that any attempt
of this sort has been made.

11. So much for my confession. I do not believe that
this is only a matter of temperament. I consider that I
have been describing the painter's temperament.

12. When I say poetry, too, I mean the warm and
steaming poetry of the earth, of Van Gogh's rich and
hypnotic sunsets, Rembrandt's specialized and golden
crowds, or Balzac's brutal *bourgeois* imagination. The
painter's especial gift is a much more exquisite, and aristo-

cratic, affair than this female bed of raw emotionality. The two together, if they can only be reconciled, produce the best genius.

E.

1. Having gone over these points, it will be easier to see what our position is towards this question of representation and non-representation, which is at the bottom of all that we are talking about.

2. If everything is representation, in one sense, even in the most "abstract" paintings, the representation of a Vorticist and of an Impressionist are in different planets.

3. What I mean, first of all, by this unavoidable representative element, is not that any possible natural scene or person is definitely co-ordinated, but that the content, in detail, must be that of the material universe: that close swarming forms approach pebbles, or corn or leaves or the objects in some shop window somewhere in the world: that ample, bland forms are intrinsically either those of clouds, or spaces of masonry, or of sand deserts.

4. Secondly, the general character of the organizing lines and masses of the picture inevitably betray it into some category or other of an organized terrestrial scene or human grouping: especially as the logic and the geometrics at the bottom of both are the same.

5. If you are enthusiastically for "pure form" and

Kandinsky you will resist this line of reasoning; if for the London group or the Leicester Galleries you will assent with a smile of indecent triumph, soon to be chastened. We will assume consent, however, to the last line of argument.

6. In that case, why not approximate your work entirely to the appearance of surrounding Nature? —landscapes, houses and men.

7. Should you have a marked fundamental attachment to the shapes of bottles, and live in a land where there are only gourds (I live in a land where there are only " gourds," in the slang sense) then realism is unnatural —if you are quite sure your love of bottles is not a romantic exoticism, but inborn and cold conceit. But these aberrations are infrequent.

8. The first reason for not imitating Nature is that you cannot convey the emotion you receive at the contact of Nature by imitating her, but only by becoming her. To sit down and copy a person or a scene with scientific exactitude is an absurd and gloomy waste of time. It would imply the most abject depths of intellectual vacuity were it not for the fact that certain compensations of professional amusement and little questions of workmanship make it into a monotonous and soothing game.

9. The essence of an object is beyond, and often in contradiction to, its simple, its representational, truth: and literal rendering in the fundamental matter of arrangement and logic will never hit the emotion intended by unintelligent imitation.

10. Not once in ten thousand times will it correspond.

155

11. It is always the POSSIBILITIES in the object, the IMAGINATION, as we say, in the spectator, that matters. Nature itself is of no importance.

12. The sense of objects, even, is a sense of the SIGNIFICANCE of the object: not its avoirdupois, its scientifically ascertainable shapes and perspectives.

13. If the material world were not empirical and matter simply for science, but were organized as in the imagination, we should live as though we were dreaming.

14. Art's business is to show how, then, life would be: but not as Flaubert, for instance, writes, to be a repose and "*d'agir à la façon de la Nature*," in giving sleep as well as dream.

15. The Imagination, not to be a ghost, but to have the vividness and warmth of life, and the atmosphere of a dream, uses, where best inspired, the pigment and material of nature.

16. For instance, because you live amongst houses, a "town-dweller," that is no reason why you should not specialize in soft forms, reminiscent of the lines of hills and trees, except that familiarity with objects gives you a psychological mastery akin to the practised mastery of the workman's hand.

17. But there is, on the other hand, no reason why you should not use this neighbouring material, that of endless masonry and mechanical shapes, if you enjoy it: and, as a practical reason, most of the best artists have exploited the plastic suggestions found in life around them.

18. If you do not use shapes and colours characteristic

of your environment, you will only use some other characteristic of somebody else's environment, and certainly no better. And if you wish to escape from this, or from any environment at all, you soar into the clouds, merely. That will only, in its turn, result in your painting what the dicky-birds would if they painted. Perhaps airmen might even conceivably share this tendency with the lark.

19. Imitation, and inherently unselective registering of impressions, is an absurdity. It will never give you even the feeling of the weight of the object, and certainly not the meaning of the object or scene, which is as it were its spiritual weight.

20. But, to put against this, attempt to avoid all representation is an equal absurdity. As much of the material poetry of Nature as the plastic vessel will stand should be taken up into the picture. Nowadays though when Nature finds itself expressed so universally in specialized mechanical counterparts, and cities have modified our emotions, the plastic vessel, paradoxically, is more fragile. The less human it becomes, the more delicate, from this point of view.

21. There is no necessity to make a sycophantish uproar about this, or to burn candles in front of your telephone apparatus or your motor car. It is even preferable to have the greatest contempt for these useful contrivances, which are no better and no worse than men.

22. Da Vinci recommends you to watch and be observant of the grains and markings of wood, the patterns found in Nature everywhere.

23. The patterned grains of stones, marble, etc., the fibres of wood, have a rightness and inevitability that is similar to the rightness with which objects arrange themselves in life—the objects upon your work-table, for instance.

24. Have your breakfast in the ordinary way, and, as the result of your hunger and unconsciousness, on getting up you will find an air of inevitability about the way the various objects, plates, coffee-pot, butter-dish, toast-rack, lie upon the table, that it would be very difficult to get consciously and deliberately. It would be still more difficult to convince yourself that the deliberate arrangement was natural.

25. IN THE SAME WAY THAT SAVAGES, ANIMALS AND CHILDREN HAVE A "RIGHT-NESS," SO HAVE OBJECTS CO-ORDINATED BY UNCONSCIOUS LIFE AND USEFUL ACTIONS.

26. Use is always primitive.

27. This quality of ACCIDENTAL RIGHTNESS is one of the principal elements in a good picture.

28. The finest artists—and this is what Art means—are those men who are so trained and sensitized that they have a perpetually renewed power of DOING WHAT NATURE DOES, only doing it with all the beauty of accident, without the certain futility that accident implies.

29. Beauty of workmanship in painting and sculpture is the appearance of Accident, in the sense of Nature's work, or rather of Growth, the best paintings being in

the same category as flowers, insects and animals. And as Nature, with its glosses, its tinting, its logical structures, is as efficient as any machine and far more wonderful; *hand-made*, as recommendation, means *done by Nature.*

30. Imperfect hands (most artists') produce what might be termed *machine-made* stuff : as men were the first machines, just as insects were the first artists.

31. The best creation, further, is only the most highly developed selection and criticism.

32. It is well to study the patterns on a surface of marble. But the really important thing is to be able to make patterns like them without the necessity of direct mechanical stimulus.

33. You must be able to organize the cups, saucers and people, in a tea-party picture, or their abstract plastic equivalent, as naturally as Nature, only with the added personal logic of Art, which gives the grouping significance.

34. What is known as "Decorative Art" is rightly despised by both the laborious and unenterprising imitators of Nature on the one hand, and the brilliant inventors, the *equals* of Nature, on the other.

35. The "Decorative" artist (as examples, the sort of spirit that animates the "Jugend," "Rhythm,"[1] Mr. Roger Fry's little belated Morris movement) is he who substitutes a banal and obvious human logic for the

[1] "Jugend" is a German popular magazine, "Rhythm" was an art-review, of "post-impressionist" type.

co-ordination and architectures that the infinite forces of Nature bring about.

36. These exterior "arrangers," not living their work, have not even the reflected life that the photographer can claim.

37. The only people who have nothing to do with Nature and who as artists are most definitely inept and in the same box as the Romantic—who is half-way between the Vegetable and the God—are these between-men, with that most odious product of man, modern DECORATION.

F.

1. To conclude: The Whole of art to-day can undoubtedly be modified in the direction of a greater imaginative freedom of work; the philosophy of art can be restated to harmonize with the present epoch of infinitely multiplied material power.

2. But I think a great deal of effort will automatically flow back into more natural forms from the barriers of the Abstract.

3. There have been so far in European painting, Portrait, Landscape, Genre, Still-life.

4. Whatever happens, there is a new section that has already justified its existence, which is bound to influence, and mingle with, the others, as they do with each other. That is, for want of a better word, the Abstract.

5. This extremely moderate claim and view of our endeavour does not, however, suggest that it would be "equally good" to paint Brangwyns, de Lazlos, or Poynters.

6. The least and most vulgar Japanese print or Pacific Island-carving is a masterpiece compared to a Brangwyn, a de Lazlo, or a Poynter.

7. The whole standard of art in our commercial, cheap, musical-comedy civilization is of the basest and most vitiated kind.

8. Practically nothing can be done, no Public formed, until these false and repulsive standards are destroyed, and our entire system of life overhauled and put in order.

9. The technique of Science, dominating our daily life, will gradually accomplish this. We should, however, hasten it.

10. What I said about only THE GOOD ARTISTS being allowed to "represent," or do recognizable things, was not a jibe.

11. Actually, if Tube Posters, Magazine Covers, Advertisement and Commercial Art, were ABSTRACT, in the sense that our paintings at present are, they would be far less harmful to the EYE, and thence to the minds, of the Public.

12. A Bill should be passed at once FORBIDDING ANY IMAGE OR RECOGNIZABLE SHAPE TO BE STUCK UP IN ANY PUBLIC PLACE; or as advertisement, or what-not, to be used in any way publicly.

13. Only after qualifying, and the examination should

be severe, and obtaining a suitable CERTIFICATE, should a man be allowed in his work to represent Human Beings, Animals, or Trees.

14. Mr. Brangwyn, Mr. de Lazlo and Sir Edward Poynter would not pass this Board: driven into the Vortex, there would be nothing left of them but a few muddy Brangwynesque bubbles upon the surface of the Abstract.

NOTES AND VORTICES
III

Editorial " Blast " No. 2

*B*LAST finds itself surrounded by a multitude of other Blasts of all sizes and descriptions. This puce-coloured cockleshell will, however, try and brave the waves of blood. But let us pass at once to the business of this "war-number," and, first, to our attitude, as artists, to the great conflict with which this country is faced.

We will not *stop* talking about Culture when the War ends! With this rather sinister reminder of responsibilities being incurred, we may pass to this War-Number.

Germany has stood for the old Poetry, for Romance, more steadfastly and profoundly than any other people in Europe. German nationalism is less realistic, is more saturated with the mechanical obsession of history, than the nationalism of England or of France.

This paper wishes to stand rigidly opposed, from start to finish, to every form that the poetry of a former condition of life, no longer existing, has foisted upon us. It seeks to oppose to this inapposite poetry, the intensest aroma of a different humanity (that is *romance*)—the Poetry which is the as yet unexpressed spirit of the present time, and of new conditions and possibilities of existence.

Under these circumstances, apart from national partizanship, it appears to us humanly desirable that

Germany should win no war against France or England.

When we say that Germany stands for Romance, this must be qualified. Official Germany stands for the Romantic Spirit—if only the *berserk* romance of battle. But unofficial Germany has done more (in the practical field) for the movement that this paper was founded to propagate, and for all branches of contemporary activity in Science and Art, than any other country. It would be the absurdest ingratitude on the part of artists to forget this.

More than *official* Germany, however, stands for Romance. The genius of the people is inherently romantic (and also official!). We are debtors to a tribe of detached individuals—and perhaps to Romance (but we hope not too much). It is for this reason that of those two figures—our own genial and realistic barbarians on the one side, and the champions of melodramatic philosophy, on the other, we dispassionately prefer our own side!

I hope that, so far, partiality has not obtruded itself too much. We have all of us had so much cause for uncomfortable laughter, at the outset of the War, in reading articles by our leading journalists proving that "the Hun" could only see *his* side of the question—that *this* was the peculiarity of "the Hun," whereas other races always saw with their neighbours' eyes and in fact were no race at all—that we feel a certain hesitation in praising England.

Germany, in the things of the spirit, was long ago

subjugated by France, as a slight acquaintance with her best young gentlemen will convince anybody. But she still mysteriously holds out in the material and political domain; (commerce the key to this enigma, of course.)

It is commonly reported that the diplomatic impossibility of a visit to Paris, from time to time, has darkened the whole life of the Kaiser. The German's love for the French is notoriously *un amour malheureux*, as it is by no means reciprocated. And the present war may be regarded in that sense as a strange, an outrageous, wooing. The Essential German *will* get to Paris, to the Café de la Paix, at all costs; if he has to go there at the head of an army and destroy a million beings in the process. The monstrous carnival of this race's thwarted desires and ambitions is what 1914 has sprung upon us, without any really fundamental issues being involved, and yet the absolute necessity to resist and definitely end this absurd aggression from the centre of Europe.

We are, in a certain sense, then, up against such a figure as I have indicated above—namely that of the fantastic arrogance of a Prussian officer engaged in an amorous adventure. The Martinet and the Coquette are mingled. He is also a Samurai. This, anyhow, is the *commis voyageur*, the accredited personal figure, that Germany's obscure commercial forces have engaged (because of his distinguished, frank, and alluring manners), to represent them, and whom they have incidentally armed very thoroughly.

The God of Sport and Blood

A FACT not generally known in England, is that the Kaiser, long before he entered into war with Great Britain, had declared merciless war upon Cubism and Expressionism. Museum directors, suspected of Cubist leanings, were removed from their posts. Exhibitions that gave shelter to Pablo Picasso, or even to Signac, were traitorous institutions.

I expect among his orders to his troops is one to "spare no Cubist prisoners, wounded or otherwise." I am not implying that this should be a bond of sympathy between the British Nation and Cubists or Vorticists. I only mention it as an interesting fact.

This good Emperor smells the Divine, the Sober and Sheet-Iron puritanism, underneath these art-manifestations, and he feels his trade will suffer if such things are allowed to go on. What would happen to me, says he to himself, if all that chilly severity, and gay and icy violence, got the upper hand; *Naja!* We'll nip that in the bud!

No one can say the Germans are not amusing in their sport. The English have their innocuous little sports; the German has his old *war*, of course. "It is not cricket," we will admit. They are inclined to gouge out people's eyes preparatory to bowling, to prevent them making a run. If they ever play Rugby football they will take knives into the scrum with them and hamstring and otherwise in its obscurity disable their opponents. They will use red pepper, and they will confuse the other side by surreptitiously slipping a second and even a third ball amongst the players. They will be very hard to beat until the team opposed to them are armed with automatics and the goalkeeper is entrenched, with barbed wire and a machine-gun. The referee's task will be a most delicate one. He will hover over the field at a safe height, in a captive-balloon, perhaps.

Most people have what is known as a sneaking admiration for this desperateness. In fact the conditions of the primeval jungle are only thoroughly unfavourable to one type of man—the best in any walk of life. "Civilization" (which means most favourable conditions for him) is of his making, and it is by his efforts that it is maintained.

But civilization, that silken fortress he has built to dream in, is not what he dreams about. (Law and righteousness are the strongest metal available, but are a useful metal: it is only in times like ours that they become material for art.) What he dreams about is the Primeval Jungle, twelve colours and a thousand forms.

The only thing that the average man has brought away from his primitive state is admiration of ferocity. The little photographic god whose yellow orb pours out light at the upper end of the Cinema Chapel—and as he gazes, scenes of intense vulgarity and foolishness stream forth one after the other, as though they were his thoughts—this god is the civilized monkey's god. His worshippers sit in smoky silence beneath him. And really—as it is my habit to insist—this modern Jungle is not without its beauty. (What do you think of the silhouette of Manhattan, or the town of Elberfeld?) It has very little that is civilized about it. It is at present, too, replete with a quaint and very scientific ferocity.

Sport and blood are inseparable, or Sport without blood is anæmic. Sport and blood again are the rich manure all our vitality battens on.

All the bustling fun of Mr. Bernard Shaw's plays, as an instance, although he wishes war away with a disgust not sham (since he considers, with a little reason, that his plays should definitely have taken its place) are based upon sport and blood. All the thrills of humorous delight that make their ratiocination bearable for an audience, are due to the Playing with Fire, the Dancing on the Crater, that that particular boisterous humour and sporting sense of his most certainly is. Mr. Shaw, to be consistent, should be as solemn as a judge. Only if he were bitter, like Swift, would his laughter not be a contradiction. He is too genial and his humour too schoolboy-like for him to be able to disclaim ferocity. It is only the hyena in the intellectual world (such as his ecclesiastical countryman just mentioned) who can speak convincingly with disgust of Krupp.

The thinkers and Lords of the Earth, then, have fortified themselves in a structure of Law. The greatest praise the really wise Lord can bestow on the man in the street is that he is "actual," "of his time," "up-to-date." Men must be penned and herded into "their Time," and prevented from dreaming, the prerogative of the Lord of the Earth. They must also be prevented from drifting back in the direction of their Jungle. And the best way to do this is to allow them to have a little contemporary Jungle of their own. Such a little up-to-date and iron Jungle is the great modern city. Its vulgarity is the sort of torture and flagellation that becomes the austere creator.

No oligarchical politician who knew his job would ever encourage the public to be conservative, in the sense of "old-fashioned," or over-sentimental about the things of the past. The only real crime, on the contrary, would be to dream or harbour memories. To be active and unconscious, to live in the moment, that would be the ideal set before the average man.

The directors of the German Empire have shown their vulgarity and democratization as clearly in their propaganda of ferocity, as in their management of medievalism and of historic consciousness. They have broken with all other rulers, and introduced a new element into the modern world with their repudiation of tacit (much more than of explicit) regulations. From this supposedly "aristocratic" Junkerish country has come the intensest exhibition of democratic feeling imaginable. It is not *we* who are the democrats.

This contempt of law, of "humanity," is popularly supposed to be the outcome of the teachings of the execrable "Neech," and to be a portion of aristocratic "haughtiness." Nietszche was much too explicit a *gentleman* to be a very typical one. And his "aristo-cratism," so gushing and desperate athwart his innumerable prefaces, raises doubts in the mind of the most enthusiastic student: for he did not merely set himself up as the philosopher of it, but discovered simultaneously the great antiquity of his Slav lineage (although Prussia, we learn, swarms with "Neeches").

German statesmen and generals are too *thoughtful* as a class. But to become anxious is to become democratic. They have become infernally philosophic and democratic, their heads naturally not being of the strongest, or being over-stiff. There is only one sort of person who can be conscious and not degenerate. Germany's rulers do not belong to that august category.

Their wicked and low degeneration, their identification of themselves with the people, will recoil on their own heads. No wonder they have an admiration for British cunning, as they describe the good old British common-sense.

Artists and the War

SOME people are of opinion that "painters should participate in these events" by representing scenes of fighting in Flanders and France. This does not appear to me incumbent even on representative painters. If out of the campaign in Flanders any material, like the spears in Uccello's *Battle* in the National Gallery, forces itself upon the artist's imagination, he will use it.

The huge German siege guns, for instance, are a stimulus to visions of power. In any event the artist's spirit is bound to reflect these turmoils, even if only by sudden golden placidity.

The Public should not suffer its men of art to die of starvation during the war, of course (for men of action could not take their places). But as the English Public lets its artists starve in peace time, there is really nothing to be said. The war has not changed things in that respect.

Under these circumstances, artists probably should paint, fight, or make a living in some trade according to their inclination or means. Still, entirely recognizing that such a thing could never happen, I will put it to some people that, could a few hundred pounds be divided up amongst those artists who in ordinary times find difficulty in selling their work, and now must be penniless, it would be a meritorious action. There are several men to whom the disbursing of such a sum as fifty pounds would be a bagatelle. For long afterwards they would feel the refreshing repercussions of this ridiculous *largesse*; such folly always pays in the long run.

As an extenuation of the *naïveté* of these remarks, I will add that I did not suggest that a supporter of the school of Mr. Wilson Steer, or Mr. Walter Sickert, should be expected to support a young man who cubed. Such a gentleman will, on the contrary, pray—with far more conviction of hatred than mere racial difference could engender, or Ernst von Lissauer express—that the war will kill off every Cubist in Western Europe, or cripple the movement and ruin its financial supporters. He will hope, even, that Paris may be invested by the Germans on the off-chance that the great stores of Cubist pictures known to exist there might be blown up or burnt to ashes. " May the mortality amongst Cubists, Fauvists and Vorticists at the Front be excessive! May those who survive have nothing but their feet left to paint with, and may those not at the Front die of starvation." This very naturally will be the feeling of very many people here.

But there remain a handful of "amateurs" whose life, or at least whose intelligence, is bound up with the latest movements in painting. They understand the value of the courage that has impelled a small number of men, without resources in money, to fling themselves into these studies. I have launched my pessimistic cockle-shell, and I wave it a distinctly mechanical adieu.

Notes and Vortices: III

That the war will in any way change the currents of contemporary art, I do not believe. They are deeper than it. An earthquake might do so. Krupps is a poor substitute for seismic fire, as the Cinemas showed at the time of the Avezzano Earthquake. The universality of the present war will limit its influence. The Germans only should be an exception to this rule; for they are alone, and its consequences will be more marked for them. It is their war in fact. The Allies are being, in a sense, only complaisant—too complaisant naturally. Victorious elation will be sobered by the fact that, in the case of each of the Allies, the victory must go all round.

For Germany, even, defeat will hardly spell such changes as judged by another time than ours (even judged by sixty years ago) it should. The humiliation of defeat against such odds can be only a matter of abnormal popular vanity. And the German populace is a very different personality to the German military *literati*, or to the boastful and crapulous cosmopolitan, the waiter or sharper the Londoner judges Germany by. If pockets are empty for some time, Germany is used to poverty. And then it certainly becomes her better than riches. A few good artists may pop up again, when the popping of the Sekt bottles dies down for a bit.

Every reactionary—political, æsthetic, journalistic— sees all sorts of rosy possibilities in this war. You would think, to listen to them, that the splendid war army of England was fighting to reinstate the tradition of Sir Frederick Leighton, to sweep away the unorthodox splendours of the Russian Ballet, or revive a faded

Kiplingesque jingoism. But the war has not resurrected Mr. Kipling's muse but only made it creak rustily and peevishly at being disturbed; nor has it produced the faintest shadow of a new Kipling. There is only one thing that would have deeply changed England, and that would have been loss of her Empire and complete defeat. That evidently is not going to happen this time.

How this war will affect English art afterwards is chiefly, then, a question of how people's pockets will be affected. And on this question, however expert an opinion you may obtain, you never get far away from a fairly universal optimism—which, if it is justified by events, will leave conditions for art very little modified.

In any case, as to painting, since Sir Edward Poynter will not be a radiant youth after the war; Augustus John not find any new tribe of gipsies kicked up by the military upheavals, to refresh his brush: since in short the æsthetic human contents of the realm will be exactly the same, it is merely a question of whether Mr. Wyndham Lewis, Mr. Brzeska, Mr. Wadsworth, Mr. Etchells, Mr. Roberts are going to recant and paint and sculpt on the mental level of Mr. Lavery or Mr. de Lazlo; or, to put it another way, whether such a terrific interest will be awakened in Mr. Lavery, Mr. Wilson Steer, and Mr. Caton Woodville that attempts at a purifying of taste and renovation of formulas will obtain no hearing.

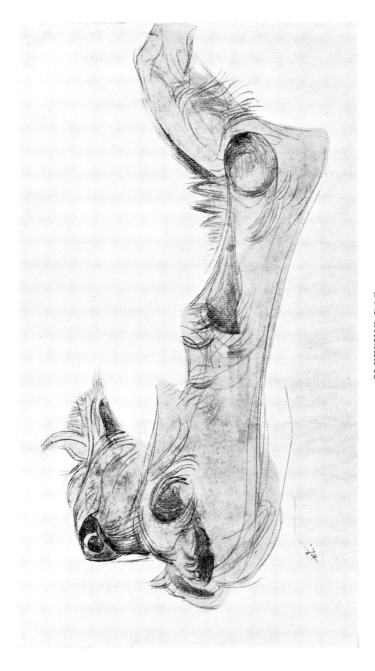

SLEEPING DOG

The Exploitation of Blood

THERE is a certain sort of blackguard that this time has produced—as an earthquake produces looters. He uses the blood of the Soldier for his own everyday domestic uses. He washes his very dirty linen in the Press with the blood of the patriot.

Scores of articles have been written in connection with Art—and I am sure that the same thing has been going on in Engineering, Plumbing, Button-making, the Church, and the Law—the purport of which, is that "this great National Event" will engulf and sweep away all that it is to the writer's business interest or inclination should be swept away. In an Earthquake or Revolution the burglar, who has long had his eye on a certain "crib"—which, however, in several raids he has been unable to "crack"—with a delighted chuckle seizes his opportunity, and pilfers at will. It is the same way with rapes and other misdemeanours.

Certain critics or journalists whose personal interests are involved on the side of lucrative and established forms of art, and who take this opportunity to attack the movement in Painting that threatens to discredit Pompierdom in this country, are an exact parallel to the burglar in the earthquake. They are what the French reporter would call a Ghoul. With many unctuous references to the "Great National Event," "before-the-War-era" separated by "gulfs" from, presumably, the orgies of vulgarity and relapses into sentiment he hopes may await us after the war, the academic partisan attempts to convince the Public that the subversive modes of painting are at an end. We are going to be purer in future and paint like Marcus Stone, Sir William Richmond, de Lazlo, the late Abbey, or Dendy Sadler.

It is conceivable that the War may affect Art deeply, for it will have a deep influence upon the mass of the people. But the reflection in Art of these changes will certainly not be in favour of any sentimentalized reactive painting; the results are not likely to please the pompier-journalist or the pompier-critic any more than the manifestation he already fumes, splutters, and weeps about.

The soldiers in France or Belgium would be the last people to relish these transactions, or to have themselves held up as intellectual crusaders. They are fighting just as animals or savages have to fight and as men have to still. We all agree in admiring the sacrifice of the patriot: but those soldiers would not suggest that their present activities should destroy the beauty of Bach's music, although it might the beauty of many a Bosche, a very different thing. If the authorities of some parochial concert-hall like to look a little askance at German music—well, that's either bestial foolishness, or a cowardliness a soldier would not admire, either. The art of to-day is a result of the life of to-day, of the appearance and vivacity of that life. Life after the War will be the same brilliant life as it was before the War.

Its appearance certainly will not be modified backwards.

The colour of granite would still be the same if every man in the world lay dead; water would form the same eddies and patterns, and the spring would break forth in the same way. The soldier would not consider it at all reasonable to assert that his most furious salvo would alter the continuity of speculation that man had undertaken, and across which this war, like many other wars, has thrown its shadow, like an angry child's.

The Six Hundred,
Verestchagin and Uccello

To the question "Why has not the present war produced fine poems, etc.? " you would reply, "What fine
poetry or literature did the Crimean War or the Franco-
Prussian War produce? " Some clever stories by Guy
de Maupassant, and Zola's *Débâcle*, were about the
only good literature 1870 has to show for itself. Tenny-
son's "Cannon to the right of them, cannon to the left
of them " is certainly not as good as Kipling's specializa-
tions in military matters, which came out of an
imperialist epoch of prolonged Peace.

Tolstoy's account of the Siege of Sebastopol is the
sort of book of notes any war or similar adventure may
be responsible for, if an observant person happens to be
among those taking part in it. The Napoleonic Wars
were different. The work of Stendhal, for instance, is a
psychological monument of that epic, in that part of it
which is the outcome of the hard and vulgar energies of
his time. But at present Germany is the only country
that harks back sufficiently to put up any show of
analogy to those energies. And she is honeycombed
with disintegration into another and more contemporary
state of mind: that is her worst enemy—not England,
as her journalists proclaim.

I have heard people say " None of our great men have

come up to scratch. Not one has said anything *adequate* about the War." Shaw, Wells, and so on, have seemingly all failed to come up to scratch. But when you consider that none of them like the War, though all are more or less agreed that England was right to fight—that they are Socialists, and do not wish to encourage and perpetuate War by saying anything "wonderful" about it, or flattering its importance—these shortcomings of theirs are hardly surprising. There is one man in Europe who must be in the seventh heaven. That is Marinetti. From every direction come to him sounds and rumours of conflict. He must be torn in mind as to which point of the compass to rush to—to drink up the booming and banging, to lap up the blood! He must be a radiant figure at this moment.

Marinetti's one and only (but very fervent and literal) disciple in this country, had seemingly not thought out, or carried to their logical conclusion, all his master's precepts. For I hear that, *de retour du Front*, this disciple's first action has been to write to the compact Milanese volcano that he no longer shares, that he REPUDIATES, all his (Marinetti's) utterances on the subject of War, to which he formerly subscribed. Marinetti's solitary English disciple has discovered that War is not *magnifique*, or that Marinetti's Guerre is not *la Guerre*.—Tant Mieux.

The dearth of "war verse" or good war literature has another reason. The quality of uniqueness is absent from the present rambling and universal campaign. There are so many actions every day, necessarily of brilliant daring, that they become impersonal. Like the multitudes of drab and colourless uniforms—these in their turn covered with still more characterless mud—there is no room, in praising the soldiers, for anything but an abstract hymn. These battles are more like anti-fights than anything we have done in this way up to now. The Censor throws further obstacles in the way of Minor and Major Verse.

Of similar interest to the question of War-Poetry is that of War-Painting. To illuminate this point I will quote an article called: "Historic Battle Pictures," in the *Daily News* of February 2nd:

"One is already asking on the continent who will be the first to immortalize on canvas or in marble the tremendous realities of 1914–15—every epoch has had its illustrious painters. Charlet drew the old soldiers of the 'Grande Armée' and the bewhiskered grenadiers; after the First Empire came the artillery officer Penguilly l'Haridon, Boissard de Boisdenier, the friend of Delacroix and creator of the *Retraite de Russie* in the Rouen gallery; Eugène Lami, Hippolyte Bellangé, Meissonier himself, Yvon, whose speciality was Zouaves, and Protais, the painter of the *chasseurs à pied*; and the names with which lovers of the priceless collection at Versailles are familiar.

"Defeat inspired the historical painters in the 'seventies. Victory will be the new theme. The famous *Les Voilà!* of Etienne Beaumetz adorns one of M. Millerand's rooms at the Ministry of War. It was Alphonse de Neuville who gave us most of the vivid details of the terrible year—the hand-to-hand encounters, the frenzied and bloody struggles of the dying, the calm portrayed on heroic countenances as death approaches, the flight and explosion of shrapnel. And after him Edouard Détaille, whose *Défense de Champigny* is one of the greatest battle-pictures of any country or any age.

A NEW VERESTCHAGIN?

" The campaign of last year and this! What masterpieces must be born! "

It is useful to quote this article because, in its tone, it reproduces the attitude of the Public to War-Art. It also supplies us with an eloquent catalogue of names.

No critic of let us say a leading Daily Paper would pretend that the " Meissonier himself " of this article, or " Yvon whose speciality was Zouaves," were very good painters; any more than to-day they would insist on the importance of Mr. Leader. Edouard Détaille, whose " *Défense de Champigny* is one of the greatest battle-pictures of any country or any age " is, in circles who discuss these matters with niceness and sympathy, considered, I believe, not so good as " Meissonier himself."

Shall we conclude from this that War-painting is in a category by itself, and distinctly inferior to several other kinds of painting? That is a vulgar modern absurdity:

painting is divided up into categories, Portrait, Landscape, Genre, etc. Portrait being "more difficult" than Landscape, and "Battle Pictures" coming in a little warlike class of their own, and admittedly not such Very High Art as representations of naked women.

Soldiers and War are as good as anything else. The Japanese did not discriminate very much between a warrior and a buttercup. The flowering and distending of an angry face and the beauty of the soldier's arms and clothes, was a similar spur to creation as the grimace of a flower. Uccello in his picture in the National Gallery formularized the spears and aggressive prancing of the fighting men of his time till every drop of reality is frozen out of them. It is the politest possible encounter. Velasquez painted the formality of a great treaty in a canvas full of soldiers. And so on.

There is no reason why very fine representative paintings of the present War should not be done. Van Gogh would have done one, had he been there. But Derain, the finest painter to my knowledge at the Front, will not paint one. Severini, on the other hand, if his lungs are better, and if Expressionism has not too far denaturalized his earlier Futurist work, should do a fine picture of a battle.

Gaudier-Brzeska, the sculptor, whose Vortex from the trenches makes his sentiments on the subject of War and Art quite clear, is fighting for France, but probably will not do statues afterwards of either Bosche or Poilu: to judge from his treatment of the Prussian rifle-butt.

Marinetti's Occupation

THE War will take Marinetti's occupation of plat-form-boomer away. The War has for the moment exhausted interest in booming and banging. I am not indulging in a sensational prophecy of the disappearance of Marinetti. He is one of the most irrepressible figures of our time; he would take a great deal to discourage. Only he will have to abandon War-noise more or less definitely, and this I feel will be a great chagrin for him.

If a human being was ever quite happy and in his element it was Marinetti imitating the guns of Adrianople at the Doré gallery with occasional answering bangs on a big drum manipulated by his faithful English disciple, Mr. Nevinson, behind the curtain in the passage. He will still be here with us, the War finished. Only there will be a little something not quite the same about him. Those golden booming days between Lule Burgas and the Aisne will be over for ever.

There is a *passéist Pathos* about this thought. It has always been plain that as artists two or three of the Futurist Painters were of more importance than their poet-impresario. Balla and Severini would, under any circumstances, be two of the most amusing painters of

185

our time. And regular military War was not their theme, as it was Marinetti's, but rather very intense and vertiginous Peace. The great poets and flashing cities will still be there as before the War. But in a couple of years the War will be behind us.

The Art of the Great Race

ALL times equally have witnessed what appeared to be a certain snobbish energy of Nature. Like a suburban Matron, men think they catch her plagiarizing their fashionable selves. They laugh faintly with a distracted vagueness, or they tug at their moustaches, and slowly shake their bottoms and trail their feet, according to the period. But Oscar Wilde publicly denounced her. In following the social syntheses that masters of fiction throw up in their works, flesh and blood appears to have transformed itself, and become a tributary, blood-relation, and even twin of the shadow.

So Wilde eventually accused Nature point-blank of plagiarism. "Nature imitates Art, not Art Nature." Let us take up this old æsthetic quip, and set ourselves the light holiday task of blasting it indolently away.

First, however, it is advisable to become fixed upon one point. Artists do not, *qua* artists, influence breathing humanity plastically. Bach moulded the respirations of his art and modified its organs; but the behaviour or appearance of the young composer was moulded by other and less precise hands. It is the human and literary side of plastic genius that affects contemporaries in this palpable way. In ideas, it is the reform element, and not the deep element (which is monotonous) that we find suddenly flinging up a host of new characters.

Goethe, with a book, set free the *Weltschmerzen* of the suicidal Teuton. The razors flashed all over the Teuton world. The pistol-smoke went up from every village. He had pressed a nerve of a definite type of Teutonic man, and made a small desperate sub-race suddenly active.

Bach stepped with the blank anonymity of Destiny. He squabbled with some little nobody, got a job with certain acumen in spite of some other somebody's efforts. But he did not turn Humanity into any new and equally futile way. No grocer talked more or less of his soul, or of his German soul, because of the music of this master.

Painting, with its persistently representative element, has always had in the modern world more ethical effect. The artist has the same moral influence as the dressmaker. A bird-like hat in process of time produces a bird. Painting to-day, in renouncing more and more the picturesque and representative element, escapes also the embarrassments of its former popular influence, and the dangers of more and more plastic compromise.

To begin with, then; about these creatures brought into being by the fiat of some artist. To-day that does not happen to the same extent as formerly: our stage is too big, and too complex. The " Rossetti woman "—the most famous of these types—was a phenomenon of the sleepy mid-Victorian literary village. The " John young woman " (the gipsified and picturesque projection of the romantic genius of Mr. Augustus John) was the last of these *tribes* suddenly thrown up by an artist. Probably there will be no more. But however that may be, such tribal units are not the issue of a pure fount apart.

What shall we say comes from a pure fount of art?

Nothing, according to our notion. The purest art is not tyrannic but is continuous, and Tourgeniev's *Six Unknown* always existed and always will exist. They make no fuss. They do not wear the uniform of a sect or faction. They are anonymous and not recognizable in the throng.

Tourgeniev, when asked whom he wrote for, said " for the Six Unknown." Tourgeniev himself was merely one of them. He wore more lightly than any of his countrymen the overpowering psychic accoutrements that are the Russian-spirited national costume. He was an independent and permanent being, not a temporary (or chronologic) half-being.

Shakespeare, again, was a mighty mirror: his figures accumulated by a natural process, and for no reason. They dragged all sorts of burdens of power with them. They were immense outcasts, silhouetted at last in the sunshine of his plays. He whistled Music Hall airs as he worked. Shakespeare was one of the Six Unknown; though well enough known to the world. He was one of the easily numbered race who were the first and only certainly future men, who are unknown to each other. His effect on morals and appearances was as non-existent as Bach's.

Montaigne, Shakespeare's master, gives, in his books,

a useless melancholy. Art is not active; it cuts away and isolates. It takes men as it finds them, a particular material, and works at it. It gets the best out of it; and it is the best that it isolates. The worst is still there too, to keep the man in touch with the world, and freer because of the separation. Perfect art insists upon this duality, and develops it. It is for this reason, and in this way, that the best art is always the nearest to its time, as surely as it is the most independent of it. It does not condescend to lead. But often, an artist, simply because he takes hold of his time impassively, impartially, without fuss, appears to be a confirmed protester; since that actuality seems eccentric to those who are defective in will.

Another question, transpiring naturally from this first one, is whether the possession of this immediate popular influence is as surely the sign of the inferior artist as an eminence and unchallengeable power like Shakespeare's, combined with that large uncanny effacement, is the mark of the finest artist? That question can be best answered at the end of this essay.

Before the blarney with Nature of the æsthete, lending itself to mock diagnosis, could be used, it was necessary to establish the value of this influence to which the æsthetic referred.

As to Nature's unoriginality then and her supposed imitation of the artist's handiwork. How long would it take Nature, in the form of her human children, to make a replica in flesh of the artist's work? She would have to begin imposing her will on the subject chosen very young. But in the case of the alleged imitation of Rossetti's type of woman by Nature, Rossetti in his young days was not known to Nature at large. It is at the moment of the artist's fame that these imitations suddenly appear. They appear at once on all hands like mushrooms. And if a painter of this human and political description be unknown one day and celebrated the next, these simulacra in flesh of his painted figures will appear as though by magic. Or such has been the case in the periods propitious for the creation of such romantic sub-species.

All goes to prove the pre-existence of these types; and that the artist only calls together, and congregates, from the abysses of common life, a hitherto scattered race, in exalting one of its most characteristic specimens into a literary or artistic canon, and giving it the authority of his special genius. Miss Siddall languished behind the counter in the Haberdasher's in Leicester Square long before the young Italian could have influenced her, or Nature have got to work on her with plagiaristic ardour. The "long necks" that Oscar Wilde speaks of, witnessed to the ideal tendency of their owners' minds centuries before Rossetti repeated them in his pictures.

I see every day in a certain A.B.C. shop at least three girls who belong to a new and unknown race. They would furnish an artist looking for an archetype with the model of a new mankind. And it would be as individual and apparently strange as that genre of Englishwoman that attracted Rossetti.

The " John young lady " poured burning oil upon the

heads of plumed assailants from the brand-new walls of Fourteenth Century castles. She was a wild camp follower in the rear of Pictish armies. The Beardsley vamp was a cause of scandal to our remotest forefathers. The Rossetti woman stretched her long, swoony Saxon neck up to be kissed long before the last Stuart sovereign died. These genres have always existed. On the promotion of their type to a position of certain consideration in art circles, and gradually in wider spheres of life itself, they all emerge from their holes, and walk proudly for a decade —or several, according to the vitality of their protector —in the public eye. We have still amongst us here and there survivals of a gentler fashion.

If you are not one of the Six, corresponding in the things here written about to the Six Hundred golden beings of the West which the Statue of Liberty sheds its rays on; if you are of an as yet uncharted race, you will some day perhaps have the opportunity of testing for yourself the validity of these assertions. Imagine yourself going out one morning, and by the hesitating yet flattering glances of your fellow citizens, and various other unmistakable signs, becoming aware that your day has come. Some artist, you at once recognize— perhaps with shrinking—is busily employed in making your type of beauty prevail. Or you believe yourself, with your *chapeau melon* and your large, but insignificant library, beyond the reach of the Creator. But the Wet Nurses of Dickens' time thought the same. The Suburbs never dreamt of being conscripted by any Mr. H. G. Wells that the old Earth could make—they are now most drab but famous armies. If numbers were the decisive factor, they would certainly rout any host brought against them, except those gathered by a Religion. They are almost the English Nation—the hosts of the Little Man.

The race that some of these political æsthetic creators call into life, overruns a city or a continent, a veritable invasion come out of the ground; risen in our midst, with the ferocious aspect of the mailed and bedizened bodyguard of a barbarian invader. Others come to us beneath the aegis of some perfumed chief, with mincing steps and languid masterfulness. The former have at times been observed to refine themselves amongst the gentle influences of the town, though preserving their outlandish costume and nomenclature; the latter have been known to learn a certain roughness from the manners of newer in-vaders. That debile and sinister race of diabolic dandies and erotically bloated diablesses and their attendant abortions, of Yellow Book fame, which tyrannized over the London mind for that *naughtiest* — though not wickedest—of all English decades, gradually withdrew from the capital, not to the delicate savagery from which it was supposed to come, but certainly to a savage clime. In Germany some years ago I observed in youthful state many figures of that naughtiest of British stocks, as vigorous and vampire-like as when the ink was still un-dried upon Smithers' catalogues.

When a man portrays and gives powerful literary ex-pression to a certain type in a nation and *milieu*, he attracts to him that element in the race which he symbolizes. That, in fine, is what occurs. These movements are occasionally accompanied with an enthusiasm that resembles a national awakening or revival: in such instances, of a race within the Race. In the case of a great writer, when it is usually a moral type that is celebrated, the commotion may be considerable. But when it is the personal appearance which is in question, the peace may be definitely disturbed.

Every nation is composed of several or many distinct types or groups. Each demands expression just as each nation does. Each of these psychic groups has, like the classes, a psychology of its own, if not a vocabulary. These groups are independent of class, too. When such freemasonries are touched into life, they exist without reference to their poet. Some creators, in fact, find themselves in the position of the Old Woman Who Lived in a Shoe. Their progeny may even turn out to be a race of cannibals and proceed to eat their poet.

There is in every nation an essentially exotic element. But this "foreign" element is usually the most energetic part of the community; that side on which the race is destined to expand and renew itself. The English have never been so insular and "English" as at the present moment. When a people first comes in touch with neighbouring races, its obstinate characteristics momentarily become more pronounced than ever. A man travelling abroad for the first time becomes conscious of his walk, his colour, his prejudices. Such peculiarities under the stress of a novel self-consciousness, become more marked. So it is with a people. In an age of ripe culture the different elements or races within a people are harmonized. It is then that the *universal* artists peacefully flourish—the universal artist, is, in fact, in the exactest sense national. He gathers into one all the types of humanity at large that each country contains. We cannot have a universal poet when we cannot have a national one.

At present, in our Press-poisoned imperialist masses, which we call nations, where all art and manners jostle in hopeless confusion, with insane waste of vitality and health, with impossibility of conviction, the types to which I am here drawing attention are more than ever sharply defined.

One may observe, in one person's flat, the taste of Paris struggling with that of Ealing; in another's next door, a scheme of decoration of the peasant-industry variety; across the street, a dwelling that is an attempt at a miniature Palladian country-house. This currently goes under the name of "individualism." Hardly anywhere is there a sign of an "actual" and contemporary state of mind or consciousness. There is not even an elementary climatic and temperamental rightness in current popular art. All this is because the "present" is chronically immature.

But there are among us some Primitives of a future equilibrium. I have praised in this paper the vulgarity and confusion of our Time. When all these vast communities have disintegrated; when economic conditions have adjusted themselves, and standards based on the necessities of our national genius have been fixed, there will be a period of balance again.

But when the balance comes, the conditions are too favourable. This Russian winter of inanity and indifference, produces a consciousness that evaporates in the Southern brilliance of good conditions. The only person who objects to uniformity and order—One art, One life —is the man who knows that under these conditions his "individuality" would not survive. Every real individuality and excellence would welcome conditions where there would be a hierarchy of power and vitality. The Best would then be Free. Under no other conditions is any true freedom at all possible.

When the races within the race (to return to them) are asserting themselves, then the Great Race is usually rotten or in bondage. And, then, perpetual local and picturesque outcroppings are phenomena of a period of transition. Often considerable poets are found at the head of these revolutions. But their art is hardly ever Great Art, which is the art of the Great Race, or an art foreshadowing it. The art of the Great Race is always an abstract and universal art, for it is the result of a welding of elements, of a synthesis of life.

In this connection, it is curious to remember that Rossetti was an Italian. That testifies to the disruption and unreality at the root of this consciousness more vividly than anything else. Rossetti, the foreigner, found in England that intensely English type of feminine beauty, the " Rossetti woman," and painted her with all the passion of the exotic sense. Yet he was supposed to have invented her. It was as if Paul Gauguin had been credited with the invention of the Tahitian belle.

One man living in a cave alone can be a universal poet. Solitude in fact is art's atmosphere, and its heaven is the Individual's. The abstract artist is the most individual, just as genius is only sanity. It is the Individual, however, and not our contemporary "individualist," whose individualism consists in saying Booh! when you say Bah! Everyone should be obliged to say Booh! only or Bah! only. And it would then depend upon the intensity of expression—the strength of his lungs, or the delicacy of his ear—alone, that would enable one man's Booh! to be more compelling than another's.

The National Poet is a folk poet. But the politically souled Artist found at the head of local revivals or type-awakenings is also a sort of Folk Poet. This is his intellectual secret.

Folk Art, along with Music Hall Songs, and Viennese Waltzes is very seducing and certainly the next best thing to the high art of the great masters. (The officially " serious " artists of any time, who practise *le grand Art*, come well below *My Home in Dixie*.) These " folk-artists " form that department of art that is attached to life, and are of the same order and importance as the decorations upon vases or carpets, ornaments, and things of use. They are the ornament and current commentary of everyday life, the beer song of the Hiring Fair, the dance of the Fiesta, the madrigal, or the war-song.

The only exactly and narrowly National Art is folk-art. All Nationality is a congealing and a conventionalizing, a necessary and delightful rest for the Many. It is Home, definitely, with its compromises and domestic routine.

The great National Poet, like Shakespeare, is not national at all in that limited sense. The Germans speak of "our Shakespeare," and play him and understand him far better than we do. But Shakespeare is not more German than English. Supposing English people became more used to using their intelligence and grew to care more for art, they would not nationalistically *possess* Shakespeare any more for that. They would play him and read him as much as the Germans, and there would be a National theatre. But a truer name for this would be Universal Theatre. Only in a universal theatre could Shakespeare be adequately staged. No country can be possessive about a man like that, although Will may have been a gentle Englishman.

Modern Caricature
and Impressionism

THE ineffectiveness of caricature, especially the English variety, is the direct result of Impressionism. The naturalistic method, with its atmospheric slop and verisimilitude, makes a drab academy study of the best comic notion. *Punch* is a national disgrace, from the standpoint of drawing. No great comic paper of France, Germany, Italy, or Russia could possibly contain anything so spiritless and silly as are, without a single exception, the drawings in any number of *Punch*. If you compare the political cartoons of the war printed side by side, where a *Punch* cartoon turns up, its rustic and laborious mirth, combined with the vilest and dullest standard of drawing, appals you. And England is famous for its comic spirit throughout the world!

On the other hand, scattered up and down papers like the *London Mail*, *Sketch*, *London Opinion*, are excellently telling drawings interpreting current events. "The German leaving Kiou-Chou," his "place in the sun" having got too hot for him, is a good example. Why does not some enterprising newspaper-proprietor gather all this scattered talent and wit together, and start an important Comic Paper to supersede *Punch?* It would be certain to pay. It is such an obviously sound enterprise that it is difficult to see why it has not been done up to the present.

To reform *Punch* from within would be impossible. It would be like an attempt to re-sculpt the Albert Memorial. There is no harm whatever in *Punch*, any more than in any other Victorian institution. But that it should represent England to-day is an absurdity.

Whether it is an abstract figure of Britannia, or of a Sportsman, or a Territorial, the method employed by the degenerate *Punch* cartoonist is always the same. A suitable model must be sent for, dressed and stuck up, and carefully copied in the required attitude. That young woman—"artist's model"—within a radius of five miles of the cartoonist's studio who, draped with a Tadema property-robe, may approximate to Britannia, must appear as our most authoritative conception of that august abstraction.

We are not attacking the method of working from Nature. If that is done without any literary objective, and only from interest in the object *as an object*, the result can be such as is found in Van Gogh, Manet, or Cézanne. This at least is respectable and inoffensive, and by accident or through the natural resources of genius, can become completely satisfying.

England produced in the matter of imaginative drawing in the Nineties, one very important figure, who had a very great influence, especially on the drawings in the best comic papers abroad. It was admitted that the influence of Aubrey Beardsley was greater than that of any other European artist who had appeared for many years. But except for ridiculously literal imitations, his effect upon graphic art in England was extremely slight.

It was entirely the *literary* side of his genius, which was the least important and which contained all his contemporary "decadent" paraphernalia, that was mainly seized upon by the English draughtsmen.

Beardsley's several versions of John Bull would be a good model to set against the endless tiresomeness and art school banalities of some Albion or Lord Kitchener by Bernard Partridge. On those lines you could get an English Comic paper which would compare not unfavourably with *Simplicissimus* or with *Le Rire*.

Or compare even John Tenniel's "Dropping the Pilot" with the latest dense attempt to revive the success of that admirable old cartoon.

Life has no Taste

THE best artist is an imperfect artist.

The PERFECT ARTIST, in the sense of "artist" *par excellence*, and nothing else, is the dilettante or taster.

"Pure art," in the same way, is dilettante art: it cannot be anything else.

It is, in fact, rather the same thing to admire *everything* in Nature around you—match-boxes, print dresses, ginger-beer bottles, lamp-posts—as to admire every æsthetic manifestation—examples of all schools of art.

Taste is dead emotion; or mentally-treated and preserved emotion. Taste is also a stronghold against barbarism of soul.

You should be emotional about everything, rather than sensitive.

You should be human about *everything*: inhuman about only a few things.

Taste should become deeper and exclusive: definitely a *stronghold*—a point and not a line.

Notes and Vortices: III

AMERICAN ART

American art, when it comes, will be Mongol, in-human, optimistic, and very much on the precious side, as opposed to European pathos and massiveness.

The characteristics of the best art so far produced north of Mexico and south of the Pole all point in the same direction.

Red-Indian

Edg. Allen Poe	(series of sincere and solemn bluffs. Heinesque lyrics, monotonously absorbed in the technique of romantic emotion.)
Whistler	(Nocturnes, lithographs, "butterfly" fastidiousness.)
Henry James	Ghost psychology of New England old maid: stately maze of imperturbable analogies.
Walt Whitman	Bland and easy braggart of a very cosmic self. He lies, salmon-coloured and serene, whittling a stick in a very eerie dawn, oceanic emotion handy at his elbow.
Ezra Pound	Demon pantechnicon driver, busy with removal of old world into new quarters. In his steel net of impeccable technique he has lately caught Li Po.
	Energy of a discriminating Element.

Wyndham Lewis Vortex No. I
Art Vortex: Be Thyself

You must talk with two tongues, if you do not wish to cause confusion.

You must also learn, Circassian horseman-like, to change tongues so to speak in mid-career without falling to earth.

You must give the impression of two persuaders, each standing on a different hip—left hip, right hip—with four eyes vacillating concentrically at different angles, upon the object chosen for subjugation.

There is nothing so impressive as the number TWO.

You must be a duet in everything.

For the Individual, the single object, and the isolated, is, you will admit, an absurdity.

Why try and give the impression of a consistent and indivisible personality?

You can establish yourself either as a Machine of two similar fraternal surfaces overlapping:

Or, more sentimentally, you may postulate the relation of object and its shadow, for your two selves.

There is Yourself: and there is the external world, that fat mass you browse upon.

Notes and Vortices: III

You knead it into an amorphous imitation of yourself —inside yourself.

Sometimes you speak through its huskier mouth, sometimes through your own.

Do not confuse yourself with it, or weaken the esoteric lines of fine original being.

Do not marry it, either, to a maiden.

Any machine then you like: but become mechanical by fundamental *dual* repetition.

For the sake of your good looks you must become a machine.

Hurry up and get into this harmonious and sane duality.

The thought of the old body-and-Soul, Male-and-Female, external duet of existence, can perhaps be of help to you, if you hesitate still to invent yourself properly.

No clear-cut lines, except on condition of being dual and prolonged.

You must catch the clearness and logic in the midst of contradictions: *not* settle down and snooze upon an acquired, easily possessed and mastered, satisfying shape.

We artists do not provide wives for you.

You have too many as it is.

THE CALIPH'S DESIGN

Architects! Where is your Vortex?

PREFACE

Preface

I HAVE assembled round my parable a series of short articles and notes. These are all related to the idea which this parable embodies. The second half of this pamphlet deals with that section of modern painting which stands to our revolutionary epoch as a legitimate offspring of great promise, but which through certain weaknesses falls short of what such a relationship demands. These weaknesses in the painting in question seem to me a diagnosis of fatigue. Such shortcomings should be defined and isolated, lest they infect succeeding generations.

The spirit that pervades a large block—cube, if you like—of the art of painting to-day is an almost purely art-for-art's-sake dilettantism. Yet you find vigour and conviction: its exponents, Picasso, Matisse, Dérain, Balla, for example, are very considerable artists, very sure of themselves and of the claims of their great craft. So you get this contradiction of what is really a very great vitality in the visual arts, and at the same time a certain sceptical discouragement, a misuse of that vitality. How far is this the result of the obtuseness and the difficulties set up by the scratch-Public upon which painters have to-day to rely? How far is it the result of a combination of the speculative agility of the dealer and of a mere technical agility among artists?

Then the pleasant amateur (the vindictive failure of more settled and splendid ages) sees his chance. He drops down into the arena from among the audience, flourishing a red pocket handkerchief. By his pranks—some pseudo-professional, skipping like any Espada; some an impudent buffoonery—he adds to the general confusion. The little bull laughs to see such sport; the crowds of degenerate and dogmatic Toreros, popping with pedantic mirth, tumble in imitation of the new-fangled clowns; the women hurl expressionist javelins torn from their hats, and transfix the bottoms of the buffoons and the billycocks of the banderilleros! The little bull, at first amused, as the Corrida ends, dropping with boredom, goes quickly aside and falls asleep. A pale urchin with side-whiskers and a hooked nose stands watching him with a dull grin. Is not that a fairly accurate picture of the bloody spectacle that we, Public and Performers, present?

It is evident that the Public is at fault. Why does it not insist on a better type of Bull in the first place, a more substantial type of art, that would be capable of driving all but the best performers from the arena? If the public cannot think of a new type of Bull at the moment, and is not willing to take a new brand of beast that we are rearing on trust, let it at least put into the Circus some fine animal from Nineveh, or rake the Nile valley for a compelling and petulant shape.

But the painter or sculptor, too, might give a hand, and the (I hide my face! I am almost too ashamed for him to utter his name) the Architect! Why does not the

The Caliph's Design: Preface

Architect (and every time I have to use that word I shall feel like apologizing to you for mentioning such a poor, forgotten, lamentable creature!)—why does not this strange absentee, this shadow, this Ghost of the great Trinity, Sculpture, Painting, and Architecture—for which I have substituted Design, from a feeling of understandable diffidence—*why does he not cheer us up by building a New Arena?* Constructing—around the new Bull that we are breeding, our new very active Art—a brand new and most beautiful Arena?

That question, I know, will remain unanswered. It was tactless of me to have asked it. But I have thought of a way out for the Architect. It has often been suggested of late that the Architect might become a department of the Engineering industry. But why should he take all his bric-à-brac over to that clean, fresh, erect institution across the road? Rather let the Engineer and the Painter fix up a meeting and talk over the sadly-involved affairs of this decayed concern. Of all the scandals in the Art-World, the most discreditable by far is the pass to which Building has come. The Painter and the Engineer could buy out the Architect, go into partnership, and produce what would neither be a world of boxes on the one hand (as it would be if the Engineer controlled house construction—*vide* skyscrapers), nor of silly antique fakes on the other, as happens when the Architect has his sweet way. Let us divide up this ramshackle empire of Architecture. We could even dispense with a Caliph. There need not be any bloodshed. It is a not quite irrational world!

Wyndham Lewis the Artist

Now, of all painters who have ever breathed ponderously under a copper-coloured Vlaminck sky, the Cubist painters of Paris, the quantities of ponderous painters to be found cubing away in that city, are the best fitted for this rôle. It is they who should supersede, in a practical liaison with the Engineer, the virtually extinct architect.

The energy at present pent up (and much too congested) in the canvas painted in the studio and sold at the dealer's, and written up with a monotonous emphasis of horror or facetiousness in the Press, must be released. It must be used in the general life of the community. Thence, from the life outside, it will come back and enrich and invigorate the Studio.

When accepted at all, modern painting is accepted as a revolutionary oasis in the settled, dreary expanse of twentieth century commercial art. It is recognized as a place where bright colours, exciting and funny forms, a little knot of extravagant people, are to be encountered, which it is amusing sometimes to visit. It was the same with the Impressionists. Whistler found himself beleaguered and interfered with in the same way: Gauguin and Van Gogh had the same experience.

Listlessness, dilettantism is the mark of studio art. *You must get Painting, Sculpture, and Design out of the studio and into life somehow or other*, if you are not going to see this new vitality desiccated in a pocket of inorganic experimentation. Then you must put the Architect, as he drags out his miserable if well-paid existence to-day, into the dustbin, *and close the lid*.

When in the course of this pamphlet I speak of the

The Caliph's Design: Preface

"movement in painting," or Modern Painting, I refer to the sort of painting done by such diverse masters as Dérain, Matisse, Picasso, Kandinsky, or Klee. These painters represent a single æsthetic current in the sense that they are none of them Impressionists, have all one synthetic intention or another, and are all roughly related in time and in enterprise. The complete non-representative character of Kandinsky's painting, or the weightiness and palpable logic of the Cézanne-evolved Cubist, belong really to the same impulse in art as do Dérain or Matisse, who are neither Cubist nor Abstract. Klee's mixed phantasy is the same.

There are bound to be within this great general movement many experiments and enterprises attempting to attract all the rest in one direction or another. One of the most powerful of these and one that has held the stage for the last few years, is the Nature-morte development of a group of Cubist painters. Picasso, Braque, and Gris are three of the best known among them. Entertaining as some of these things are, I can see nothing of permanent interest deriving from them. Meantime, this exercise pursued over so long a period by these painters denotes, so it seems to me, a weak spot in the Abstract armour. Again, Picasso, great artist as he is, and much as I admire him, has an equivocal and unsatisfactory look. To an adverse analysis of this aspect of the general movement, I devote considerable space. But it is because I believe so much in the wider movement, and because the spirit of this *Nature-mortism*—also the David-Raphael eclectic classic wave—contradicts what I have written this pamphlet to propose, that I deal with it so thoroughly.

One other point in this preamble. I have no fault to find with Cézannism. Any faithful discipleship of that master is sure to be sound art. All the same, Cézanne is such a lonely figure, and he has such a weight of pups around him! No one man, even Cézanne, should have on his shoulders such a huge effort of initiation as was his. There should have been several men. Ungrateful as that sounds, one cannot but regard it as a misfortune that all the diversity of art and human talent of a generation should have depended upon this one old man, as has been the case since he was unearthed.

THE CALIPH'S DESIGN
PART I

The Parable of
The Caliph's Design

ONE day the Caliph rose gingerly and stealthily from his bed of gold and placed himself at a window of his palace. He then took a pen of turquoise, and for some hours traced hieroglyphs upon a piece of paper. They consisted of patches and of lines, and it was impossible to say what he was doing. Apparently exhausted by the effort, he sank back upon his bed of gold and slept heavily for ten hours. Waking up in the small hours of the morning, he summoned a messenger and despatched him in search of Mahmed and Hassan, respectively the most ingenious engineer and the most experienced architect in his dominions.

The Caliph was in fine fettle when they arrived. He pointed with a certain facetiousness to his design lying outspread on a table. Then he addressed them as follows: —" I am extremely dissatisfied with the shape of my city, so I have done a design of a new city, or rather of a typical street in a new city. It is a little vorticist bagatelle that I threw off while I was dressing this morning." He negligently curled the tips of his beard. " I want you to look at it and tell me what you think of my skill."

Mahmed and Hassan bent over the design, and, noticing that their lord's eye was dancing, they indulged

217

in a few hurried guffaws, scraping their feet and pushing and nudging each other.

The Caliph then observed, stroking down the sumptuous brocade of his new dressing-gown: " Oh, Mahmed and Hassan, that is a very funny design. But it is my will that such a street should rise beneath the windows of my palace. Work shall start on it at ten o clock to-morrow morning. It is your unpleasant duty to invent the forms and conditions that would make it possible to realize my design. You have till ten to-morrow morning in which to produce the requisite plans and instructions for such a work. Should you fail to do so your heads will fall as soon as I have been informed of your failure; between, that is, ten and eleven to-morrow. Good-night, oh Mahmed and oh Hassan."

Those two tremendously able men burst into a cold sweat. Their eyes protruded from their intelligent faces. They clicked their tongues, shrugged their shoulders, and shuffled out with gestures of despair. After a half-hour of complete paralysis of their brilliant faculties, they pulled themselves together. By ten o'clock the following morning a series of the most beautiful plans that had yet been made in Baghdad (retaining with a scrupulous fidelity the masses and directions of the potentate's design) were ready for their master. And within a month a strange street transfigured the heart of that cultivated city.

The Bull Sounds

WE are all agreed as to the lamentable nature of the form-content and colour-content around us. There is no one found to deny the hideous foolishness of our buildings, our statues, our interiors. The prevalent imbecility of Demos is a commonplace. But there agreement ends.

Divergence of opinion centres round the following points. Here is point one. Is it not preferable to have every manifestation of the vulgar and stupid constantly, in an appetizing, delicious form (something like the "highness" of game), at the disposal of our superiority and wit?

What would Flaubert have done had France not bred Bouvards and Péchuchets with rabbit-like fecundity? Can nature ever be thanked enough for Sir Sampson Legend, Mantalini, Boswell's Johnson, Falstaff or any such types of Comedy, composed often of the nastiest excrement, the washiest imbecilities? No one would cut down these supplies of offal by so much as an ounce, which are the approved diet for so much that is good in art. No one would see folly or deformity, gluttony or cruelty, reduced by one single unit; or no one who recognizes the great benefits that have accrued, in the field of art, from their abundance in nature!

A less self-indulgent satirist, like Aristophanes, it is

true, will attach a stink or some disgusting attribute to his absurd *bonhomme*, relying on the squeamishness of his audience: sending his characters about like skunks. But most authors are not so moral as to poison our pleasure with these gases.

Now a stupid form is for the painter the same food as a stupid man for a Gogol or for a Flaubert. So it is questionable whether without the stimulation of stupidity, or every beastly, ill-made, or tasteless object that abounds in life to-day, the artist would be as well off, as well *nourished*. Would he not be in the position of a satirist, like Flaubert, without a Bouvard, or of an artist like Boswell without his rich and very unusual dish? The irritation with the particular French folly that surrounded him, and that Flaubert's eyes devoured every day as regularly as he ate his breakfast; the consequent pessimism that became the favourite manure for his thoughts; we cannot see Flaubert without that, any more than we can conceive of Rousseau the Douanier without his squab little bourgeois, and blank, paunchy little villa and silly little pony, in an ugly little cart.

The point rather lies in the *attitude* that was respectively that of Flaubert and that of the Douanier. Flaubert hated Bouvard: he considered the vulgarity and idiocy that he witnessed a very sad and improper thing. The Douanier, on the other hand, probably admired *his* Bouvards very much. It was with a naïvely respectful eye, it may be assumed, that he surveyed the bourgeois on Sunday, and noted his peculiarities like a child directly; without judging.

The Caliph's Design: I

Shakespeare, it is true, must have relished the absurd or deformed more consciously. Dickens made a cult of it. But with Shakespeare it was against a vast background of other matter: as comic relief, or used in farces, and so labelled. It has never amounted to what has practically become, in our day, a *rejection* of anything as dull or useless *unless* it lend itself to our appetite for the comic or the "queer."

But Butler's, or Chesterton's, or Shaw's antithetic glitter, when used in journalism, may become the most wearisome thing. We long, confronted by such a monotony of inversion as we get in Mr. G. K. Chesterton, for a plain "dull" statement of fact. Similarly, there *could* be such a thing as too much ugliness, or foolishness. Since the beginning of time the imbecile has been the rule, the intelligent the exception. Yet if imbecility should become as it were the religion of the educated, its pursuit and enjoyment the main end of cultivated life —just as foxes, dogs, and horses monopolize the mind of the country gentleman—would not people begin to sigh for the old variety? The hero, the villain, the distressed maiden, the vamp and the 'comic-relief' would have their turn again. Should we not also, were we embedded in some bric-à-brac of stuffed birds and wax flowers, the languors of the "æsthetic period" of the article I cite later in this pamphlet, look towards Karnak, a plain French provincial town, or almost anywhere, with eyes of longing provided there were no wax flowers or stuffed birds?

Surely all this sensibility of the "queer," the

"amusing," the divinely ugly, the exquisitely vulgar, will date, and date very quickly.

There would to-day, in the "modern" section of the art-world, be as great an outcry if some philistine proposed that the lovely embellishments of our streets, coloured signs, posters, beautiful police-stations and bewitching tiled Tube stations should be pulled down, as there would have been formerly—and is still by the "beauty-loving public"—when some "picturesque old bit" or decaying cottage was removed.

With men trying their hardest to eliminate ugliness, injustice, or imbecility from the world, has there ever been any absence of these commodities for the delectation of the artist? Is there ever likely to be? It is true that the artist can gorge himself to-day probably as never before. But is that the best thing for his talent?

If twenty Christs charged abreast anywhere in the world, you would still get in a remarkably short time, and within a half-hour's walk of their super-calvary, some such monument as the First Pyramid, the result of such a block of egotism as had never been seen before, to demonstrate the futility of the humane corrective. But I do not believe you would ever get a pyramid builder without Christian hysteria.

Even in order to appreciate the "banal" you must not have too much of it. And you must *pretend* that you do not like it, even if you are incapable of liking anything else. The reactionary Prussian theorists of war (*la bonne guerre*) of political tyranny, of "functional" aristocracy, were less useful than the Pacifist, and less intelligent.

The approved arrangement seems to be this: you spend half your time destroying the cheap, the foolish, the repellent; the other half you spend destroying what is left over after your efforts! Such evidently being the way we are intended to live, there is no excuse for slackness in the performance of your unpleasant duty: that is, to desire equity, mansuetude, in human relations, to fight against violence, to work for formal beauty, for more intelligent significance in the ordering of our lives.

But to conclude. The great line, the creative line; the fine, the exultant mass; the gaiety that snaps and clacks like a well-braced instrument string; the sweep of great tragedy; the immense, the simple satisfaction of the completest art, you could not get if you succeeded in eliminating passion. Nor could you get it if you crowned imbecility, or made an idol of the weak. Whereas you can always get enough silliness, a sufficiency of obnoxious form, or of vulgar flavour to satisfy the most gargantuan appetite.

The Politician's Apathy

BUT what is this ugliness, this commonness and squalor, to which we have been referring? It is what meets the eye in any London street, in any railway, bus, teashop, restaurant or hotel in our capital city, or in the official art which is to be found annually displayed in Burlington House. What influences go to the making of this repulsive form-content and colour-content of all the images that assail our eye—for which we may either offer up a prayer of thanks, or take no notice of, according to our temperament? What lassitude, or what ill-directed energy of mind, working through unnumbered channels, and multitudes of people, is responsible for the designs on match boxes, the ornamental metal-work on the lamp-posts, gates, knife-handles, sepulchral enclosures, serviette-rings; for most posters, menu-cards, the scenery in our musical spectacles, chapter-headings and tailpieces, brooches, bangles, embossments on watches, clocks, cruets; pendants in Asprey's, in Dobson's, in Hancock's windows in Bond Street; in fact, every stitch and scrap of art-work that indefatigably spreads its blight all over a modern city, invading every nook, befouling the most attractive necks, waists, ears, and bosoms; defiling even the doormat—climbing up, even, and making absurd and vapid the chimney pot—which

THE SURRENDER OF BARCELONA

you would have thought was inaccessible and out-of-sight enough for Art not to reach—for the cheap modern thousand-headed devil of design not to find it out or think it worth while to spoil?

We are all perfectly agreed, are we not, that practically any house, railing, monument, thoroughfare, in this city should be instantly pulled down, were it not (and there's the rub) for the "amusement" and stimulus that the painter may desire.

A complete reform (were it not for the needs of the painter who *must* have his bit of banality, bless his little heart!) of every notion or lack of notion on the significance of the appearance of the London scene should be instituted. A gusto, a consciousness should imbue the placing and the shaping of every brick. A central spectacle, such a street as Regent Street, should be worked out in the smallest detail. It should not grow like a weed, without any impulse but the drifting and accident of commerce. A great thoroughfare like Regent Street develops and sluggishly gets upon its ill-articulated legs: blankly it looks at us with its silly face.—There exist Bouvards and Pécuchets in brick and stone. So there are Flauberts in paint and crayon.

Do politicians understand so little the influence of the Human Scene, or the effect of Nature, that they can be as indifferent as they are to the aspect of the capital of a wealthy and powerful community? Would not a more imaginative Cecil Rhodes have seen that the only way an Empire such as he imagined could impress itself upon the consciousness of a people would be to make the individual citizen aware of his privileges? All ambitious nations have understood this. Whether in the weight of a rhetoric of buildings, in the subtler ways of beauty signifying the delights and rewards of success won by toil and adventure; in a thousand ways the imagination of the public would be captured and fixed. But beyond the obvious policy of not having a mean and slipshod surrounding for the capital of what sets out to be an "Empire," simply for human life at all—*in order to increase gusto and belief in that life*—it is of the first importance that the senses should be directed into such channels, be appealed to in such ways, as to induce this state of mind of relish, of fullness, if not of exultation.

It is life about which, obviously, the legislator should be concerned: and full satisfaction of life is reached through the fancy and the senses. The latter must be stimulated and not depressed. But the streets of a modern English city are exceedingly depressing. They are so aimless, so painfully unplanned, that the mind and senses jog on their way like passengers in a slow train, with blinds down, in an overcrowded carriage.

This is worse, again, for the crowd than for the more fortunate few. The life of the crowd, of the Plain Man, is external: he can live only through others and outside himself. Then he, in a sense, *is* the houses, the railings, the statues, the churches, the roadhouses. His beauty and justification is in the superficial life of all that he *sees*. He dwindles, grows restless and sick, when not given the opportunities to live and enjoy in the simple, communal manner. He has just sense enough to know

226

that he is living or not living: give him a rich type of life, a bit dashing perhaps, with clothes on his back that enhance his personality instead of killing it, with a glamour about it, and he is gladdened, if his stomach is not too empty. Give him processions and proper holidays; provide him with military display, if he lives under a military system. Yes, but there is something we were going to omit. He recognizes that the plaster objects stuck up in Oxford Street outside Selfridges for Peace Day are not a symbol of anything but commerce —in which he equally, though not so successfully, is engaged. There is nothing there to nourish his imagination. Similarly, it is not such a tremendous critical flight as you would imagine for him to connect in some subtle way in his mind these plaster statues with the more careful but even more effusively mean Albert Memorial, or any other monument that meets his eye. Yet these are the monuments that celebrate and advertise the society of which he is a unit. The putrescent dullness, that deadly and vacuous stare with which he is confronted in those images—the symbols provided by his masters, who in their own persons are no more stimulating, can hardly be expected to excite him either to buoyancy, obedience, or anything but boredom.

So if there are a hundred good reasons why Painters should oppose any modification of the appearance of our modern world, which in the quaintness of its stupidity is as relishable as a Limberger cheese, there is no reason at all, that I can see, why the politician should feel obliged to protect it.

How the fact of Style Obstructs

THE parable of the Caliph's design describes the state of mind which must be that of every true artist living in the midst of the blasphemous stupidity, too much so even for mere animal health, by which we are to-day surrounded. Alas! although, like the Caliph, a vorticist, I have not the power of life and death over the Mahmeds and Hassans of this city. Otherwise I should have no compunction in having every London architect's head struck from his body at ten o'clock to-morrow morning, unless he grappled with the problems of his art and endeavoured to improve his understanding of it. I would flood those indolent offices, where architects pursue their trade, with abstract designs. I am sure the result would be to cram the modern scene with form and purpose, where to-day, in so far as it is beholden to the architect, it has no discernible significance of any sort.

There is no reason whatever why we should not have a number of interesting architects. I can also see no reason why this pamphlet should not bring them forth. I should be very proud of that. It is, I think, such a modest optimism, that you will, I am sure, allow it. I should like to see the entire city rebuilt upon a more conscious pattern. But this automatically would happen, should an architect of genius make his appearance: he would invent an architecture for our time and climate which was at once a creative and fertilising art-form. The first great modern building that arose in this city would soon carry everything before it. Hand in hand with the engineer by force of circumstances, his problems so exactly modern ones, this surprising building of our new architect would provide a new form-content for our everyday vision. All we want therefore is one single architect with brains. Him we will regard when he arises, with unbounded optimism.

Now the question of the form-content of the every-day scene is obviously one that concerns every painter. Almost any authentic painter, sculptor, or designer will agree that Cheapside, Piccadilly, Russell Square, Mary-lebone Road, are thoroughly dull and discreditable masses of brick and mortar; that they are laid out according to no coherent plan; are fearfully vulgar in their detailed ornament; are in every way calling for instant demolishment. Similarly, he will agree that any large and expensive West-End restaurant is the nastiest of sham palaces which ever vulgarised the eye of an unfortunate Demos.

But when you say to an artist that it is about time something was done to get rid of the whole graceless and stupid spectacle, he will *agree*, yes, but will quickly change the subject. Every law of common-sense pre-cludes any possibility of modification of this detestable sight, assailing all our eyes. He will either imagine that you are proposing some Utopia (as you are) or he will think that your notions hardly agree with the fashionable idea that all is for the best in the best of all possible worlds: that *whatever* reality, accident (or your neighbour) flings at your head, your head should respond to in hollow acquiescence.

Of course there are good arguments that can be brought against you. I have made use of these arguments myself. We have just been adumbrating them in the section of this pamphlet entitled, "The Bull Sounds." But we will proceed to sift out with more thoroughness the Painter's argument; this time the argument of *any* painter.

Style, he will say, can transform anything whatever into gold. Take a convenient example. Suppose that Rembrandt had had a more interesting type of architecture before him, for subject matter, in place of the homely mills by the side of the Dutch canals: would this better form-content have made one of his pen-drawings better drawings? To that there is only one answer "No. It would not."

But a windmill is a rough and simple contrivance, and there is a sad difference between the rough beauty and fitness of such objects stuck up centuries ago in Holland, and similar rough and simple objects built in the modern age in Great Britain. One would do better to imagine Rembrandt, working in the same way that he worked—doing similar drawings—in an industrial country like ours, in the Twentieth Century instead of the Sixteenth.

Still you have to admit that as fine an artist as Rembrandt, by the magic use of the medium he chose, by his thick painterly line, by his tact of simplification and of elimination, would make a new thing of whatever it was, however poor the original. Look at Van Gogh— though France, where he worked, was very different to industrial England. So in considering if it is worth while to change a single brick, even, or the most trifling ornament, however offensive, you would be obliged to admit that, as regards the production of pictures of great beauty, you would be no better off. The best half-dozen artists of any country, as regards the actual beauty and significance of their work, do not depend upon the objective world at all, for their stimulus to creation. Subject-matter you have to dismiss as unimportant. -

As to all the thousands of artists, not amongst the most able or imaginative, but capable of something passably good, it is another story. *They* depend upon Nature, upon the objective world, from which their stimulus to work or their taste derives. Set a rather poor artist down on a camp stool out of doors, ask him to paint a picture of a street of houses in front of him. If the houses are of a good and significant build, he will be more likely to do a good and significant painting than if they are such clumsy, lineless, massless, things as we invariably find ourselves beset by to-day. If he has no invention or vision, the artist depends upon Nature. Nature must do at least half the work, then perhaps he will do the rest.

But the fallacy in the contention about *the good artist*, independent of subject-matter (for there is a fallacy) is this. Although he does not depend on Nature, he certainly depends upon *life*. He is subject to its conditions, and this surely re-acts upon his painting. If he is hungry, is disturbed in his work, or has to do some detestable type of commercial painting or designing to make a living, then this independence of external form and colour-content of his is clearly of little use to him.

Where the Painter would benefit

U PON this subject of *what we see*—of what our eyes are compelled to dwell upon, day in, day out, owing to the unsatisfactory way in which our cities are built and adorned—I have my views, as you see. I can perhaps help you to understand better what the problem is by stating it in the following terms.—Consider how I, or an artist like me, stands towards this problem. You see what my views are. What is the practical import of those views to me? It reduces itself to this: I have nothing materially to gain by your adopting this outlook. You are perplexed. Painters are everywhere perplexed. I make you and them a present of this analysis of these perplexities.

I see, at all times, the shapes that you would see, were the applied arts and the art of building in better shape than at present is the case. I do not need to have a house built with significant forms, lines, or masses, and planted squarely before my eyes, to know that such significance exists, or to have my belief in its reality stimulated.

You, on the other hand, do require that. I am obviously here to be of use to you: I am at your disposal in this matter. But that is primarily your business and not mine. I can get on quite well, the artist always can, *without this material realisation*. Theoretically, even, a creative painter or designer should be able to exist quite satisfactorily without paper, stone or paints, or without so much as lifting a finger to translate into forms and colours his creative impulse. It should be the same with the painter, the architect, or the sculptor as it is with the composer. (The Interpreter is really in the same category as the bricklayer, or at best a foreman of works).

Still, I suffer somewhat all the same. This lack of readiness, or really of aptitude, on your part, to employ me usefully is none too good—and every true artist I know, painter or sculptor, is in the same box. Here is the trouble: it does not matter what objective Nature supplies. The inventive artist is his own purveyor. But the society of which he forms a part, can, by its backwardness, indolence, or obtuseness, cause him a great deal of inconvenience; affect his pocket adversely, cause him to waste an absurd amount of time.

In his final decrepitude—when he is old, and grey, and full of sleep—it would not be a waste of time for a painter or for a writer to lecture, or suchlike, upon the subject of his craft. Palsied and half-blind, that would be very proper. But the propaganda, explanatory pamphlets, and the rest, in which we, in this country, are obliged to indulge, is so much time out of our active life which would normally be spent as every artist wishes to spend his time, namely in producing pictures.

Yet were one's ideas of painting not formulated, and given out in the shape of a lecture, a pamphlet, or a critical essay, impossible conditions would result for an artist desirous of experimenting. Half his time at least, must be spent in these extraneous activities.

So when I say that I should like to see a completely transfigured world, it is not because I want to *look* at it. It would be a great mistake to suppose that. It is you who would look at it. It would be you who would benefit by this exhilarating spectacle. *I* should merely benefit, I and other Painters like me, by no longer finding myself in the position of a freak—the queer wild men of cubes—the terrible *faures* or wild beasts—or any other rubbish that the Yellow Press invents to amuse the nerves of its readers. Do you suppose that the art-man who reports on the present exhibition of French modernist pictures and describes the "horror" of these canvases, really *thinks* that they are in any way hair-raising? Not a bit of it. He knows that for every extra thrill he makes an extra quid. Naturally it does not please me, or any other painter who paints pictures which appear extravagant, according to the pretty and facetious standard of this time, to be described as a wild man, or a "man-eater" in paint. No pleasurable thrill accompanies these words when used about one's own very normal proceedings—rational transactions, since they appear to the painter the *only* rational transactions in the midst of the capers of the mild lunatic asylum it is our lot to inhabit.

The Public chosen

THE Public I should like for this pamphlet is a rather different one from that to which painters usually consider it worth while to address themselves. In the first place, any rank and file Royal Academy artist is fond of regarding himself as "a craftsman"; as a specialist, of the most dyed-in-the-wool, horribly professional order. He is the romantic guildsman of the Brush. The more furibundly ignoble his paintings, the farther he retires into the technical mysteries of his craft. Lay opinion consequently he scorns.

Then another pale exists, an even funnier one. Beyond that stand those multitudes who have not been taught a delightful faintness, a cheap catch in the voice, and the few dozen snobbish tricks of thought and hand coined in each decade for the lucky children of the rich. A board school master, an excise clerk, a douanier, for that matter, are usually approached if at all with every nuance of amused condescension that a stereotyped education can breed.

How sick such men must get with the wearisome and endless trifling that they have come to associate with the word Artist! I write in these notes for a socially wider, a not necessarily specialist, public. I write for the factory-

236

hand, if by good luck this book should manage to reach him, as much as for the Cambridge æsthete or the Fashionplates of Mayfair. The "educated" are of course generally unteachable. Heaven forbid that I should aspire to educate the "educated"!

Architecture

ARCHITECTURE is the weakest of the arts, in so far as it is the most dependent upon the collective sensibility of its period. It is so involved, too, in utility, and so much a portion of public life, that it is far more helpless than painting and literature in the face of public indifference. Sculpture shares with it some of this helplessness. There are many good sculptors wasted to-day as thoroughly as anyone can be, through the absence of such conditions as are required to give them their chance of natural expression.

Had Gaudier Brzeska lived, he would be doing an odd door-knocker or two, an occasional paper-weight, or portrait bust, for a living, with all the limiting circumstances that personal vanity sets to the art of portraiture, whether in the flat or in the round. There only remains for the sculptor, as for the painter, the art exhibition, and the freak-selling or commercial selling of the dealer's shop. A man like Archipenko, for instance, quite capable of finer things, is reduced to stunt-sculpting of a dilettante sort, upon a small scale, and it may be assumed very ill-paid at that.

Have you ever met an Architect? I do not mean a prosperous *pasticheur*, who restores a house or runs one up, in Tudor, Italian, or any other style. I mean a creative architect, or a man with some new power in his craft, concerned with the æsthetic as well as the practical needs of the mass sensibility of his period? I never have, I may say at once. And what is more, should you wish to approach this neglected subject and learn more about it, you will find nothing but a dismal series of very stupid books, for your information and reference.

The best treatise I have come across is W. K. Lethaby's handbook, *An introduction to the History and Theory of the Art of Building.* It appears to me to be an uncommonly sound book: if everybody were of Mr. Lethaby's way of thinking we should soon find that the aspect of this lifeless scene had changed for the better. Furthermore this voice for the right and active vision comes from the unlikeliest quarter. For Mr. Lethaby, I understand, is Chief Lecturer on Architecture in the South Kensington School.

But listen to this recognized authority of academic status:

" Modern armoured concrete is only a higher power of the Roman system of construction. If we could sweep away our fear that it is an inartistic material, and boldly build a railway station, a museum, or a cathedral, wide and simple, amply lighted, and call in our painters to finish the walls, we might be interested in building again almost at once. This building interest must be aroused.

" We cannot forget our historical knowledge, nor would we if we might. The important question is, Can it be organised and directed, or must we continue to be betrayed by it? The only agreement that seems possible is agreement on a scientific basis, on an endeavour after perfect structural efficiency. If we could agree on this we need not trouble about beauty, for that would take care of itself.

"Experience must be brought back once more as the centre of architecture, and architects must be trained as engineers are trained.

"The modern way of building must be flexible and vigorous, even smart and hard. We must give up designing the broken-down picturesque which is part of· the ideal of make believe. The enemy is not science, but vulgarity, a pretence to beauty at second hand."

What do you make of that? "Must be . . . even smart and hard!" Does not Mr. Lethaby, Professor of Architecture in the South Kensington Schools, speak to you in a tone seldom heard in the art-schools? What English Professor of painting would you find recommending his pupil to paint in a manner "smart and hard"?

Such books as C. H. Caffin's contain nothing very useful. He refers to the Woolworth buildings in New York in the following way:

"Up to the present, the noblest example of this new movement is the Woolworth Building, which is not only the tallest of the tall buildings, but a monument of arresting and persuasive dignity. Such a building supplies an uplift to the spirit." Etc.

The Woolworth Building, one of the tallest in New York, consisting of 51 storeys, is a piece of rudimen-

THE ENEMY

tary ecclesiastical nonsense, 25 of its storeys being a spire. It is in every way less interesting than the less ambitious skyscrapers, which are at least enormously tall boxes, and by their scale "uplift the spirit," that wishes to soar so high, far more than this Anglican monstrosity: which is not a church, however, and has not even that excuse for its stupid spire.

In this connection, we hear a great deal of claptrap talked about the sky-scraper. The sky-scraper, for the most part, is a tall box. So far it has been nothing but that; except where, as in the Schiller Theatre Building in Chicago, or the famous Woolworth Building, some dreadful intervention of "the beautiful" has converted it into an acre-high advertisement of the modern architect's fatuity.

It has been a fashion lately to admire the sky-scraper in its purely engineering capacity, along with other forms of simple engineering. But a box is always a box, however high. And when you think of the things that could have been done by a liaison of the artist's fancy, once more, with all these works of engineering genius, you wonder that there is not one single example which one can quote of such a structure.

In the case of a dynamic shape like an aeroplane there is neither any reason nor any need for the collaboration of engineer and artist. All such machines, except for their colouring, or some surface design, to modify their shape, develop in accordance with a law of efficient evolution as absolute as that determining the shape of the tiger, the wasp, or the swallow. They are definitely,

Wyndham Lewis the Artist

for the artist, in the category of animals. When we come to the static cell-structures in which we pass our lives there is far more latitude and opportunity for his inventiveness.

To begin with, let us by all means reduce everything to the box. Let us banish absolutely the stylistic architectural rubbish. But as to the shaping of the box or series of boxes let the artist be used.

For if you say that the surface design or ornaments which comprise the outer shell of the building is the same as the clothes on a man's back, there is still something to be said about the naked shape of the man or even about his skeleton. The nature of the nude body or of the skeleton will decide what the character of the clothes must be. So the artist should come into the picture long before he usually does, or give a new consciousness to the shaping of the skeleton of the Engineer. This should be invariable, not occasional: that is to say of course when the first painters or sculptors have come to be used for this purpose, instead of the horrible stock architect.

Remy de Gourmont expresses himself as follows on the subject of the decay of architecture in our time:

" Voilà le point capital de l'explication pourquoi on avait au moyen-age le sens de l'architecture: on ignorait la nature. Incapables de jouir de la terre telle qu'elle est, des fleuves, des montagnes, de la mer, des arbres, ils étaient obligés, pour exciter leur sensibilité, de se créer, un monde factice, d'ériger des forêts de pierre.

242

The Caliph's Design : I

" La nature s'ouvrit à l'homme parce que la France et
le centre de l'Europe furent sillonés de routes, parce que
les campagnes devinrent sures et d'un commode accès."

And he goes on to fancy that perhaps when nature
has become too cheap, through its general accessibility,
and men tire of it, that Art and Architecture will once
more have their turn.

Since a narrow belt of land like the Nile Valley is
more crowded with buildings, or their remains, than any
other territory, and since the character of those buildings, the source of all subsequent constructions, was
evidently determined by the nature of the landscape of
Egypt, the hills, palms, and so forth, with which,
further, the builders were at least as familiar as any
men could be with nature, de Gourmont's theory would
appear to be nonsense. It displays the listless and dull eye
that a usually keen journalist can turn upon this Cin-
derella of a subject.

Child Art and the Naif

THE Child and the Naif are two of the principal mainstays of dilettante criticism in this country—and practically all art-criticism in England is dilettante criticism, for art is an intellectual exercise, not a passion, for the English. This "phenomenon" with all the sentimentality of which its exploitation clearly is susceptible, is one of the trump cards in the Amateur's game, and a fruitful source of confusion. It is one of the most obvious avenues by which the thoroughly undeserving can slip through into a position of artificial respect.

The Young Visiters is swelling into fabulous editions. Pamela Bianco, a child of nine, is fawned on by the hoary great. The Omega workshops have had an exhibition of children's drawings. The Naif is another doll-like dummy that the trader on sentiment pushes in front of him in stalking the public. The Naif is an elastic phenomenon: it is of earlier date, as regards its boom, than the child.

The Slade School produces regularly a certain number of professional naifs. They are frequently the most sophisticated individuals it is possible to meet. Beyond the fact that they wrestle with a slight incompetence, in addition to possessing a pretty feeling for the sentimentalities of rustic prints, they are no more naïve than

244

Mr. Horatio Bottomley. None are half as good at manu-
facturing naïvetés as are the French. Their graces and
queernesses pall as swiftly as the tiresome mannerisms of
a child, exploiting its childishness.

There are two types of Naif : the child-naif, and the
primitive-naif. It is difficult to decide which is the more
tiresome of the two.

The child-naif usually starts with a happy combination of an ingrained technical incompetence and of a
feeling for the graces in the arts. Distressed that this
feeling should be wasted owing to lack of power, he
hits on the happy idea of bringing his lack of painter's
prowess and his nice feeling for the arts together, and
producing the very marketable commodity, Naïveté!

Or he may be a bit more definitely naïve than that.
The woodenness of his figures or trees, his rickety line,
may really have a pathetic charm for him. He genuinely
pities his little wooden figures for being so wooden and
silly-looking (a manner of pitying himself). He is
sorry for himself through them. And this sensation
grows upon him until it gets a hold; he goes on painting
the little wooden figures. If he has been touched enough
or, more likely, if he is a theatrical self-love, other people
are touched: and the little wooden figures find a market.

The more literary pathos may be absent. That is
another variety. The weak pathetic line, the meaning-
less forms, the unreal colour, are the object of a certain
emotion: something that I can only describe as a technical pity, a professional pathos. The best is made of
unfortunate limitation. This Naif may even become

extremely bumptious in course of time, by the same process that produces the infantile swank of the deformed.

The Primitive-Naif may evolve rather in the same way as the Child-Naif, or he may not. It may be a refuge of incompetence. Or it may be a romantic mode, Teutonic in character. Then the Child-Naif and the Primitive-Naif sometimes come together in the same artist.

There is no such thing as the *born Primitive*. There is the *Primitive* in point of view of date, the product of a period. And there is the *Primitive voulu*, who is simply a pasticheur and stylist; invariably a sentimentalist, when not a rogue. When he is not specially an *Italian* or *Flemish Primitive*, but just a *Primitive* (whatever period he flits into *always* a Primitive), he is on the same errand and has the same physiognomy as the Period-taster, or any other form of dilettante or of pasticheur. The Primitive *voulu* acrobatically adapts himself to the mentality of a different stage of social development. The pasticheur, *en touriste*, visits different times and places merely, without so much readjustment of his mind as of his hand.

As to the Child proper. Of course the success of *The Young Visiters* was partly due to its domestic appeal. Partly it was a sentimental curiosity. The distillation of Middle-class snobbery played its part as well.

Pamela Bianca, whose drawings are to be found in several fashionable periodicals, is like Daisy Ashford at

least in one respect, namely: *she is not a child*. She may
be nine years old, and *The Young Visiters* may have
been written by a child of two. But they both have the
sad relaxed quality of the average adult mind. They are
as unfresh as that. Pamela Bianca's sensibility has naïvely
devoured the Douanier's *Fête National*. But that is the
nearest she has come to naïveté. Otherwise she imitates
Beardsley or Botticelli, or some fellow-child, with as
sophisticated a competence as any South Kensington
student. She is very exactly the æsthetist peer of the professional painter engaged in the same sweet make-believe.

The growth of the mind and of the body is so often
not parallel, some people's "mature" lives so long,
others almost non-existent, that it is difficult to know
where you are dealing with the art-product of the child,
or, on the other hand, the child-like art of the adult.

Theoretically, a powerful nature should develop at
once, disregarding the schedules of human growth and
laws of probation. William Blake was a case in point: he
took little notice of the dawdling ritual of intellectual
expansion. But many individuals as adults have shown
no precocity at all. Genius no doubt has its system of individual evolution appropriate to the character of the gift
to be hatched out.

As regards the Naif—the real thing—Rousseau the
Douanier is the only great Naif as far as I know. In
his case Nature made on the one hand of his Douanier's
calling a water-tight case against sophistication; then
put something divinely graceful and simple—which we
associate with "childhood" and which that abstraction

sometimes has—at his disposal for the term of his natural life.

Nothing seemingly could corrupt or diminish it; and it brought with it, like a very practical fairy, or like a sardine tin with its little key, an instrument with which to extract all the genius from within this Douanier of forty or fifty years old.

To return to the Child proper. The only case in which the drawing of a child is of value, is when it possesses the same outstripping or unusual quality that the work of a very few adult artists possess. Then what it does is not " child-art ". That rare bird, the adult who is a true artist, may have accomplished nothing himself as a child: but the drawing of the gifted child would seem perhaps to be his work at a more immature stage. It is not a question of Child or Adult then. It is a question simply of the *better being*. Both belong to an exceptional human type.

There is also a fresh and delicate charm of very young life that some children, not many, have the power of infusing into their drawings. And then there remains the melancholy fact that no infant's pictures could be duller than the average adult's. Consequently there is every bit as much justification for exhibiting any twenty children's scribbles as there is for exhibiting those of any twenty professional painting adults.

Machinery and Lions

THE Italian Futurists had in their "dynamic" *idée
fixe* a great pull over the sentimental and sluggish
eclecticism, the deadness and preciosity, of the artists
working in Paris. But they accepted objective nature
wholesale, or the objective world of mechanical industry.—Their pæans to machinery were stupid. It involved a mythical attitude towards a racing-car, or workshop where big guns (or Teddy-bears) are made—not a
rational enthusiasm for the possibilities that lie in this new
spectacle of machinery; of the technical uses to which
it can be put in the arts. Machinery should be regarded
as a new pictorial resource, as with a new mineral or oil,
there to be exploited. A plant for the manufacture of
the parts of a six-inch Mk 19 gun should be regarded
apart from its function. Absorbed into the æsthetic consciousness, it would no longer *make* so much as a pop-
gun.

Thenceforward its function would change. Through
its agency emotions would be manufactured, related, it
is true, to its primitive efficiency, shinyness, swiftness or
slowness, elegance or power. But its meaning would be
transformed. It is of exactly the same importance, and
in exactly the same category, as a wave upon a screen

by Korin, an Odalisque of Ingres, the beetle of a sculptor of the XVIII. Dynasty.

Ingres lived among people consumed with a great appetite for the pseudo-classic: the Egyptian sculptor lived in the presence of a great veneration for the Beetle. Korin's contemporaries possessed a high susceptibility and sentiment for objects of the natural world. Korin's formal wave-lines is the same impulse as Balla's *Linee andamentali*. The Beetle and the Odalisque are both sleek and solid objects.

Ingres probably did not believe in the Odalisque as an Odalisque, although realizing the admirable uses to which an Odalisque could be put. The Egyptian probably found the beetle objectionable until transformed into stone. And there should be no obligation to behave like a religious fanatic about a sausage-machine or a locomotive. Other people can make parade of such mystical emotions—perhaps it is proper that they should: not the artist. If the world *would only build temples to machinery in the abstract* then everything would be perfect. The painter and sculptor would have plenty to do: they could, in complete peace, and suitably honoured, pursue their trade without further trouble. Else where is the sense in taking all the useful Gods and Goddesses away, and leaving the artist without any communal rôle at all, except that of an entertainer, or perhaps a business man?

Imagine Koyetzu, Signorelli, or the sculptor who carved the head of Akhenaton or of the wife of the Sheik-el-Beled, alive, painting and carving, to-day.

The Caliph's Design: I

They would have been in the profoundest sense the same artists. But just as a painter may use one medium one day and another the next; so far more than mere traces of the fact that they had seen with their eyes the machines that play such a great part in contemporary life would be found in their inventions. Just as the sculptors of Nineveh put the lions that were such immediate objects of their daily environment to good use in their reliefs, or the painters of the Sung period the birds and landscapes found by them in their wilful seclusion; so it was inevitable to-day that artists should get into their inventions (figures, landscapes, or abstractions) something of the lineaments and character of machinery. An artist could excel, no doubt, who never in his pictures revealed an acquaintance with anything more ferreous than a mushroom. But you would not be liable, I suppose, to pick a quarrel with the artists of Asshur because they used the lions at their doors?

The Artist's Luck

THE best artists of the Sung period lived a secluded life, very luckily for them. It was considered incumbent upon them, in accordance with contemporary feeling, to inhabit the fairly distant country and live in intercourse with the objects of Nature. When this fashion passed, and a painter had to live within hailing distance of the court, the pictures produced showed an immediate decline in quality. That is *one* lesson.

The scenes in the Assyrian bas-reliefs from Nineveh were produced by an artist who led an unlucky kind of life. He was hurried about by the king in his *razzias* and hunts: no sooner had the party (a marauding or a hunting one) returned to the city than the harassed sculptors had to rush to their workrooms and produce by the next morning a complete series of bas-reliefs describing in flattering guise the exploits of their diabolical idiot of a master. For no sooner had he slept off the fatigue induced by the last of an incessant series of displacements, than he insisted upon seeing what he had looked like to his band of performing sculptors during the last week or two. Their heads probably fell like apples in an autumn wind; though there is seemingly no record of his ever having had sculptors enough to build up their skulls into a pyramid which is what he liked to do with heads, when there were enough of them. How these craftsmen succeeded in doing such good lions it is difficult to say. Perhaps the ones who did the good lions were left in a privileged peace sometimes. But on the whole, a sculptor fated to work for Asshur's deputy would no doubt have regarded the Sung hermit, his opposite number in China, as the luckiest old yellow crab that ever painted.

It has occurred to me that we might be worse off than we are. But I can see no reason why we should not be better off still: hence, partly, this pamphlet.

THE CALIPH'S DESIGN
PART II

The Artist Older than the Fish

THE artist goes back to the fish. The few centuries that separate him from the savage are a mere flea-bite to the distance his memory must stretch if it is to strike the fundamental slime of creation. And those are the conditions—the very first gusto of creation in this scale of life in which we are set—that he must reach, before he, in his turn, can create!

The creation of a work of art is an act of the same description as the evolution of wings on the sides of a fish, the feathering of its fins; or the invention of a weapon within the body of a hymenopter to enable it to meet the terrible needs of its life. The ghostly and burning growths—the walking twigs and flying stones— the two anguished notes that are the voice of a being— the vapid twitter; the bellows of age-long insurrection and discontent—the complacent screech—all these may be considered as types of art, all equally perfect, but not all equally desirable.

The attitude of instructed people as regards "the artist" has changed. It is mixed up with, and depends a good deal upon, the precision with which they apply this term. With the grotesque prostitution of the word Artist, and its loose and paltry meaning in this country, I will deal in a separate section. A German philosopher,

R   257

living in the heyday of last century German music, propounded the theory of an *æsthetic* justification of the universe. Many people play with this notion, just as they play with Art; but we should have to disembarrass "art" of a good deal of cheap adhesive matter, and cheap and pretty adhesive people, before it could appear a justification for anything at all; much less for such a gigantic and, from every point of view, dubious concern as the Universe!

The artist's function is to create—to make something; *not to make something pretty*, as dowagers, dreamers, and art-dealers here suppose. In any synthesis of the universe, the harsh, the hirsute, the enemies of the rose, must be built in for the purposes as much of a fine æsthetic, as of a fine logical structure. And having removed the sentimental gulf that often has, in the course of their chequered career, kept Sense and Beauty apart, we may at this stage of the proceedings even refer to their purposes as one.

Fabre describes the creative capabilities of certain beetles, realizable in their own bodies; beasts with a record capacity for turning their form and colour impulses into living flesh. These beetles can convert their faces into hideously carved and detestable masks, can grow out of their bodies menacing spikes, and throw up on top of their heads sinister head-dresses, overnight. Such changes in their personal appearance, destined to inspire terror in their adversaries, is possibly not a very profound or useful invention, but it is surely a considerable creative feat. Any art worth the name is, at the least, a feat of that order. The New Guinea barred and whitewashed masks are an obvious parallel. But any invention or phantasy in painting or carving is such. As to the wing mechanism that first lifted a creature off the ground, and set it spinning or floating through the air, you must call Shakespeare in to compete with it. Ma Yuan we can consider, roughly speaking, as the creator of the first tree; or substitute for him the best artist, who has painted the best tree, that you can call to mind.

The more sensible we grow about the world, the more sensible we grow about the artist. We are really more in sympathy with a bird or a fish to-day than we have been for a considerable period. And while people at large are being forced, by snobbery, into a less anthropomorphic mood, they find, with some awakening of respect, traces and odd indications of the artist's presence everywhere they go beyond their simian pale. The artist, we all agree, was the first scientist! His "inhumanity" is so old that he looks with an understandable contempt upon that upstart growth of the Machine Age.

We have got out of our anthropomorphism, then, to this extent: that it is to-day as respectable to be a fish, as it was in the latter part of the last century to be a "savage". The Robert Louis Stevenson, George Borrow, "back to Nature" Englishman (not an artist-type at all) is as dead as a door-nail. It is the artist-type, even, that has prevailed in the philosopher's mind, the latter's dogmatism correcting itself by a careful liaison with the spirit of the artist.

Wyndham Lewis the Artist

We no longer dream about earlier communities, since we know more about them, or long for some pristine animal fierceness, or abundant and unblemished health. We realize how every good thing dates; we grasp better the complexities of life's compensations. That does not mean that we are satisfied with to-day's conditions any more than we covet those of the Hereros or Hawaiian natives to a morbid degree. Generally speaking, an intelligent modern man does not place his paradise in the Prairie or in the heart of some wild Highland clan, although envying the great and simple assets that such plain conditions imply. He has caught a glimpse of something more subtle and to him more satisfying. He really at last has a vision of his own; it plunges him back to more refreshing energies and oblivions than the noisy and snarling claptrap of tribe and clan.

"The artist" formerly was identified with the savage or the school-boy to a disobliging extent. This was in the main by thinkers impatient with the gushings and heroics of a type of rhyming or picture-painting crétin, or subman. Chelsea and Montmartre were romantic names. This disagreeable bohemian was as conservative as a woman, full of noisy protest at the draining and rebuilding of slums, which he would have "saved" on account of their paintability and picturesqueness. Clearly this masquerader, this bechevelured nonentity loaded with rusty broadswords, Spanish knives, sombreros, oaths —the arch-priest of the romantic Bottle—was not an artist-type. Gauguin was not an artist-type. He was a savage type addicted to painting. He was in reality very like his sunny friends in the Marquesas Islands. He was in as limited a way a savage as an American negro. Such people are savages who go in for art for motives of vanity or of disguised sex. Theorists build their generalizations about the artist upon such human bric-à-brac. Gauguin appears like a vulgar tripper by the side of Cézanne.

The music of *Carmen*, the *Prince Igor* ballet, all the " savage stuff " that always gets the audience, is where the artist is supposed to have his home. The truth is this: in the trek of the imagination, of however feeble powers, from any man's Present outwards in whatever direction, the first region struck is the Savage time—clash of cymbals, howl of clansmen, voluptuous belly-dance, Caucasian cartridge-pockets, castanettes, and vendettas. That is about as far as a respectable Public-school fancy takes you. It is like a scene from the more boring of the Russian ballets or a Victory Ball. There *all* the " Chelsea artists " are to be found, every form of artist— far too many artists, in fact, and far too few straight savages. But the on occasion festive philosopher is a bit of an " artist " of that sort himself. And it has been from such regions and hobnobbings that he has borne away his stereotyped convictions as to the nature of " artists," and their abode in time. It is only since more adventurous men have pushed out beyond this sententious belt of savage life into less tawdry regions, that a new type of " artist " has arisen, demanding a new classification. Incidentally he has disposed already of much of the prestige of the falsely labelled herds of submen.

The Physiognomy of our Time

LIFE, simply, however vivid and tangible, is too material to be anything but a mechanism, and the seagull is not far removed from the hydroplane. Whether a stone flies and copulates, or remains respectably in its place, half hiding the violet from the eye, is little matter. It is just as remarkable to be so hard and big as to be so busy and passionate; though owing to our busyness and passion we have a shoppy interest in the hurrying insect that we do not display for the stone.

Life has begun, as language, for instance, begins, with a crowding and redundance which must be thinned out if the powerfullest instincts of life, even, are to triumph. Where everything is mutually destructive, and where immense multitudes of activities and modes of life have to be scrapped, it is important not to linger in ecstasy over *everything*, simply because it *is*. Nor should we sentimentalize about Life where creation is still possible and urgent; where much life, although pretty, powerful or bewitching, interferes with and opposes the life of something still more bewitching and strong.

The genius of the executant in art, as much as the curiosity of the amateur, assume in their promiscuous tasting an equal perfection in everything that succeeds in living, happens to move as swiftly, or far more swiftly, for its size, than the swiftest motor-car; or to fly as infallibly as the most perfected plane we can imagine. And the impresario of the Futurists (with his Caruso tenor-instincts of inflation, of tiptoe tirade), involved himself, in his rant about *speed*, in the same position. He might, ten thousand years ago, have ranted about the lizard or the dragon-fly, with a deeper wonder at the necessities and triumphs their powers of displacement implied.

An act of creation in art is as far removed from the life of the fashionable chattering animal as is the amœba from the monkey. Truth is as strange a bird as ever flew in a Chinese forest. What shall we do with it? Does it require a drab and fickle world to shine in? Can it thrive in anything but a rich and abundant setting? Shall it be allowed to become extinct, made war on by some ill-favoured reptile? Should it be caught and dispatched to the Zoo and fed by horrible Cockney brats upon stale buns? It is in any case difficult to admit the claims of the stuffed birds we have occasion to mention, to peck at and to refill themselves on the carcase of this more splendid creature.

We know that all intellectual effort indicates a desire to perfect and continue to create; to order, regulate, disinfect and stabilize our life. What I am proposing is activity, more deliberate and more intense, upon the material we know and upon our present very fallible stock. But that stock must be developed, not in the sense of the prize bullock, not simply fattened and made sleek with ideas proper to a ruminant species. It should become the soul of things in this universe; until as a bird a man would be a first-rate organism, and, even as a bullock, be stalled in a palace. Let us everywhere substitute ourselves for the animal world; replace the tiger and the cormorant with some invention of our mind, so that we can control this new Creation. The danger, as it would appear at present, and in our first flight of substitution and re-mounting, is evidently that we should become over-powered by our creation. Our society might become as mechanical as a tremendous insect.

When I assert that the aspect of life, the forms that surround us, *might*, perchance—without too great a sacrifice on the part of the painter, without too great a disturbance for our dear conservatisms and delicate obstructionisms—be modified, I start from Buddha rather than from Lipton, Vickers, or Fokker. But I start from Buddha with so much of passion and of Zeit-geist as he would have developed living in our midst to-day; familiar with and delighting in the pleasant inventions and local colour of our age—drinking Buchanan's Scotch whisky, smoking Navy Cut or Three Nuns; familiar with the smell of Harris tweeds, Euthymol, and the hot pestiferous Tube wind.

I do not recommend any abstraction of our mental structure. No more definite unclothing than to strip till we come to the energetic lines is desirable.

Supposing that we destroyed every vestige of animal and insect life upon this planet, and substituted machines of our invention, under immediate human control, for that mass of mechanisms that we had wiped out, what would be the guiding principle of these new species? The same as at present, the wild animal and insect forms? Would we domesticate the universe, and make it an immense hive working for our will; scavenging, honey-making, fetching and carrying for man? Or what?

It is not a bird-like act for a man to set himself coldly to solve the riddle of the bird and understand it; just as it is human to humanize it. So we do not wish to become a vulture or a swallow. We desire to enjoy our consciousness, but to enjoy it in all forms of life, and employ all modes and processes for our satisfaction. Having said *all* forms, we get back once more to the indiscriminate, mechanical and unprogressive world that we first considered. Only now we have substituted, in fancy, an approximate human invention for every form of animate existence. It is evidently not this hungry, frigid and devouring ethos of the scorpion, the wild cat or the eagle that we are disposed to perpetuate. However, every living form is a miraculous mechanism, and every sanguinary, vicious or twisted need produces in Nature's workshop a series of mechanical gadgets extremely suggestive and interesting for the engineer, and almost invariably beautiful or interesting for the artist.

The rant around machinery is really, at bottom, adulation for the universe of creatures, and especially the world of insects. So the froth of a Futurist at the mere sight of a warplane or a tank is the same as a foaming ode to the dragon-fly or the sea-gull; not for any super-mechanical attribute of the fly or the bird, but simply because one is a flying insect and the other a bird. And this all-inclusiveness of the direction of our thought is the result, primarily, of the all-inclusiveness of our knowledge.

The Gothic stonemason, whose acquaintance with other forms of art than those he practised was no doubt nil, was better off than we are. Similarly, the Modern Man, the abstraction that we all go to make up, in absorbing the universe of beings into himself and his immediate life with his mechanical inventions, is equally in the position of the dilettante.

What is his synthesis going to be? So far it has been endless imitation; he has done nothing with his machinery but that. Will he arrive where there is no power or enjoyment of which other living beings have been capable which he will not, in his turn, and by a huge mechanical effort, possess himself? If he is amused enough with his intellect to give that *carte blanche*, his individual existence as an ape-like animal will grow less and less important.

As already man's body in no way indicates the scope of his personal existence (as the bear's or the spider's indicates theirs) it cannot any more in pictorial art be used as his effective expression. But that is not to say that a plate of apples, a piece of cheese or a coal scuttle can. (This choice of objects is with reference, of course, to the subject matter of much current painting, which is *too* unheroic in its ingenious tastefulness.

There is in the inorganic world an organism that is *his*: and which, as much as his partially superseded body, is in a position of mastery and of higher significance over the cheese, the coal-scuttle, or the plate of Provençal apples.

Fashion

Fashion is of the nature of an aperient. It is a patent stimulus of use only to the constipated and the sluggish: it is the specific for the second rate, to correct the stagnations that are perpetually gathering where life is poor and inactive.

The Victorian age produced a morass of sugary comfort and amiableness, indulged men so much that they became guys of sentiment—or sentimental guys. Against this "sentimentality" people of course reacted. So the brutal tap was turned on. For fifty years it will be the thing to be brutal, "unemotional." Against the absurdities that this "inhuman" fashion does inevitably breed, you will in due course need some powerful corrective.

Such are in fact our *fashions*, as we call them: a matter of the cold or the hot tap, simply. The majority of people, the Intellectuals, the Art World, are perpetually in some raw extreme. They are "of their time" as a man is typically of his country—truculently Prussian or delightfully French. So there are some people who like cold in its place and hot in its place, or cold and hot *out* of their place; or the bath mixed to some exact nuance.

Actually how this phenomenon of *fashion*, in the art of painting, works out is that Van Gogh, Praxiteles,

Giotto, the best stone carver of the VII. Dynasty in Egypt, or the Hottentot of talent, are far more alike and nearer to each other than any well-defined type-man of the contiguous ages of Queen Victoria and George V, separated by no more than sixty years. It is at no time unnecessary to point out that what takes the glamour and starch out of the Chinese pigtail and the white hood of the Carmelite is when the pigtail proceeds from the scalp of Lao-Tse and the nun's coif surrounds the adorable features of Saint Theresa. East is East and West is West, and upon a Macaroni meeting a post-Georgian swell both would bristle with horror, and behave like cat and dog. But some men have the luck to possess a considerable release from these material attachments. They are blessed with a powerful hearing which enables them, like a woman in a restaurant, to overhear the conversations at all the neighbouring tables. They can gaze at a number of revolutions at once, and catch the static and unvarying eye of Aristotle, a few revolutions away, or the later and more heterodox orb of Christ.

THE CALIPH'S DESIGN
PART III

French Realism

THE French talent is not quite happy nor satisfactory in either its "classic," its "romantic," or its "scientific" manifestations. As a great "classic" or traditional artist you get an Ingres. About Ingres at present a considerable cult is in process of springing up: whether it is a dealer's ramp or a piece of French (and Allied) sentiment it is difficult to say. Probably it is both. But in the teeth of any fashion it should be easy to discern that Ingres, with all his dreary theatrical costume pieces of the classical genre, is not as satisfactory an artist as Giotto, let us say, nor, for that matter, as Raphael. His malicious and meticulous portraits give him a permanent and peculiar place. But it is not the place, nor quite the kind of place, that is being prepared for him. To admire Racine or Corneille, similarly, is an amusing affection in an Englishman, but those dramatists are trivial beside the Greeks. If it is true, for instance, that Racine should be praised for his psychological insight, I prefer to find psychological insight without going into such a barren region to look for it. As a Romantic, again, the Frenchman is a failure. Compared with the better equipped romantics of more romantic nations he falls a little short. Delacroix and Géricault are great romantics,

but Burne-Jones, Böcklin and Turner have them beat:
or in the literary field, Victor Hugo has to hand it to Hoffman, Dostoievsky, or Scott.

When he becomes scientific in a reaction against
Romance or Traditionalism, as in the case of the Impressionists, or Pointillistes, in painting, the Frenchman
becomes *too* scientific. This is, of course, to be thoroughly
carping: but that is what we are doing, so let us be
thorough. The next thing you notice, having come
to these disobliging conclusions, is that a variety of
Frenchmen, Stendhal, Flaubert, Villon, Cézanne,
Pascal, a big list, do not fit into the French national cadre.
They have less local colour than the successes of the other
European countries. Dostoievsky, the most intoxicated
of his worshippers must concede, has the blemish of
being sometimes altogether too " Russian " to be bearable; too epileptic and heavy-souled. Turner had too
much of the national prettiness of the " dreamy "
Englishman. Even Goethe is much too German.

French Realism means, if it has a meaning, what
these best Frenchmen had. They were almost more *real*
than anything in the modern world. They have made
France the true leader-country. But it is not what people
generally mean, in this land or elsewhere, when they
talk about the " realism of the French." Reality is the
desideratum, not " realism "; and to find that, you must
watch for some happy blending of the vitality of
" romance," the coldness of " science," and the moderation of the classic mind.

The Uses of Fashion

How are we to regard the European movement in the visual arts that has succeeded the Impressionist movement? As the revenge of Raphael, a pilgrimage to Dahomey, a reawakening of austerity—as a barbarous or a civilized event? Creative Line once more asserts itself; the rather formless naturalism of the Impressionist evolves into what once more are synthetic and constructed works. The tenets of catching the Moment on the hop; of snapshotting that Moment of Nature with the eye, and so forth, gave way before the onslaught of Invention, recuperated, and come out of its disgrace. Impressionism was really a period of decay, or one of humdrum activity. It was a scavenging the ground after the riots and too popular festivities of the Romantics.

But then your view of these movements will depend on what latitude you allow to human enterprise: how closely you examine the possibilities of any short individual life: and whether fanciful claims of Progress excite you or not.

Three or four main human types—about as many as there are large sub-divisions of the human race—Yellow, White, and Black—wrestle about with each other, rise, flourish and decay, then once more ascend.

The only flaw in this parallel is that the Black race may die out, the Yellow predominate, or all races mingle in a resultant grey-yellow mixture. But the types of mind are likelier stubbornly to persist and maintain their struggle for mastery.

There are different kinds of Romantics, different sorts of Classics, and so forth. But in any movement you may be sure that one of these great warring sub-divisions is at the bottom of the disturbance. It may be composite. A movement at once Scientific and Classic is possible for instance. And all individuals are so mixed in any case.

Cézanne, considering himself probably an Impressionist, as nominally he was (only with, he would tell himself, a way of his own of doing Impressionism) has turned out to be something like a pure classic mind. Dérain, one of the two or three most conspicuous figures in French painting to-day, is almost a pure Romantic, in feeling, and capable of every sentimentality. This is natural in a man for so long a disciple of Gauguin, and the pasticheur of Rousseau the douanier, as we find him in his ballet, "La Boutique Fantasque." Yet he has a deep classic strain. Picasso has dealt, in earlier periods of his work, in every sentimental and romantic flavour. Most men with energy and illusion enough in them to do the finest work have something of the complete, composite character that I have in the preceding section attributed to the most representative Frenchmen.

But a perfectly balanced, divinely composite, *movement* is an impossibility. Anything so intelligent or so good as that is out of the question.

The Caliph's Design: III

In the first place, that class of universal minds is such a small one, that the rare existence of such individuals is quite independent of movements. In the second place, were there numbers of such men co-existing their aggregate of work would not be a *movement*. It would be the reverse of that. Any movement of such an obvious sort as we are considering would bring them away from their centre. And for that they are disinclined.

So any movement is largely either a Romantic invasion, or Romantic reaction: a Classical or a Scientific one. It usually will have the character of these limiting sub-divisions. It is the swing of the pendulum from extreme to extreme: it is the superficial corrective and fashionable play of the general sea of men. So all men must wear black in one generation, green in the next, then white, then black again: for that uniformity is a law that cannot be contradicted. Fashion is the sort of useful substitute for conviction. At present it is the substitute for religion.

So you get the cry against tradition, the cry against emotion; or against superstition, or against science. Men's consciousness can grasp one of these ideas only at a time: they cannot work except under the spell of Fashion—that is, the particular conformity prescribed for their own particular generation.

The work of any artist under this spell of fashion, unable to function without this stimulus, and to see beyond this convention, dates very·quickly and is seldom remembered after his death, except through some prank of the erudite, or some accident of history. But this slavery to fashion is a different thing from the acceptance of the data and atmosphere of a time. Rowlandson could evidently have existed, from the testimony of his work, in no other period than the eighteenth century. He *used* the spirit, the form-content, the dress, the impressionability of his time with an uncanny completeness. But had he been one dependent upon fashion he could have done nothing of the sort; for then he would have been far too afraid of what he handled, and far too obliged to it, to develop it in that bold and that *personal* way.

I would apply this analysis of the general character of "movements" in order to present events in the art of painting.

To a good painter, with some good work to do in this world (if you will excuse this Carlylean way of putting it) the only point of the "new movement" that he finds there when he comes on the scene (for there is *always* a new movement) is quite cynically recognized to be a movement that suits *him*. To look for anything more than the swing of the pendulum would be an absurdity. That *more* is supplied at the moment of every movement by the individual. And the painter who is at the same time an individual and the possessor of that "more," is not likely to try and find in a movement what he has in himself. It is for the public to take "movements" seriously—not for the artist.

Still, the individual, although ideally independent of the flux and reflux, is beholden to conditions and to the society in which he finds himself, for the possibility to deploy his gifts. So the "movement" in art, like the attitude of the community to art, is not a thing to be superior about, though it is a thing to which you may be superior. And really it is the same type of man who advertises a sceptical aloofness as regards any activity directed to *improve* the conditions around us (*i.e.*, our own condition) who shows himself the most unimaginative and cringingly fashionable in respect of what he produces as an artist—the most assiduously up-to-date, the most afraid of opinion.

This movement in painting which was making such a stir in the civilised centres of Europe in 1914, just before the Great War hit us, really looked as though it were going to be the goods from the standpoint of its uses for the best talents. Opportunities, through the successful, even victorious, progress with which the campaign began, seemed to be indicated, for the full inventiveness of the human mind to get once more into painting. This was at least a refreshing prospect, after the Impressionist years, during which this full inventiveness could show itself in painting only in some ingenious disguise, or risk denunciation: or else pretend that it had really come to examine the gas meter, to grind colours, or to scrub the floor. All seemed for the best: very much for the best! But naturally the ragtag and bobtail of the "movement" would not regard it in that severe light; for them it would be Le Mouvement, as who should say the Social Revolution, presided over by God Fashion, who is another form of the Goddess of Liberty.

Wyndham Lewis the Artist

So, has the worst happened? As far as Paris is concerned, has the revolution turned into a joke, as it is always liable to do in a Latin city? Or into some crafty bourgeois reaction?

Let us recapitulate the reasons that would induce an individual painter to support this movement, engage in it, and use it as a medium—optimistically. The creative line, the massive structure, imagination untrammelled by any pedantry of form or of naturalist taboo; a more vigorous and permanent shaping of the work undertaken; these were the inducements and the prizes. The movement also developed a cult of experiment which allowed of any combinations and inventive phantasies. All the notions of the scientist as they came along could be employed without a foolish outcry. But this liberty and these opportunities also begot a necessity for moderation, or rather *concentration*, which would have been a vice in any age of repressive and academic tyranny. The painters have been thankful for this disembarrassing of the ground, for these splendid opportunities. They do not want to *lose* what has been won as a consequence of the infatuation for some effete mode, that there is no rhyme or reason to succumb to, apart from the megalomania of an individual artist, or the promptings of his business sense.

They do not in fine wish to be involved in the mere *acrobatics* of freedom. Freedom bristles with unexpected tyrannies. It would not have been easy for Cézanne, the laborious innovator and giver of this freedom, to do so; but any very able and at the same time resourceful artist could invent you a new mode every week-end without any difficulty. Some new stylistic twist can be thought up; some new adaptation of a scientific notion. Such a volatile and protean technique has its attractions. This is not, however, what is needed. If he can do nothing *else* than that, he must be allowed to go his way in peace, his chief praise a pæan to his agility.

How we *need* and can *use* this freedom that we have is to invent a mode that will answer to the mass sensibility of our time with one voice, not with a hundred voices. We want to construct hardily and profoundly without a hard-dying autocratic convention to dog us and interfere with our proceedings. But we want *one* mode. For there *is* only one mode for any one time, and all the other modes are for other times. Except as objects of technical interest and indirect stimulus, they have nothing to do with us. And it is not on the sensibility of the amateur, which is always corrupt, weak, and at the mercy of any wind that blows, that the painter should wish to build. It is on the block sensibility, the profoundest foundations of his particular time.

What we really require are a few men who will *use* Fashion—Fashion understood as the ruler-principle in any age, the avenue through which alone that age can be approached. We desire that there should be a few men to build something in Fashion's atmosphere which can best flourish there, and which is the right thing for that particular chronological climate.

Wyndham Lewis the Artist

Picasso and the men associated with him appear to have taken their liberty at once too seriously and not seriously enough. Picasso has turned painting into an affair of *modes*—we should not turn the blind eye to that fact. He has impregnated the art of painting with the spirit of the Rue de la Paix. He really has settled down to turn out a new brood of *latest models* every few months, which are imposed upon the world by the dealers and their journalistic satellites, just as a dress-fashion is. This, obviously for painting at large, is a bad thing. Picasso's output is something like brilliant journalism of the brush. But a highbrow fashion-expert, *obliged* to seek for an obvious novelty every season, or half-season, is an unsatisfactory sun for a system to have. A less inconstant source of energy would be preferable.— But, of course, all this is in all likelihood not Picasso's *fault*.

Cézanne

WHEN that very useful process of reaction occurred in the art centres of Europe twenty years ago, the Impressionists came in for the customary heavy reversal of opinion. But the root theories of the Impressionists remained in the consciousness of the new men. Completely as they might imagine they had discarded Impressionism, Naturalism, and the rest of that movement, Impressionist compunctions and Impressionist fetishes could be found at every turn in the new painting.

There was nothing wrong with this. The Impressionists did much good work, their experience was a useful one to inherit. This would not be apparent to the rank and file of the new movement probably, but must have been to the leaders. And it was these leaders who cast round and went through their immediate heritage once more before finally discarding it. In turn the familiar faces of Dégas, Manet, Rénoir came up for inspection. Also Cézanne.

Cézanne came up rather crabbed and reluctant: a little aloof, and with something in his eye liable to awake distrust. And sure enough suspicion awoke—in fact, what the journalist would describe as a "shrewd" suspicion grew up that this still second-class artist, as it had been thought—a rather incompetent, though well-meaning old fellow—had something very useful and new in him. He was probably more a portion of the new sensibility, and possibly of more intrinsic importance altogether, it was decided, than any of his Impressionist contemporaries put together.

This suspicion grew into a furious conviction, that a very great artist had been unearthed. Cézanne became the most fashionable art figure in the world. So much so that it is impossible to write three lines about painting to-day without mentioning his name.

Matisse has not much to do with Cézanne. But the whole cubist movement comes out of him. Picasso is described by André Lhote as "the Interpreter of Cézanne." More apples have been painted during the last fifteen years than have been eaten by painters in as many centuries. But—for we must study the *buts*. It is a pity that this figure is so solitary. The only advantage is that at least there you have a condition favourable to homogeneity—to concentration of effort.

This one, very narrow, personality; enamoured of bulk, of simplicity, of constructive vision; sombre and plain as could be found surely *he* should be a boulder against diffusion—against the inroad of anything like a dilettante, undiscriminating sensibility.

But possibly the weakness inherent in this first condition, that of a *lonely source*, has left a loophole for the irresponsible, disintegrating passage of the eclectic. I do not feel that Cézanne would have agreed to Ingres, much less to David. But he would be asked to-day to agree to Everything—five minutes devoted to each item.

The Caliph's Design: III

Cézanne remains the father and prime source of all contemporary inspiration in the art of painting. And it is the oddest of ironies that such a one-track intelligence as Cézanne should be responsible for such a chaotic fusillade of styles and stunts: that this great monogamist—this man of *one Muse* if ever there was one—should have ushered in a period of unexampled pictorial promiscuity, and universal philandering.

The General Tendency in Paris

IN Paris there is a great profusion of "advanced" work being done, in the art of Painting and Design, which can roughly be classified as follows (not necessarily chronological). Inevitably the degree in which a painting at present is considered "modern" is decided simply by its relative "abstractness." This follows from the very physique, as it were, the startling properties of Abstraction. Whereas formerly it was a mere question as to whether you should paint a naked female refined to some Greek type of the "beautiful" animal, or on the other hand should choose her coarse, and give the Public a bit of the "real stuff"—some lumpy Flemish frame squatting upon the edge of a dingy bathtub (the undraped Saskia, or Dégas, or the facile Japanese realists); and whereas over periods of fifty years these opposing females were bandied about, and it took half a century for the "Modern Art" of the time reluctantly to espouse one beauty, having laboriously divorced the last; *to-day* it has been found possible and expedient, within the trivial space of ten years, entirely to eliminate from the face of the earth the naked, clothed or other female —every vestige or tatter even of a human being at all, from the horizon of the purest, of the latest, art.

This is how the public views this matter. And the

public, the ruffled, shaken, gasping but rather pleased, though not very helpful public, influences in its turn the Artist; and so back again.

Among the few hundred painters who form the façade of the temple of Fashion in Art, according to the above criterion of "modernness" it is Kandinsky who is the most advanced artist in Europe. Matisse, I suppose, of the same elect *avantgarde,* is the most leisurely, or the least furibundly outstripping. His "funniness" consists in distortion, of a simplicity akin to the facile images of French caricature, and a certain vivacity of tint, often, in his pictures, nothing more.

To proceed with these classifications Cézannism is by far the most widespread Paris mode. As Cézanne is at the bottom of "Cubism," he has really effected, by the tremendous sincerity and certainty of his work, a revolution in painting, and has made new eyes for a crowd of men. In the recent French exhibition fifty per cent. of the work was monotonously Cézannesque. In the best respected painter there, Modigliana, the heads of his sitters inclined to this side or that, because Mrs. Cézanne, during the interminable sittings she must have undergone, drooped her head stoically and brutally in that fashion. She is, as it were, the leader of a chorus of (from the standpoint of the theatre queue) very plain and even preposterous females. Similarly, the hands meet and are crossed in the lap: in a Modigliani: and that is because this was a trick or habit in the search for the compact and simple, that was Cézanne's occupation. Was there any lack of apples on tables? Did jugs abound? Were rigid napkins and tablecloths in evidence? Yes, they were ubiquitous in that exhibition, as in every other modern exhibition of the last eight years. Most of these things are a little more garishly coloured than were Cézanne's still-lifes, and side currents arrive in the midst of the bed of apples and crockery, from Vuillard, from Matisse or from Van Gogh. But Cézanne is at the bottom of it, and will be for many a day.

The Futurists, and their French followers, have as the basis of their æsthetic the Impressionists generally. They are simply a rather abstruse and complex form of the 1880 French Impressionists. Their dogma is a brutal rhetorical Zolaism, on its creative side, saturated with the voyou respect and gush about Science—the romance of machinery engraven on their florid banner.

GIRL READING

Matisse and Dérain

Matisse at his best is certainly as good a painter as any working in Paris to-day. He possesses more vitality than Picasso; and he appears to have more stability—as a result possibly of that. Matisse has had far less influence than Picasso; he is in every way a different mentality. Dérain, similarly, beyond influencing Picasso at a certain period, does not come within the scope of my immediate purpose.

Of the names of artists working in Paris well known to us here, most are those of foreigners, not Frenchmen. Matisse, Picasso, Gris, Modigliani are Belgian, Spanish, Italian. This is a new thing in France—that all its representative artists should be foreign. But outside of the large groups of artists working in Paris there are other European artists, some of equal note, and of equal importance in the history of this movement. Kandinsky among them, was, I believe, the first painter to make pictures of purely non-representative forms and colours. Kandinsky, with his Expressionism, is probably the most logical of the artists directing their attention to abstract experiment. He is not obsessed by Natures Mortes; nor does one find in him the rather obvious obsession with common objects simply because they are common (which is a similarly limiting mode

T   289

to the predilection for important and obviously significant objects). He differs from the Paris group in his
interest for the disembodied world, and the importance
he attaches to this new avenue of rescarch and inspiration. Actually his pictures possess too much of the
vagueness, of the effect of a drunken tracery, that spirit
drawings have.

The painters working in England find no place in this
pamphlet, but not because I do not esteem them. Nothing but a stupid parochial snobbism could make a half-
dozen English names I can think of, seem any less
weighty than a half-dozen French (which as a fact are
not French, as I have said). As to the Jewish painters,
they are evidently of the same race and talent everywhere. And there are at least as many here as in Paris.

First, this is not a review of painting in Europe. Rather
it plots the direction for painting to take to-day, if it is not
to fizzle out in a fireworks of ingenious pseudo-scientific
stunts, and a ringing of stylistic changes on this mode and
on that.

The emotional impulse of the latest phases of the
movement in Paris looks to me contradictory to the
creative impulse in painting. And more clearly, it seems to
preclude the development of any sensibility but that of
an exasperated egotism. The eye becomes a little glut-
tonous instrument of enjoyment. Or it watches from the
centre of its abstract brain-web for more flies and yet
more flies. It would eventually become as mechanical
and stupid as a spider, if it is not already that.

An effete and hysterical automatism certainly threatens

every art. A sorrowful Eastern fatigue wedded to a diabolical energy for materialist responses; a showy and desiccated scepticism, wedded to a tearful sentimentality, as sweet and heavy as molasses. What is to be done about that? But that is a problem for another day.

Well, then, what I propose is that as much attention might be given—it would end by being as concrete—to the masses and entire form-content of life as has been given by the Nature-morte school to the objects upon a studio table. If architecture and every related—as we say, applied—art were drawn in—were woken up, then the same thing would be accomplished upon a big scale as is at present attempted upon a small scale. All the energies of art would not be centred and congested in a few exasperated spots of energy in a few individual minds. But the individual, even, would lose nothing as a consequence: the quality of his pictures would not suffer. And a nobility and cohesion would be attained that under present conditions it is difficult to visualize. Most people grasping at such a notion have stopped short at some fantastic Utopian picture.

But to enable you to arrive at a fair estimate of my conclusions, I must give you the analysis through which I come by them in detail. And I cannot avoid some investigation of the record, both technical and emotional, of Picasso. For Picasso is the recognised pictorial dictator of Paris. So the character and intellect of that one individual signifies a very great deal to all artists at the present time.

Picasso

P ABLO PICASSO is to start with one of the ablest living painters and draughtsmen; indeed it would be impossible to display more ability. In addition to this, he is extremely resourceful and inventive. The back of his talent is too broad to suffer from even an avalanche of criticism—it is the consciousness of this that makes it more easy for me to state plainly his case as I see it. For he is such a fine artist that criticism, except between painters, should be avoided. But this pamphlet *is* between painters more or less.

It is out of scholarship that this revolutionary intelligence came armed to the teeth with the heaviest academic artillery. Picasso was equipped for the great battle of wits that goes on in Paris with a thousand technical gadgets, of the most respected antiquity, which he often has put to the strangest uses. The exact analogue to this is the art of Ragtime or Jazz. Picasso stands now against the Parthenon in the same relation that a great jazz composer stands to Beethoven. Even Cézanne Picasso stands on his head. He takes Cézanne at his word: when Cézanne says (as he did) "tout est sphérique et cylindrique," Picasso parodies this paradox.

With remarkable power Picasso has refertilized many extinct modes, and authenticated interesting new and specially scientific notions. He has given El Greco a new lease of life on the Catalan hills in his painting of Spanish shepherds, oxherds and vagrants. He has revivified a great artist's line there, another's colour combinations here, and has played the most dexterous variations upon great classical themes. Since every great creative painter must at the same time have great executive ability—the more dexterity he can command the better—it is always difficult to decide where this hand-training does or should leave off, and where imaginative invention (apart from the delights and triumphs of execution) may or does begin.

Briefly, Picasso's periods are as follows. His earliest work contained a variety of experiments: women sitting in cafés in reds (the " red period "); Daumier-like scenes, but more fragile and unpleasantly sentimentalized; then a painting of a poor family drooping by the side of a mournful bit of sea, their bones appearing through their clothes, their faces romantically haggard and hyper-delicate—a general air of Maeterlinck or some modern German " poet-painter." The best known has been widely reproduced. (Title: " Pauvres au bord de la Mer.") Then came a period during which Dérain's Gauguinism appealed to Picasso. El Greco was a still more prolonged infatuation and source of study. Lastly Cézanne makes his appearance in his paintings; the portraits of Miss Stein and of Monsieur Sagot are of that time. And Cézanne and all the things to which Cézanne leads—was the great influence.

African carvings must next be mentioned in conjunction with the Marquesas Islands and André Dérain. These solid and static models—African, Polynesian, Aix en-Provence—drove out the Grecos, the Maeterlincks and the Puvises. Braque appears to have been the innovator in Cubism. The brown brand of mandoline, man's eye, and bottle, are his: lately, through Picasso's gayer agency, taking on brighter and purer colours. Futurism once more gave this Wandering Jew from not far from the Sierras a further marching order. Off his talent leapt into little gimcrack contrivances. *Natures-mortes*, in fact, stick out from the canvas; little pieces of *nature-morte* sculpture—nature as the artist sees her; the bottle, the mandoline and the copy of *La Presse* reappearing out of art transfigured (after passing at first through the artist's eye, spending a bit of time in the busy workshop of his brain, and so abiding for a year or so) into the flat world of the artist's canvas. After this series of hairbreadth adventures it is natural that this docile collection of objects should no longer remind the casual observer of any category of objects known to him.

In considering the future of painting, Picasso is the figure upon which you have to fix your attention. But it is the uncertain and mercurial quality of his genius that makes him *the symptomatic object* for your study and watchfulness. It is with some anxiety that the attention must be fixed upon this Jack-in-the-Box or *Spring-heeled Jack*. Everything comes out in the superb virtuoso perfectly defined. Every influence in his sensitive intelligence burns up and shows itself to good advantage. There is nothing, as I have said, with regard to technical achievement, that he cannot do. Picasso appears to me to have a similar genius to Charlie Chaplin's; that of a gnome-like child. His clock stopped at fifteen summers (and he has seen more winters than Charles, although Charles is not averse to a Dickens scene of the Poor Orphan in the Snow), with all the shallowness of a very apt, facile, and fanciful youngster and the miraculous skill you might expect in an exquisitely trained infant prodigy. As to what judgment you should arrive at, at the end of your critical survey, there the issue is quite clear. It will all depend upon whether this mercurial vitality, so adaptable as to be flesh-creeping, seems to you preferable to a vertical source of power, like the sour and volcanic old *crétin*, Cézanne. It is which manner of life you most prize, or admire, really. I consider Pablo Picasso as a very serious and beautiful performer in oil-paint, Italian chalk, Antoine ink, pastel, wax, cardboard, glue—anything, in fact. But he appears to me to be definitely in the category of *executants*, like Paganini, or Pachmann, or Moiseivitch; whereas Cézanne is clearly a brother of Bach, and the Douanier was a cousin of Chardin.

That his more immediate and unwavering friends are dimly conscious of this fact is proved by a statement I have just read, in the current number of the *Athenæum*, by the French painter, M. André Lhote:

"Cézanne embodies, through the romanticism with which he was impregnated, the avenging voice of Greece and Raphael. He constitutes the first recall to classical order. It was necessary, in order that the lesson he gave us might be understood, that an *interpreter* should appear. This was Picasso.

"The young Spanish painter deciphered the multiple enigma, translated the mysterious language, spelt out, word by word, the stiff phrases. Picasso illuminates in the sunshine of his imagination the thousand facets of Cézanne's rich and restrained personality."

What a performer on a pianoforte does in his concerts is to give you a selection of the works of a variety of musical composers. Now, apart from giving us very complete interpretations of Cézanne, Daumier, El Greco, Ingres, Puvis, as Picasso has done, there are other ways and far more convincing ones, in which a painter can betray the distinctively interpretive character of his gift.

What do all these "periods" and very serious liaisons of Picasso imply? To dash uneasily from one personal revolutionary mode to another may be a diagnostic of the same highly sensitive but non-centralized talent as you would think that a playing first in the mode of El Greco and then of David would imply. An inconstancy in the scholarly vein, might be matched by an inconstancy in the revolutionary. These are difficult things to decide, since painters are, through the nature of their art, at the same time composers and executants.

What has happened in this volatile and many-phased career of Picasso's? Has he got bored with a thing the moment it was within his grasp? (And he certainly has arrived on occasion at the possessive stage.) If it is boredom, associated with so much power, one is compelled to wonder whether this power does not derive from a source infected with automatism. He does not perhaps *believe* in what he has made. Is that it? And yet he is tirelessly compelled to go on consummating these images, immediately to be discarded.

But when we consider, one by one, with a detailed scrutiny, the best types of work of his various periods, we must admit that Picasso had certain reason in abandoning them. However good a pastiche of El Greco may be, it is not worth prolonging indefinitely such an exercise. The same applies to his Daumieresque period. Splendid such paintings as the *Miss Stein* and *Monsieur Sagot* undoubtedly are. Still they are Cézanne. And although many artists, among his dilettante admirers or his lesser brethren, would give their heads to produce such almost first-hand Cézannes, once you *can* do this as easily as Picasso, it can hardly seem worth while to continue to do it.

Very likely, at the present moment, his Ingres or David paintings will induce the same sensations of boredom in him (I can imagine David inducing *very* dismal feelings in an interpreter), and will have a similar fate. All that remain to be considered are the less easily deciphered works of his more abstract periods. I think his effort of initiation, and obstinacy in that brand of work, showed a different temper. But these innovatory abstractions, again, are open to question. They reduce themselves to three principal phases. The first, or Cubist phase—really a dogmatic and savage development *interpretation* of Cézanne's idiosyncrasy (example: " Dame jouant de la mandoline ") is in a way the most satisfactory. But I am not convinced that Cézanne gains anything by what is so violent an interpretation of his vision. On the other hand, the Lady with the Mandoline appears to me as interesting as a typical Cézanne portrait, and it is a powerful and inventive variation on Cézanne.

About the next step—fourth dimensional preoccupations and new syntheses added to the earlier ones ("Dame assise") and the first Braque-like contrivances: these probably are more important as grammatical experiments than as works of an artistic consummation. But the whole character of these things: the noble structural and ascetic quality, the feeling that the artist was doing something at last worth while, and worthy of his superb painter's gift—this makes them a more serious contribution to painting than anything else done by him so far. All the admiration that you feel for the really great artist in Picasso finds its most substantial footing in the extraordinary series of works beginning with the paintings of the time of the Miss Stein portrait, and finishing somewhere in the beginning of his Braque period.

I have been analysing this work according to the highest standards of artistic excellence. In the light of his more recent work, with which I entirely disagree (and for the purpose of combating the tendencies that must inevitably result from its influence), I have underlined Picasso's shortcomings. They could only result in the mechanical eclecticism that I describe in the next section of this pamphlet (The Studio Game).

THE CALIPH'S DESIGN
PART IV

Foreword

Two things have conspired to exalt indifference on the part of the painter to the life around him, to the forms that life takes, into a virtue. For a specialized visual interest in the débris on your table, or the mandoline you have just bought—in copying the colours from your garret-studio—is *not* the creative interest required for art. It is a parasitic interest. Your interest in the forms around you should be one liable to transfigure and constantly renew them: that would be the creative approach. To use the grand masses of surrounding life, in fact, as the painter uses the objects on his table. He does not approach those objects as though he were a photographer. He arranges, simplifies, and changes them for his picture. So it should be with the larger form-content of general and public life.

Braque and Picasso have *changed*, indeed, the form-content before them. Witness their little Nature-morte concoctions. But it has only been the débris of their rooms. Had they devoted as much of their attention to changing our common life—in every way not only the bigger, but the more vital and vivid, game—they would have been finer and more useful figures. They would have been less precious, but not less good, artists.

Two things, then, have made this indifference displayed by most artists to their form-content come to be regarded as a virtue. One is the general scepticism and discouragement, the natural result of the conditions of our time. Intellectual exhaustion is the order of the day; and the work most likely to find acceptance with men in their present mood is that work that most vigorously and plainly announces the general bankruptcy and their own perdition. For the need of expression is, in a sense, never more acute than when people are imperturbably convinced of its futility. So the most alive become the most life-like waxworks of the dead.

The painter stands in this year in Europe like an actor without a stage. Russia is a chaos; whether a good one or a bad one remains to be seen. Writing in Paris has fallen among the lowest talents. Painting is plunged into a tired orgy of colour-matching. A tessaract broods over Cézanne's apples. A fatuous and clownish mandoline has been brought from Spain; an illusive guitarist twangs formal airs amid the débris. Germany has been stunned and changed; for the better, pious hope says. But for the present art is not likely to revive there.

A number of the younger painters are embarked upon an enterprise that involves considerable sacrifices and discomforts, an immense amount of application, and an eager belief. This effort has to contend with the scepticism of a shallow, tired and uncertain time. There is no great communal or personal force in the Western World of to-day, unless some new political hegemony supply it, for art to build on and to which to relate itself.

It is of importance, therefore, to a variety of painters,

who have to put their lives into this adventure, that it should not be—through the mistakes, the cupidity, or the scepticism of their leaders, or one mischance or another —brought to wreck.

This part of my pamphlet deals with a path which should have a *Danger* board every ten yards; or rather two paths. For the Braque Nature-morte phase, and the David-Ingres phase, in which painters in Paris are at present indulging, is the same sort of thing, different as the results (a small abstract Nature-morte, and a large painting à la David) may appear.

Our Æsthetes and Plank-Art

THERE are two attitudes towards the material world
which are especially significant for the artist: which-
ever of these manifests itself in him, designates him as
belonging to one side of a definite creative pale. These
attitudes can be approximated to the rôles of the sexes,
and contain, no doubt, all the paradoxes of the great
arbitrary sexual divisions of the race.

An artist can Interpret, or he can Create. There is for
him, according to his temperament and kind, the alternative of the Receptive attitude, or of the Active and
Creative one. One artist you see sitting ecstatic on his
chair and gazing at a lily, at a portion of the wall-paper,
stained and attractive, on the wall of his delightfully
fortuitous room. He is enraptured by all the witty accidents that life, any life, brings to him. He sits before
these phenomena in ecstatic contemplation, deliciously
moved to an exquisite approval of the very happy juxta-
position of just that section of greenish wall-paper, and
his beautiful shabby brown trousers hanging from a
nail beneath it. He notices in a gush of rapture that the
white plate on the table intercepting the lower portion
of the trousers cuts them in a white, determined, and
well-meaning way. He purrs for some time (he is, Mr.
Clive Bell will tell you, in a state of sensitive agitation

304

WOMAN'S HEAD

By permission of *The Carlisle Museum*

of an indescribable nature). And then he paints his picture.

About everything he sees he will gush, in a timorous lisp. He is enraptured at the quality of the clumsy country print found on the lodging-house wall; at the beauty of cheap china ornaments; a stupid chair, obviously made for a stupid person; a staring, mean, pretentious little seaside villa. When with anybody, he will titter or blink or faintly giggle when his attention is drawn to such a queerly seductive object.

I am, you will perceive, drawing a picture of the English variety of art-man. The most frequently used epithet will be " jolly " for the beautiful; and its pursuit invariably will be described as " fun." So we have before us, all said and done, a very playful fellow indeed, who quite enters into the spirit of this " amusing " life, and who is as true a " sportsman " as any redcoated squire; only, for the pursuit of " jolly " little objects like stuffed birds, apples, or plates, areas of decayed wall-paper, and the form of game that he wishes rather smirkingly and naughtily to devour, he must be as cunning, languid, and untidy as his distinguished brother-sportsman is alert, hearty, and coloured like a letter-box. For stalking a stuffed bird you have, in the first place, to be a little bit dead yourself.

I have been portraying to the best of my ability the heir to the æsthete of the Wilde period: the sort of man who is in the direct *ligné* of Burne Jones, Morris, and Kate Greenaway. And he is a very good example of how to *receive* rather than to *give*.

Wyndham Lewis the Artist

Now all the colour-matching, match-box making, dressmaking, chair-painting game, carried on in a spirit of distinguished amateurish gallantry and refinement at the Omega workshops, before that institution became extinct, was really *precisely the same thing*, only conducted with less vigour and intelligence, as the burst of abstract *nature-mortism* which has marked the last phase of the Cubist, or Braquish, movement in Paris. These assemblings of bits of newspaper, cloth, paint, buttons, tin, and other débris, stuck on to a plank, are more " amusing " than were the rather jaded and amateur tastefulness of the Omega workshops. But as regards the Nature-mortists and Fitzroy tinkerers and tasters, one or other have recognized the affinity. Both equally are the opposite pole to the reality and intensity of creative art.

The Bawdy Critic

UNDER a series of promptings from Picasso, then, painting in Paris has been engineered into a certain position, that appears to me to bear far too striking a family likeness (in its spirit if not in its workmanship) to the sensibility of our English Amateur not to arouse the deepest misgivings. In this analysis of what I see as a deep weakness, and a scholarly, receptive and tasteful trend, rather than a creative one, I must provide chapter and verse, and devote some space to what are otherwise thoroughly unimportant people. The important thing is obviously the painting in Paris—not the type of English dilettante mind to which I relate it. But if I can make you see this striking community of temperament, you will know better where you are when you find yourself in front of an arrangement of bits of newspaper, cloth, cheese parings, bird's feathers and tin. You might not otherwise arrive at the heart of this mystery at once. For the law that assembled these objects together will appear, and indeed is, more daring and abstruse than the more nerveless and slovenly colour-matching and cushion-making to which I relate it.

Again, it is really only what happens in a picture which is not organised to attract the objects that it depicts. Whether you stick a bit of wall-paper and a patch of trouser-leg side by side on a piece of wood, or use these objects in a picture painted on a piece of canvas, it is much the same. The only thing that can be said of these particular experiments is that they demonstrate an exasperated interest in media, and the shop-side of painting, and a certain mental liveliness. But there the life stops.

A desire to accept and enjoy; to accept what is already in the world, rather than to put something new there: to be in a state of permanent *pamoison* about everything; the odder the thing, the *queerer* that you should find yourself fainting and ecstatic about it—the *funnier*, you see? It is in the possession of this spirit, at bottom, that these two sets of otherwise so dissimilar people betray their relationship.

A composer of music does not, in his best moments, fling himself into a luxurious ecstasy at a musical performance. The painter, similarly, does not derive from his own paintings, or other people's, æsthetical ecstasies or anything nice like that. He derives from the production of his own paintings, or should do so, a hundred times more pleasure than any hysterical amateur is likely to experience in front of *any* work of art. As a matter of fact, in most cases it is out of *himself*, not from the picture, or the art object, that the amateur gets his satisfaction. Hence the tone in which some of them chant in the newspapers of their experiences. " Connoisseurs in pleasure—of whom I count myself one— know that nothing is more intensely delightful than the æsthetic thrill," etc., croons one.

The Caliph's Design: IV

Unsatisfied sex may account for much: you wonder if it is really a picture, after all, and not a woman or something else that is wanted, for the purposes of such a luxurious thrill. Is not most emotional interest in Music or Pictures, unaccompanied by the practice of the art enjoyed, sex? In fact, the painter or the musician are the only people for whom it is *not* sex. These bawdy connoisseurs should really be kept out of the galleries. I can see a fine Rénoir, some day, being mutilated: or an Augustus John being raped!

"We Fell in Love with the Beautiful Tiles in the South Kensington Museum Refreshment Room"

IF we intend thoroughly to pursue our Pablo into the deplorable corner into which his agile genius has led him, and others at his heels, we cannot do better than marry him, in our minds, for the moment, to the erudite form of Mr. Roger Fry. And if I devote a little space to the latter gentleman, it is only to use him as a glow-worm by which we can the better investigate Pablo's peculiar plight.

I will give you a passage from an article of Mr. Fry's which appeared in the *Athenæum* of July 11 of this year (1919).

"Objects of the most despised periods, or objects saturated for the ordinary man with the most vulgar and repulsive associations, may be grist to his (the artist's) mill. And so it happened that while the man of culture and the connoisseur firmly believed that art ended with the brothers Adam, Mr. Walter Sickert *was already getting hold of stuffed birds and wax flowers just for his own queer game of tones and colours.* And now the collector and the art-dealer will be knocking at Mr. Sickert's door to buy the treasures at twenty times the price the artist paid for them. *Perhaps there are already young artists who are getting excited about the tiles in the refreshment room at South Kensington,* and when the social legend has gathered round the names of Sir Arthur Sullivan and Connie Gilchrist, will inspire in the cultured a deep admiration for the ' æsthetic ' period."

Mr. Sickert you find embedded in the midst of this useful passage. He is a living and genuine painter; and is in that galère, therefore, you can take it, fortuitously and through no fault of their own. Notice, first, the stuffed birds got hold of by Mr. Fry's artist " for his queer game of tones and colours." Mr. Fry's artist's " queer game " is the same as Picasso's or Braque's ingenious sport. Then we have a luxurious picture of " the collector and the art-dealer " knocking at the artist's door, and asking to buy his " treasures " (more luxury)—the stuffed birds that have been used in his " queer game "—for *Twenty Times the Price* paid for them. Next we have a little vignette of the young students of the South Kensington School eating buns and milk in the Museum Refreshment room, and oozing infatuated lispings about the tiles they find there; and going back with naughty, defiant minds to their academic lessons, their dear little heads full of the beautiful tiles they have seen while at lunch. " WE FELL IN LOVE with the beautiful tiles in the South Kensington Refreshment room," to parody the famous advertisement. We think of the sugary poster-couple on the walls of the Tube, who utter their melancholy joke and lure you to the saloons of the Hornsey Furnishing

Company; and we know that Mr. Fry's picture is as sentimental a one as that—the student " getting excited " —the gush, the buns, *the tiles.*

The last sentence of the passage I cite prophesies that " the cultured will at some future date conceive a deep admiration for the æsthetic period." After the tiles of South Kensington Museum, the faded delights of the æsthetic period! Mr. Fry chooses the æsthetic period as the subject of his prophetic vision because of a natural predilection that he no doubt has for it, because he is a little bit in advance of his time in this respect. Already he experiences the thrill of such an admiration.

But you are to understand first that there is no mode of the human mind, no " period," no object of any sort or description, that will not have its turn, and be en- thused about either by the art-student, or the " cul- tured." Secondly, that this is very much as it should be, and that this universal tasting and appreciation is all for the best; quite the most suitable way of envisaging the art of painting, sculpture and design.

It was no doubt, in the first place, a very naughty piece of fun for this scholarly and fastidious art-critic, with a name in Europe for his taste, his deep knowledge of Italian pictures, to find himself exclaiming in rapture over some object as *trivial* as most of the objects he had up till then dealt in had been *rare.* He naturally might get a kick out of that.

Theoretically this honey-bee had no predilections. All flowers are the same. But an especially *conscious* plant on which he should chance to alight would recognize from his method of settling, the character of his *tâtonne-ments*, that he had not alighted for the purpose of extract-ing honey at all. Such a critic, at the same time a dilettante, is not curious about the *object* that his mind approaches, but is entirely engrossed with *himself*, and his own sensations. It is amusing to flit from petal to petal; the grace with which you alight is amusing; it is amusing that people should suppose that you are engaged in such a beautiful business as gathering honey; to bask in a slightly intoxicating pollen-thickened atmosphere is delicious. But the fun is *only to pretend* to be a bee. To be a *real* bee would be a frightful bore.·

The eclecticism, then, as regards modes and periods of art, finds its natural development in an eclecticism as regards *objects*. "A man's head is no more and no less important than a pumpkin," from the article already quoted. "Objects of the most despised periods may be grist to his (the artist's) mill." Should art connoisseurs and dilettantes all turn painters, the sort of art move-ment they would like to find themselves in the midst of (we are supposing them fashionably-minded, as many are) would be such a giant amateurism and carnival of the eclectic sensibility as we are in for, if the dealers' riot in Paris succeeds, and if the votaries of Nature-mortism and the champions of the eclectic sensibility here, are to be believed.

We see exhibitions of French painting written about in the tone of an intellectual tourist—as though they con-stituted an entirely new thing in the way of pornographic side-shows, to which the English tripper is immediately led on his arrival in Paris. The "æsthetic thrill" obtained at these shows is described in an eager and salacious key, and with many a chuckle. The truth is that for the amateur turned critic, or the amateur painter, these modern painter's experiments still remain imbued, as they do, for the public, with a great deal of naughtiness. The English philandering flapper-sensibility transpires in every sentence.—There we have then our indigenous æsthete spreadeagled for our leisurely observation.

I will now give you a few lines of an interview with Picasso, which appeared in the *Weekly Dispatch* of June 1 of this year:—

"Picasso was enchanted with our metropolis (London). He waxed excited over our colourful motor-omnibuses.

"And Picasso had a thrill of joy on discovering a pavement artist. 'This good man knelt down and drew in coloured chalks on the stone. I assure you, they are admirable.'"

The motor buses are the same as the tiles in the Refreshment Room. The pavement artist is the eternal Naif or the Gifted Child. When will the Naif, the Pavement Artist and the Child resume their places, *quâ* Child or Naif simply: the very good Naif, like the very good child, as rare as anything else very good, alone remaining in our foregrounds?

And it is easy to see how Picasso, wonderful artist as he is—the great professional—has encouraged this hope of a thoroughly detestable state of amateurish philandering—naughtiness, scepticism, and sham. Here and in Paris Cézannism is being side-tracked into a pretty studio-game. Certainly no painter who does not want to be turned into a tasting-machine should allow his delight in technical acrobatics to run away with him. He should turn a deaf ear to the twanging of the deliciously cracked guitar.

The Vengeance of Raphael

DAVID is the order of the day. David, the stiffest, the dreariest pseudo-classic that ever stepped, has been seized upon (as a savage tribe might take one of their idols by the heels and drag him out), and has been told in frenzied and theatrical accents that *he must avenge himself*! And, being probably a rather peppery and sanguine little Frenchman, revenge himself he will, if he is not stopped! Or, rather, M. Lhote, his self-appointed executioner, will do the job for him. Picasso, alleged to be doing portraits in the manner of Ingres, is the cloaked and consenting, the sinisterly Spanish figure in the background of this "classical" razzia. "Raphael shall be avenged!" shrieks M. Lhote. I have heard from people who have seen this artist in Paris in the last month or so that he is very excited. The Madonna-like face of the Florentine master inspires him to very great fury: a fury of Mariolatry, a determination to make short work of those who have played ducks and drakes with their inheritance of Greek and Roman beauty.

The parrot-like echo of all this turmoil turns up punctually in our Press. I saw this week in a current art article the first tinkle of the eulogistic thunder that is shortly to burst, everything indicates, around the Parthenon Frieze in the British Museum. Nasir Pal's square Semitic shoulders may get a pat or two in passing. But it will be in the Greek Gallery where all the fun of the fair will rage. These draped idealities have already been described as *distorted*, to bring them into line!

Ingres, David, Raphael! Poussin and Claude! Easter Island carvings, El Greco, Byzantium! But there is a vast field yet to cover: the friezes from Nineveh, the heart of Sung, Koyetzu and Sotetzu, the Ajanta caves, Peru, Benin; and the Polar regions have their unhappy dolls, their harpoon handles, and the Midnight Sun for some future ballet!

This is leaving out of count *the tiles in the South Kensington refreshment room* and the "æsthetic period," and a million other things. What incredible distances the art-parasite travels! How he does see the world!

Is Western Europe too uncertain of to-morrow, the collapse of religion too dislocating, Great Wars too untimely, for us to have an art that is any more than locally or individually constructive? I am convinced that the sooner the general European destiny of painting gets out of the hands of the dealers' ring in Paris the better for it. Also the hysterical second-rate Frenchman, with his morbid hankering after his mother-tradition—the eternal Græco-Roman—should be discouraged. And if Picasso, with all his native Catalan freshness and *sans-gêne*, succumbs to the classical influences of the French capital, he should be momentarily disowned.

General Nature and the
Specialized Sense

WHEN it was necessary in this country and elsewhere to undertake a rapid education of a public of some sort, exaggeration—that was unavoidable—had to be indulged in. The position had to be posed *too logically* for reality, or too altogether exact. Also everything in the innovation that contradicted the tenets of the prevalent and tired sensibility had to be thrown into a crude salience.

But to-day this necessity no longer exists.

Yet writers supporting, more or less, the great European movement in painting still repeat the lesson as it was given them. The statement, for instance, that a man's head is no more and no less important than a pumpkin, indicates a considerable truth: it depends in what connection, only, it is advanced, and how, of course, applied. The ideal *pure visual* obviously has no preoccupations but formal and colour ones. But when you say that Cézanne, an heroic *visual pure*, in his portrait of the two men playing cards was emotionally moved only by the form and colour, you are omitting a great sub-conscious travail of the emotion which fashioned, along with the pure painter's sense, what he did; dyeing, with a sombreness and rough vitality, everything. There is no painter's sense, admittedly, so "unbiological" that it can be independent of this extra-

318

sensual activity of the painter's nature. His disposition, his temper, his stubbornness, or his natural gaiety are all there in his specialized sense. Given the undoubted and fundamental rightness of this sense, it is an open question how far the emotional non-specialized activity of the mind should be stimulated, and how explicit its participation should be in a painter's work.

The important thing is that the individual should be born a painter. Once he is that, it appears to me that the latitude he may consider his is almost without limit. Such powerful specialized senses as he must have are not likely to be overriden by anything. He would laugh at you if you came along with your "head and pumpkin" dogmatizing.

To sum up: On the subject of eclecticism, if there were no painters and therefore no art, the dilettante would have nothing to be eclectic about. Secondly, no great painter has ever been eclectic, or very fickle, in the matter of his work. His subject-matter has tended to be constant. His manner he could change no more easily than his *name*. And if the complexity and scepticism of their time drives artists into the rôle of the dilettante, or interpretive performer merely, that is unlucky for them, that is all one can say.

ESSAY ON THE OBJECTIVE OF ART IN OUR TIME

Art Subject to Laws of Life

FROM what, in my preamble addressed to the public, I have said as to the tremendous ultimate effect that art has on all our lives, it might seem that I was claiming for such painting as I advocate merely a usefulness, regarding it as, in the usual sense, a means to an end. When I claimed that a man painting a plate of apples in his studio could influence, by the way he treated those apples—the æsthetic principle involved in his vision—the art of the architect, commercial designer and so forth, that might seem to be evading an affirmation of the absolute value of the painting productive of such far-reaching effects.

To begin with, I hold that there is never an *end*; everything of which our life is composed, pictures and books as much as anything else, is a means only, in the sense that the work of art exists in the body of the movement of life. It may be a strong factor of progress and direction, but we cannot say that it is the end or reason of things, for it is so much implicated with them; and when we are speaking of art we suddenly find that we are talking of life all the time. The end that we set ourselves, again, and that we are able to imagine but not to compass and possess, is so relative, that we are operating in a purely conventional system of our own.

Wyndham Lewis the Artist

A picture, in the interminable series of pictures, is in the same position, in one way, as is a scientific theory. Let us take a concrete example of that. Professor Sir W. H. Bragg (to name, I think, the best authority) suggests to-day that we may have to return to the corpuscular theory of light, abandoning the wave theory that has passed as the likeliest for so long, and which superseded Newton's theory of a bombardment of particles. But it would not be the *same* corpuscular theory that would then be arrived at, but one that had passed through the ether waves, so to speak. It is quite possible that the wave theory may come in for another lease of life, with the constant arrival of new factors of knowledge, beyond the revised Newtonian view of the matter, if such once more prevails. And so it will go on, an ascending see-saw of hypothesis.

Is there a culmination to that series, and whither do those speculations tend? Whatever the answer may be to that, art is in the same position as science, in one sense: that is, it has the same experimental character, and exhibits the same spectacle of constant evolution. To see this evolution at work life-size, we will take the painting of our own times. The French impressionist picture of the last century provided a new experience in the historic chain. This success was taken over by the school that succeeded the impressionist, other elements were introduced, and again a new thing was the result. This "newness" in both cases possesses the merit of being what the painter of the preceding school would have evolved had he been given a double term of life.

The Objective of Art in Our Time

It did not mean the death of a good thing, but its fecundation. The inexhaustible material of life, as it comes along, suggests constantly a readjustment and revision of what is there when it arrives. The new thing in art, is not *better* than the thing that preceded it, except at the turn of the tide in a period of great impoverishment and decadence, when a dissolution and death is occurring. It *may* be better, though never better than the best already recorded or existing. It may be worse. But it is a growth out of its immediate predecessor, and is marching in time, also, with the life with which it is environed. A form of it becomes extinct, perhaps, in one race, and is taken up in another.

The way in which science differs, at first sight, from art, is that the progress of scientific knowledge seems a positive and illimitable progression; in the sense that we know more to-day about the phenomenon of electricity, for example, or of disease, or the structure of the world, than men are recorded ever to have known. There is reason to believe that we shall soon be still better informed. In painting, on the other hand, a masterpiece of Sung or of the best sculpture of Dynastic Egypt is, as art, impossible to improve on, and very little has been produced in our time that could bear comparison with it.

But art is a valuation: in its relation to science it is somewhat in the position philosophy has so far occupied. Science presents men with more and more perfected instruments, and the means of material ascendancy: these appliances are used, and the use of them reacts on the user, and on his estimate of the meaning and possibilities of life. These estimates and beliefs are chalked up, and more or less critically signalled, in the works of the artist, and assessed sometimes by the philosopher. So science, in a sense, is criticised by art at the same time as is man.

The popular current belittlement of the function of what, since Socrates, has been called philosophy, tends, as is always the case, to become vindictive; to thrust too harshly some hero of the moment into the empty throne. No doubt philosophy must become something else to survive, though the character of mind that has heretofore made of a man a philosopher will still be operative. The pseudo-scientific element in philosophy, with the growth of exact specialized science, has brought it to its present pass. That unbridled emotional element found in it, which has discredited most speculation in retrospect, is proper to art, where it can be usefully organized and controlled. All that side of the philosopher has its legitimate outlet there. And the man of science, so long as he remains ideally that, is a servant and not a master. He is the perfect self-effacing highly technical valet of our immediate life. The philosopher as such shows every sign of distintegrating into something like (1) the artist, (2) the man of science, and (3) the psychologist. The artist gets a good share, it is certain, of the booty attending this demise.

At the moment of this break-up it is perhaps natural that art and science should both be momentarily swollen with the riches of this neighbouring province suffering partition. The disinherited spirit of the philosopher finds asylum in these related activities. The philosopher, that hybrid of the religious teacher, man of science, and artist, was always, certainly, a more artificial and vulnerable figure than his neighbours. Yet neither the artist nor the man of science can take his place.

When, however, the definitely intellectual character of art to-day is complained of, and artists are accused of theorizing too much on the subject of their books and pictures, one cannot do better than quote David Hume where, in the process of relating morals to the æsthetic sense, he writes: "But in many orders of beauty, particularly those of the finer arts, it is requisite to employ much reasoning, in order to feel the proper sentiment; and a false relish may frequently be corrected by argument and reflection. There are just grounds to conclude that moral beauty partakes much of this latter species, and demands the assistance of our intellectual faculties, in order to give it a suitable influence on the human mind."

The finer the art, the more extended the rôle the intellectual faculties Hume speaks of are called upon to play.

The concatenation and growth of scientific theories (to return to our earlier argument) may be like the growth of a tree, which from the start is destined for a certain height, volume and longevity. The human mind, evolving its theorizing chain, may have such a circumscribed and restricted destiny. It certainly is as irretrievably rooted in its soil, and on any at present ascertainable base it cannot balance itself more than a certain height in its atmosphere. If you take this restricted point of view (and all human life is lived upon some such assumption) art then will always be its ultimate necessity: it is what the philosopher comes to out of the discomforture of his system; what, for the man in the street, cannot with impunity be divorced from the attitudes and very form of his religious beliefs; and it is the ideal check on the mechanical encroachments of science.

ART AND GAMES

The game of cricket, or of tennis, is an ingenious test of our relative, but indeed quite clumsy and laughable, physical prowess. These games depend for their motive on the physical difficulties that our circumscribed extension and capacities entail. It is out of the discrepancy between *absolute* equilibrium, power, and so on, of which our mind is conscious, and the pitiable reality, that the stuff of these games is made. Art is cut out of a similar substance.

The charm of a game consists partly in our inordinate satisfaction with ourselves when we succeed in some trivial physical manœuvre. Such satisfaction would be impossible without the existence of the humorous philosophy of sport. This British invention has produced what is called the "sporting" attitude. Fundamentally that is nothing but a humorous (an artistic or a philosophic) acknowledgment of our grotesque and prodigious limitation. Why we are able to embrace this philosophy without abjectness, is evidently on account of the great discrepancy that our consciousness of this

situation predicates between what we can perfectly well
imagine, and what, in the limited time, conditions, and
space at our disposal, we can accomplish. The man, as
"sportsman," says, to all intents and purposes, when he
is administering the sporting spirit: "Steady, steady!
Easy, e-a-s-y! It'll all be the same a hundred years
hence. Don't fling yourself on that ball as though it
were a chocolate-ice in the tropics, or a loaf of bread
let loose upon a famine. It's only a little leather balloon.
It's only a game you're playing. We all know you're a
very wonderful player, my friend, but don't murder that
man, or commit suicide: it's only a game after all." Or
if he is being "a sport" at the moment, himself, his
gesture of restraint or abnegation will declare: "This
is not *real* life. We're only exercising our bodies, laughing at ourselves a little, for the funny little machines that
we are; being deliberately children. That is all."

The Englishman is justly proud of this invention, the
"sporting" spirit. His attitude, and his games, are a
great practical contribution to human life: though they
are also peculiarly his own, and it is doubtful if his
formula can be satisfactorily used by any one else. The
revers de la médaille I will not go into here; though it
evidently consists in the fact that, in the aggregate, the
Englishman has not a "reality" good enough to place
against his "game": or rather he has it, but omits to use
it. His achievement is an analytic and practical one; a
slowing down, a sedative pill for too harsh vitality. In
Taine's description of the English, he refers to the
abnormal checks required for so much egotism as he

found among them. Turn the coin round, and back to back with the philosophic athlete you will find nothing more than—Queen Victoria (whose name I hesitated to mention, on account of the *lèse* Strachey it entails). The national aggregate sports, on its currency, the athlete: but it has not, as it should have, Shakespeare or Newton upon the other side, but some sceptred symbol of the middle class snob.

According to my view, all intellectual endeavour is in the same contingent category as a game of cricket or of tennis. It is remarkable what can be done with the mind, and the doing it is stimulating: just as it is surprising, or so it is felt to be, that we should be able to leap so high and as far as we do, run a hundred yards under ten seconds, defend our wicket for so many overs, and so forth. But, although the mind possesses immensely more scope and resource, and its exercise is vastly more complex and exciting, it ultimately is marking time as much as the body, it has the movements of marching forward, but does not march, but is energetically drumming one spot all the while. Its method is built up, like that of a game, on the same reservations; and even like the appetite for the game, is mixed with a sense of the weak and the ridiculous.

The art impulse reposes upon a conviction that the state of limitation of the human being is more desirable than the state of the automaton; or a feeling of the gain and significance residing in this human fallibility for us. It is to feel that our consciousness is bound up with this non-mechanical phenomenon of life; that, although helpless in face of the material world, we are in some way superior to and independent of it; and that our mechanical imperfection is the symbol of that. In art we are in a sense playing at being what we designate as matter. We are entering the forms of the mighty phenomena around us, and seeing how near we can get to being a river or a star, without actually *becoming* that. Or we are placing ourselves somewhere behind the contradictions of matter and of mind, where an identity (such as the school of American realists, William James, for example, has fancied) may more primitively exist.

Our modern "impersonality" and "coldness" is in this sense a constant playing with the fire; with solar fire, perhaps, and the chill of interstellar space—where the art impulse of the astronomer comes in, for instance.

But an astronomer, confronted with a whole drove of universes, is by no means abashed. They are his game merely, and he knows it. He regards the stars as the cattle of his mind, and space as his meadow. He must do, even to the simplest observation; or else he would not be so jolly even as he is.

Some adjustment, then, between the approach of a conscious being to that mechanical perfection, and the fact of his mechanical incompetence (since mechanical perfection will not tally with the human thing) is the situation that produces art. The game consists in *seeing how near you can get*, without the sudden extinction and neutralization that awaits you as matter, or as the machine. In our bodies we have got already so near to extinction. And with these portions of mountain and of star, in which we remain with such hardihood and even insolence—playing fast and loose daily with our bacillus-ridden, terribly exposed *pied-a-terre*—we are in a daily æsthetic relation. The delight in physical danger, another ingredient of our games, the major motive of the switchback, of mountain climbing and other dangerous pastimes, is the more extreme form of our flirtation with extinction, or matter, if you like. All the thrill that we obtain from an exercise of the sense of humour is based on this phenomenon.

In a great deal of art you find its motive in the assertion of the beauty and significance of the human as opposed to the mechanical; a virtuoso display of its opposite. But this virtuosity, in its precision even in being imprecise, is not so removed from a mechanical perfection as would at first sight appear.

There is a passage in Dostoevsky's *Letters from the Underworld* quoted by Lavrin, that has a bearing on this point. I will quote it before leaving this part of my argument. "If ever a formula is discovered which shall exactly express our wills and whims, make it clear what they are governed by, what means of diffusion they possess: a formula mathematical in its precision, then man will have ceased even to exist. Who would care to exercise his will-power according to a table of logarithms? A man would become, in such circumstances, not a human being, but an organ-handle or something of the sort."

The Objective of Art in Our Time

The difficulty of standards in art is very great. But it is not more difficult in art than in anything else; science alone, with its standards of weight, can, in its dealing with dead matter, pretend to a certain finality. No one controverts the velocity of light, established for us by Römer, though its constancy may be questioned: little facts like the distance of the Earth from Saturn remain quiet and unchallenged. Once these things have been *measured*, there is an end to the matter. The science consists solely in inventing the most satisfactory means of effecting these measurements.

Metaphysics, on the other hand, is in a chronic state of flux and chaos; so much so that to-day the metaphysician seems to have been driven off the field. As I have said already, I think he will reappear in some rather different form; and he will reappear all the better for his holiday among the hospitable arts and sciences. (For he *must* be somewhere: and I do not believe that he has become a stockbroker, in disgust, or a commission agent.) Kant, in his *Prolegomena*, writes of his science of metaphysics: " In this domain there is as yet no standard weight and measure to distinguish sound knowledge from shallow talk." And, again, " It seems almost ridiculous, while every other science is certainly advancing, that in this, which pretends to be wisdom incarnate, we should constantly move round the same spot, without gaining a single step. And so its followers have melted away: we do not find men confident of

333

their ability to shine in other sciences venturing their reputations here." At least a standard in art is not more difficult to fix than it is in this constantly discomfited sister science.

What has happened to philosophy has also, to some degree, happened to the fine arts. The incessant disputes between schools, the impossibility in which the public finds itself of establishing an interest (whether commercial or snobbish) anywhere, has ended by exhausting its patience, and it falls back on Rolls-Royces and whiskies and sodas with a vicious and defiant glance at the artist. "I hate books," "I hate pictures," or "I hate music," is a remark not infrequently heard on the lips of people who formerly would have derived some satisfaction from supporting the arts. They have backed too many "duds": they know that there is nothing they can encourage or identify themselves with that will not involve them almost in abuse, that will not be violently attacked. It will be almost as though they had done the beastly thing themselves! Such pictures, music or books as would *not* involve them in this, are too stupid and clearly insignificant to waste time about. So, desiring a quiet life, they fight shy of the arts altogether.

And yet, because this produces a vacuum, which as true children of nature they abhor, in their existence as social beings, and makes their life shrink to a valueless and less excusable affair, all this leaves them a little ashamed and worried. All science can give them, and to it they repeatedly turn, in the shape of values, is a scepticism of which they have enough and to spare, and accumulations of animal luxury, which they feel, in its naked effrontery, should in some way be clothed with values, and the intellectual disguises in which their selfishness has always formerly been wrapped.

This question of a criterion is forever the ultimate difficulty where art is concerned. When the social life on which art depends becomes especially diseased and directionless, it appears with more insistence than ever, forced out of the contradictions beneath. This is because the picture, statue or book is in effect a living and active thing, evolving with other living things, and suffering their checks and distresses.

You can have a perfect snowball: what you expect of it is that it be made of snow and nothing but snow. That is all you mean by "perfect" in this case. All snow is the same, and so you get easily enough your perfect snowball.

But the book or the picture again not only is living but gives an account of life. The work of art is produced by means of an instrument not originally shaped for performing these literary or other feats, and one that has to be employed concurrently at a variety of blunting tasks—it may be, even, making a living in a bank, or livery stable. The mind, hybrid as it is, with no end and no beginning, with no nice boundary at which it could be said: "Up to this mark you can depend on a perfect result, and all that arises you are competent to deal with": from this mind nothing can be awaited but such productions as may cause us to say: "That is the work of a good specimen of human intelligence"; just as you say

" an attractive woman," " a fine cat," or in French, "*un beau nègre*." Calderon de la Barca, Voltaire, or Plotinus are good human specimens. There is nothing " perfect " about their plays, novels, or treatises. They are good in relation to the ineptitude around them. Strengthen this ineptitude, isolate it, into a potion of some body, and you get one of these striking men. But you must not mix it *too* strongly, or vitalize it too much: for he who sees God, dies. Gather into one personality all the graces and virtues of the three men I have taken, and you would have no further need of any one of the three, theoretically. But then a synthesis of their prowesses would be less stimulating for us than one really lively specimen of such a distinguished triad. Amalgamated, they would be a pale shadow of their separate selves.

Perfection, therefore, from this standpoint, appears as a platonic ideal, and is a thing with which we have not very much to do on our present road. With perfect snowballs or with perfect lightning conductors, we have some commerce; but not with " perfect " works of art or perfect human beings. The next point is this: could you distintegrate Voltaire or Plotinus still further; and would you get a still further improvement? I should rather say that Voltaire, etc., were the exact degree of distintegration from some all-inclusive intelligence needed to arrive at what we are adapted to comprehend. And that any further distintegration results in the dispersion of mediocrity—of little Voltaires: and anything more universal must progressively cancel itself.

If you conclude from this that I am treading the road

THE ENEMY

to the platonic heaven, my particular road is deliberately chosen for the immanent satisfactions that may be found by the way. You may know Schopenhauer's eloquent and resounding words, where, in his forcible fashion, he is speaking of what art accomplishes: "It therefore pauses at this particular thing: the course of time stops: the relations vanish for it: only the essential, the idea, is its object."

That might be a splendid description of what the great work of plastic or pictorial art achieves. It "pauses at this *particular thing*," whether that thing be an olive-tree that Van Gogh saw; a burgher of Rembrandt or the person of Miss Stein. "The course of time stops." A sort of immortality descends upon these objects. It is an immortality, which, in the case of the painting, they have to pay for with death, or at least with its coldness and immobility.

Those words are, however, part of a passage in *The World as Will and Idea* that it may be useful to quote fully:

"While science, following the unresting and inconstant stream of the fourfold forms of reason and consequently, with each end attained sees further, and can never reach a final goal nor attain full satisfaction, any more than by running we can reach the place where the clouds touch the horizon; art, on the contrary, is everywhere at its goal. For it plucks the object of its contemplation out of the stream of the world's course, and has it isolated before it."

We might contrast this with a Bergsonian impressionism, which would urge you to leave the object in its vital *milieu*. Again, the "presence of mind" in the midst of the empirical reality which Schopenhauer cites as the characteristic of genius, this coldness is a self-isolation, in any case; for he who opens his eyes wide enough will always find himself alone. Where the isolation occurs, of subject or object, outside or inside the vortex, is the same thing. The impressionist doctrine, with its interpenetrations, its tragic literalness, its wavy contours, its fashionable fuss, points always to one end: the state in which life itself supersedes art: which as Schopenhauer points out, would be excellent if people knew how to use their eyes. But if they did it would no longer be "life" as we commonly mean it.

To continue the above passage, omitting several lines: "This last method of considering things (that of experience and science) may be compared to a line infinitely extended in a horizontal direction and the former to a vertical line which cuts it at any point. The method of viewing things which proceeds in accordance with the principle of sufficient reason is the rational method, and it alone is valid and of use in practical life and in science. The method which looks away from the content of this principle is the method of genius, which is only valid and of use in art. The first is the method of Aristotle; the second is, on the whole, that of Plato."

The act of creation, of which a book or picture is one form, is always an act of the human will, like poisoning your business rival, or setting your cap at somebody; the complete existence and exercise of this will entails much human imperfection, which will be incorporated in the book or picture, giving it the nervousness of its contours, and the rich odours, the sanguine or pallid appearance, which recommends it to us.

In art there are no laws, as there are in science. There is the general law to sharpen your taste and your intelligence in every way that you can. John Constable, in writing of an exhibition, said: "Turner's light, whether it emanates from sun or moon, is always exquisite. Collins' skies and shores are true. His horizons are always pretty." That is about as far as any painter gets, except Leonardo or a very few, in analysis of what he understands so well but about which, on the side of direct concrete appraisement, there is so little to be said beyond affixing a rough epithet.

All that we can definitely say—and we know that, surely, as much as we know anything—is that Bach's music is better than that of Irving Berlin, or that the Sistine chapel is better art than the Nurse Cavell monument, with relation to any end that we can conceive. Only a few people are able to discriminate, it is true, between these respective works of art. A freak might be found who would derive identically the same intellectual satisfaction from gazing at the Nurse Cavell monument that Picasso would from gazing at Michelangelo's paintings in Rome. And for this freak there would be no difference between them. But if that were so, it would be Michelangelo that he would be looking at, in reality, or what is Michelangelo for us. And in that case he would be mad.

Wyndham Lewis the Artist

Every time has its appointed end, and its means are proportioned to it. Beauty occurs in the way that is met in motor-car construction or the human body. No more in pictures than in anything else can it be isolated from some organic principle. It is a portion of the Means, nothing else.

A THIRD METHOD, BETWEEN SUBJECT AND OBJECT

The function of the artist being to show you the world, only a realler one than you would see, unaided, the delicate point in his task is to keep as near to you as possible, at the same time getting as far away as our faculties will stretch. The motive of this contradictory manœuvre is as follows. He is obliged, before he can show you reality, to dissociate himself from the objective world entirely, and to approach it as a stranger or (which is the same thing) a child. He, ideally, must not take any of the acquired practical information of daily life with him, to the point from which his observations are to be made. Any of the fever of combat (where he is at his task) would impair the equilibrium of his instrument.

When anyone says, however, a "realler" world, not only an intenser and more compact statement of it than the usual working of our senses provides, is meant, but also a different world.

For what the artist's public also has to be brought to do is to see its world, and the people in it, as a *stranger* would. There have been so far principally two methods of achieving this. One is to display a *strange* world to the spectator, and yet one that has so many analogies to his that, as he looks, startled into attention by an impressive novelty, he sees his own reality through this veil, as it were, momentarily in truer colours. The other method is the less objective one of luring the spectator to the point from which, inevitably, the world will appear as the artist sees it, and the spectator from that point of vantage paints the picture for himself, but with the artist's colours and his more expert eyes. The first of these methods can be described very roughly as the impersonal and objective method, and the second the personal and subjective one. The latter method (contrary to what is sometimes supposed) seems to be more assured of a positive result: for a lesser effort of intelligence is required on the part of the public. It is the method that usually characterizes the art of an undeveloped society. The former, in which everyone participates more fully, is proper to a "civilized" time. The civilized man again is less willing or less able to abandon his personality sufficiently. He is (each member of the thronging audience) a little artist himself. He will not be meddled with: he must be addressed and moved, if at all, in the capacity of critic. He is not adventurous enough to go far afield. It is a case of the mountain going away from Mahomet where Mahomet will not budge himself, if it is desired that the mountain should not be so near to the spectator.

The artist, unless of a very lucky or privileged

description, can only exist, even, by pretending to be one of the audience. Nothing less democratic than that will be tolerated.

By this description of what we call a "civilized" public you may gather that I am not very enthusiastic about it. In that you will be right: but it is not because I contrast it nostalgically with its opposite. A sort of undisciplined raw democracy of the intellect is what "civilized" describes in our time. It is the revolt of the not naturally very wise or sensitive against any intellectual rule or order (parodying or marching in sympathy with political revolution).

What I consider that a certain amount of contemporary art presages, is the development of a new method—a third, if you like—that should not, if it comes, resemble the religious tyranny of the subjective method, and would escape from the half sophistication that the other method begets or for which, partly, it is designed. This point I will develop later, however; showing more fully, I hope, what I find unsatisfactory in these opposing methods, how the reconcilement might be effected: and how I see in some work of to-day an indication of the approach of a time when it may be used.

THE SENSE OF THE FUTURE

Bergson's view that the permanence of the work of art, or its continued interest for us, depends on its uniqueness, on the fact that such and such a thing will *never happen again*, would make of everything in life a work of art. This uniqueness is a portion of everything, and need not be invoked for the definition of art. In fact, the other factors of the work of art of an opposite and general description are those that distinguish it from the rest of life, cancelling as far as possible its uniqueness. Indeed, as I have shown, it would seem that successful expression occurs exactly at the point where, should this uniqueness be diminished any further, it would lose in force as human expression. Even one of the only standards of measurement we have is the distance to which a personality can penetrate into the general or the abstract, without losing its force and reality for us.

The object, in Schopenhauer's words, "Plucked out of the stream," also is only plucked so far as will still enable it to breathe and live. Or rather—to dispense with the metaphor—the "plucking" consists just in *abstracting* it. When it has been abstracted it is not quite what it was when in the stream. It is always a *different* thing, as we have said, when conveyed to us as an object of contemplation. And yet, it is that particular thing, still, that it was in the stream. For the distance it has traversed in the process of abstraction is insignificant if compared with the distances involved were it to reach an ultimate abstraction.

The question of uniqueness is bound up with that of the "present time" for the "present" is the essence of the unique, or of *our* unique. I will deal with this later on, only considering for the moment our relation to the *future*, which must be considered at this point.

If it is true that all the past is in us, that it is this

past, in terms of the present, that the artist shows you when he excites you most;—where, we must ask, in all this, does the future come in? Tragedy drags to the surface your wild monsters, gives them a few hours' frolic, and they are then driven back quietly to their dens. There is another sort of artist (of which the Italian Futurist, now deceased, is an excellent specimen) who should really be called a Presentist. He is closely related to the pure Impressionist. He pretends to live, and really succeeds sometimes, a sort of spiritual hand-to-mouth existence. He has tried with frenzy to identify himself with matter—with the whizzing, shrieking body, the smooth rolling machine, the leaping gun. And his life is such an eternal present as is matter's: only, being a machine, he wears out: but with his death nothing comes to an end, or is supposed to come to an end, but the matter of which his dynamic present is composed.

There are, however, some men who seem to contain the future as others contain the past. These are, in the profoundest sense, also our men of action, if you admire that term: for, as the hosts of the unlived thing, they are the personification of action. I think that every poet, painter or philosopher worth the name has in his composition a large proportion of *future* as well as of past. The more he has, the more prophetic intuition, and the more his energy appears to arrive from another direction to that of the majority of men (namely, the past), the better poet, painter or philosopher he will be.

A space must be cleared, all said and done, round the

hurly-burly of the present. No man can reflect or create, in the intellectual sense, while he is acting— fighting, playing tennis, or making love. *The present man in all of us is the machine.* The farther away from the present, though not too far, the more free. So the choice must be between the past and the future. Every man has to choose, or rather the choice is early made for each of us.

We all know people, and not necessarily old people, who live in the past. The past that they survey is only a prolonged present, stretching back as far as their mind's eye can reach. We know a great many more, the majority, of machine-like, restless and hard individuals, who positively rattle with a small, hollow, shaken ego; or, less objectionably, throb and purr with the present vibration of a plodding and complacent mechanism.

The man of the future, the man who is in league with time, is as engrossed *away* from the actual as the first man is in his dear past. There is not such a sad light over the future: it is not infected with so many old murders, and stale sweetheartings, and therefore the man accustomed to its landscapes is of a more cheerful disposition than his neighbour the other way round.

I must leave this attractive figure, and once more hurry on, hoping to deal with him more fully before this essay is completed.

Upon this theme, however, before departing from it, I must offer an exhortation.

You handle with curiosity and reverence a fragment belonging to some civilization developed three millenia ago. Why cannot you treat the future with as much respect? Even if the Future is such a distant one that the thing you hold in your hand, or the picture you look at, has something of the mutilation and imperfection that the fragment coming to you from the past also has, is not the case a similar one? May it not actually possess as well the "charm" you allow to your antiquarian sense? I think we should begin to regard ourselves all more in this light—as drawing near to a remote future, rather than receding from an historic past. The time has perhaps arrived to do that! Have not a few of us been preparing?

The future possesses its history as well as the past, indeed. All living art is the history of the future. The greatest artists, men of science and political thinkers, come to us from the future—from the opposite direction to the past.

THE FUNCTION OF THE EYE

The practical and, as we say, "prosaic" character of the function of our visual sense does not enable us to experience through it normally a full emotional impression. We cannot dream with our eyes open. Association is too strong for us. We are all, in a sense even, so thoroughly hidden from each other because we *see* each other.

It is more difficult to exercise our imagination when the eye is functioning. (The ear, being *blind*, is in that respect better off.) The practical and very necessary belittlement accomplished for us by the eye at the same time invalidates its claim to priority as the king organ where imaginative expression is concerned, although in every other sense it is so supreme. Even the eye cannot have the apple and eat it too; or be the apple of the mind's eye, and Nature's as well. The eye has to pay, emotionally, for its practical empire over our lives.

In dreams, however, the eye is in every way supreme. Our dreams arc so muffled (or are such dreams only a painter's?) that they are nearly as silent as the silent film. There the mind, by arranging things as it requires them for its own delight or horror, can get the full emotional shock, the purely visionary quality that early in life becomes dissociated from our exercise of the visual sense.

In what does this "emotional" quality, the stripping of things and people by the eye of their more significant and complete emotional vesture, consist? Simply in an incessant analysis of the objects presented to us for the practical purposes of our lives. We are given by the eye *too much*: a surfeit of information and "hard fact," which does not, taken literally, tally with our completer values for the objects in question. To make up, from the picture presented to us by the eye, a synthesis of a person or a thing, we must modify the order for which the eye is responsible, and eliminate much of the physical chaos that only serves to separate us from the imaginative truth we are seeking.

The eye, in itself, is a stupid organ. Or shall we say a *stolid* one? It is robust to a fault, where the ear is, if anything, hypersensitive. Everything received through the eye from the outside world has to be " treated " before it can be presented to the imagination with a chance of moving it. The law of this " treatment " is, first, a process of *generalization*. An intense particularization may, however, on the principle of extremes meeting, have the same effect. But, broadly, it is by a *generalizing* of the subject-matter that you arrive at the rendering likely to be accepted by the imagination. I am using the word " imagination " to stand for that function of the mind that assesses and enjoys the purely useful work performed by the other faculties; the artist-principle in the mind, in short.

In traditional psychology the distinction between imagination and memory is said to be, that, with the former, the sensations are arbitrarily re-ordered; whereas " memory " is the term we apply to a fainter picture of something already experienced, but the sensations occurring in the same order, in the order of nature. Dreams are an example of sensations evolved, with great complexity, in a new order, and with new emotional stresses and juxtapositions. The work of the dramatist or novelist is in this category, and that of most painters whose work is remembered. But the work of art does the re-ordering in the interests of the intellect as well as of the emotions.

It is by studying the nature of this process of organization in art, taking several concrete examples, that I shall begin the search for the laws that govern this form of invention.

Why "Abstract" Paintings?

THE present number of *The Tyro* contains, as regards the pictures reproduced, a large majority of radical experimental work. The question will arise naturally to what extent the European movement that these things typify has succeeded, how the war has affected it, and what its future may be. During the last ten years, at regular intervals, writers and people in conversation have said: "Cubism, Futurism, Vorticism, and all the rest of that revolutionary phase of art, is dead." Whenever a picture dealer, who had been a courageous supporter of this movement, has failed, or appeared to be failing, or whenever a painter conspicuously associated with this movement has exhibited pictures of a more orthodox tendency, the same thing has been confidently announced. A great innovating movement is not, however, so easily destroyed. The quality of its vitality is certain to be so much truer and harder than that of its multitudes of opponents, that the world would have to penetrate further into chaos than it has done, or is likely to be allowed to go, to make such manifestations impossible.

Also, if you contrast it with the modes of expression that depend for their existence on the precarious remains of a past order of society and life, you will see that, depending as this other one does on a mentality in course

349

of formation, whose roots, literally, are in the future, its chances of survival are better than its more immediately traditional rivals. Yet those voices that are repeatedly raised announcing the decease of that troublesome innovation, are always gladly acclaimed. Everyone (or rather the great majority of the educated public) would welcome the disappearance of something that wounds their vanity, because it is not a thing that can be readily assimilated by their intelligence; which does not reach their sentimental nature; and which does not appeal to them commercially. Regarding the last point, they reflect that it is hardly likely that such "freaks" will ever find people more responsive than the public in front of them to-day. They say, with an appearance of justice: "Art is an expression of life. I live, and there are millions like me. These so-called pictures mean nothing to me. It may be good mathematics or good engineering, but it is not *art*. Art expression has always been based upon our general susceptibility to *beauty*. There is nothing that I recognize as beauty in these things."

And these things do not contain, it is true, the perfumes of the songs of Hafiz, the ineffable human gracefulness of Botticelli, the athletic youthful perfection of Greek sculpture, which is what is usually indicated by the word "beauty." But neither does Signorelli's nightmare of the damned; nor Rembrandt's heavy burghers and their wives; nor Goya's witches; nor Daumier's laundresses. The "beauty" objection is really easily overcome. (I think that an abstract design may contain, in

The Objective of Art in Our Time

every sense, the flowering of beauty. But as this would merely hold us up on a point, the elucidation of which involves a great deal of time and attention, we will ignore it.)

The next objection that I must meet will run somewhat as follows. "You mention Rembrandt's burghers. They were at least immediate and understandable images. They were *realism*. They meant something to everybody."

"Realism" it may be well to interpolate, as it is used in popular art criticism, is a fine manly practical word that appeals to everyone as being safe and satisfactory. After having been annoyed by some form of art remote from their daily city or Bridge experience, they fall back with relief and defiance upon it. It thus sounds the call of sanity-and-no-high-brow-nonsense for them, affording them promise of things as immediately appetizing and as easily assimilated as the Sunday newspapers' murder or divorce tales, or speculation on a beauty competition. Art, however, the greatest art even, has it in its power to influence everybody. Actually the shapes of the objects (houses, cars, dresses and so forth) by which he is surrounded have a very profound subconscious effect on the average citizen. A man might be unacquainted with the very existence of a certain movement in art, and yet his life would be modified directly if the street he walked down took a certain shape, at the dictates of an architect under the spell of that movement, whatever it were. Its forms and colours would have a tonic or a debilitating effect on him, an emotional value. Just as he is affected by the changes of the atmosphere, without taking the least interest in the cyclonic machinery that controls it, so he would be directly affected by any change in his physical milieu.

A man goes to choose a house. He is attracted by it or not, often, not for sentimental or practical reasons, but for some reason that he does not seek to explain, and which yet is of sufficient force to prevent him from taking it, or to decide him to buy it on the spot. This is usually an example of the functioning of the æsthetic sense (however undeveloped it may be in him) of which we are talking.

The painting, sculpture and general design of to-day, such as can be included in the movement we support, aims at nothing short of a physical reconstruction and reordering of the visible part of our world. Pretentious as this assertion sounds, it is an aim that appears to many of us as feasible as it is necessary, and it has not had its birth in an æsthetic megalomania, any more than in the volcano of political revolution.

The way the effect of a painter's or sculptor's vision works is this. Every educated man in any age must acquaint himself and know a certain amount about the innovations in art, science and so on that are in progress. According to the susceptibility of the individual, when, if he is an architect, for example, or an engineer, he comes to carry out some commission, you will find that certain things will enter into his design which would not have been there if he had not acquainted himself in that way with contemporary thought. To take a

SUNSET-ATLAS

smaller example, the posters on the hoardings and in the tubes to-day would not be quite what they are (the same applies to the designs on magazine covers, caricatures, and advertisements) if painters and draughtsmen in their studios had not done paintings (principally of apples and mandolines too!) of a certain type, during these last ten years.

The result is *never* (in art as in politics) the equivalent in intensity of the ideal implied in the work of the original mind. But great changes are effected, accompanied by their attendant human compromise.

When people assert, therefore, that the movement in painting about which I am writing, is *dead*, you only have to ask yourself what is going to take place, and you see the unreality of the position occupied by the speaker. *You* may want everything except Bridge, dancing, whiskey and the Mystery Story to end to-morrow; and you may even be fool enough to pay a man to write that for you in your daily paper. But you will not have to reflect very much to see that as life has never been confined to those things, but always outspeeded the jazz, overflowed the whiskey, and transcended intellectually the Mystery Story, that there is a good chance of its always doing so. It is in fact precisely as impossible to destroy Einstein, a picture of a mandoline by Picasso, or Marcel Proust, as it would be to exterminate Bridge, Johnny Walker and the rest of that.

So then, if you succeed even in destroying one abstruse and tiresome phenomenon, another one instantly will pop up in its place. And as our time is crystallizing more or less, the new phenomenon will, round about these centuries, present a distressing resemblance to the last.

For example, at this moment let us assume that all this disagreeable Vorticism and Cubism is at an end. What do you expect is going to be there in its place? Nothing but photographic portraits of interminable beauties, never-ending slap-dash flower-pieces, the monarch laying a foundation stone, a mother (terribly anxious "to be like" a mother) washing a baby that is resolved to be a baby for ever and at all costs? Or shall we all return to Degas (whom we have recently seen at a London Gallery): return to Rodin, taking Gaugin on the way? Or shall we go slowly and historically back, beginning with the nineties, and passing majestically through the reign of Queen Victoria, till we arrive (with a sigh) on the fringes of the dark ages? Would it not be better to develop a plastic and pictorial art in harmony with the innovations (that is the living existence, merely) of science and political thought, which is, in our time, real enough?

Is not *our* reality not alone the motor-buses where there were once sedan chairs, soft felt hats where there were black chimney pots, but also what our age politically and intellectually is struggling towards: its "beliefs" in what we do not possess, and disgusts with what we have, as well as the accidents of our moment? If, as a reply to all this, I get an answer, "Yes, you need not return to the French Impressionists, or our own later Tonks or Steer, nor the *Blue Boy* nor the *White Girl*. But *must* you do these abstract things?" Then I should say: " Would you *really* understand a Gainsborough or a Whistler any more than an 'abstract' canvas? If nature had bestowed on you some terrific dose of native honesty, would you not have to admit, that, apart from a snobbish working-up and stimulation, the *Blue Boy* was neither better nor worse for you (although worse if anything) than an enlarged photograph would be of the same blue-clad lad? And, that being so, would it be desirable (practical questions apart) for a painter to abandon his imperious vision, and promise to satisfy you in the way that a photograph could? "

To that you would no doubt retort (I am assuming that we have not arrived at the stage where you say " Do anything you damned well please! "): " But what then *is* an artist, if he is not an individual who gives pleasure or does *something* to somebody in addition to specialists of his own craft? "

Well, I do not for my part believe that a painter or sculptor has been understood, ever, by anyone except a painter or a sculptor: any more than the astronomical mathematics with which Einstein plays are to be understood by anyone but a specialist in that branch of mathematics. Specialists in the art of painting, sculpture and architecture were naturally given the job of building Buru Budur, or a temple at Thebes, or Chartres. The artists performed those tasks superbly; unnecessarily superbly from the point of view of taste, perfection of workmanship, and value for money. Once the job was handed over to them, got into their hands, a quite new factor was introduced, which had

355

nothing to do with the particular dogma involved. The people, and their rulers, were thinking of some great abstraction; not luckily, at the moment, of their own domestic æsthetic, with the result that the unnecessarily noble achievement was acclaimed. And certain periods have possessed a fervour, dignity and honesty that ours can hardly boast; there would, in such a period, certainly be something in the æsthetically unenlightened mass that responded to the endeavour of the artist.

To return for a moment to the substitute for our present European movement away, so far away, from representative truth. " Representative " painting (with luck, of a good type) must always exist. The painter's function of putting a *bonhomme* on canvas is too fundamental a one to lapse; no other form of artist, except the camera, can take his place. And he will always outpoint the camera. There is no reason why such work of even the highest conceivable type should not co-exist with a great output of experimental work of all sorts, more specialized and more scientific, in which intenser field the æsthetic incubation of a new mentality could be achieved. Why should not the Royal Academy practitioner, to his enduring benefit, perhaps, work out his yearly Burlington House masterpiece in cubist or expressionist form first? A provincial mayor might be greatly impressed in watching the evolution of the ultimate rosy photograph from the cylindrical and egg-like shapes that first made their appearance upon the canvas.

A painter's sketch, some rough affair with the forms

The Objective of Art in Our Time

indicated rather than achieved, has always had a fascination for people, other than painters; and an "impressionistic bit of work" has for a good many years had its appeal for a public that soon got over the shock of seeing pictures exhibited that were not really "finished" (Monet, Degas, Manet and their followers and successors). This fascination appears to me to be of a fundamental sort. People feel that the polished, pretentiously completed work may lack some "charm" (and is not that the same as "beauty") which the shorthand of the sketch possesses. This is not a legitimate, but may it not be an easy way (developing this feeling a few stages farther) to the understanding of "abstract" art?

Still, you will say, I have not answered the question, "Why *abstract* paintings? Why not variations on Manet, Gainsborough, Raphael—such as are indicated, however, by an absence of demand for Madonnas, great difference in contemporary dress, social style and the rest, without such a radical cutting adrift from the normal visual understanding as is implied in a Vorticist, Cubist or Expressionist picture?"

My answer to that will be found in another place. There I have begun an essay which I hope to continue in subsequent numbers of *The Tyro*, and in which I have set out to elucidate fully the points popularly raised in this preamble, and to assemble my views of *The objective of art in our times*.

357

Recent Paintings in London
The Finance Expert

THE landscape of art in London has not much changed since the appearance of the first number of *The Tyro*. A few structures damaged by the war have been still further repaired; the usual graceful floraisons have occurred. Otherwise the profoundest lethargy prevails. There are the usual French Impressionist shows (French and British dealers have such large stocks of these masters, and they must be cleared before contemporary pictures can be seriously considered). The London Group has had an exhibition, and has engaged the services of an illustrious professional economist.

The London Group has grown into a large miscellaneous collection of the younger painters of "modern" tendency. There are friends of mine amongst them and several whose work I admire. But that sect of militant amateurs—banded together to defeat nature's ends, since nature distributes talent with an unfair bias for those who have no money apparently—called, for want of a better word, Bloomsburies, infest this over too large society like a strangely-privileged fungus. There are too many of these jealous sectaries altogether in the London Group.

The financial expert called in proved to the public, in the catalogue, that if they bought a Bloomsbury picture to-day for two and sixpence, they might find someone fool enough to pay five shillings for it twenty years hence—*if* trade had revived by that time. I may have got the figures a little wrong, but this was the sense of it. Which extremely brilliant example of imaginative finance is credited with having swept off their feet a certain number of people to the tune of a few pounds. All of which enables one to predict what the catalogue of the art exhibition of the future will be like.

Everything but " pure commerce " (to pair with pure painting) will be banned. Several economic experts may be called in, to get the thing right to a halfpenny. The small and Bateman-like purchaser of the future will stand, pencil and notebook in hand, amid masses of figures. Before risking a rather large sum (say a fiver) upon such a thing as an oil-painting, he will have acquired the habit of expecting exhaustive information: expense involved in painting the picture; financial record of similar pictures during the preceding century; predictions from an accredited art finance expert. Thus, if it is winter, so much for R.S. and C.'s silkstone, or the best anthracite nuts, to warm for five-and-a-half hours the anæmic sitter, immobilized for the purpose of the imitation. 2/2 an hour for professional immobilization. If the sitter's motive is to be classed as love, vanity or weak-minded-ness, then 3/4 all told must be allowed for *Rich Tippy Pekoe*, and at least 2/- for a good brand of Turks. So much for mixed flax-and-cotton, extra for all-flax, canvas, round £2 3*s.* 6*d.*, that is 3ft. 2in. by 3ft 10in. Pigment roughly 17/-; wear of eleven hog brushes 8/3; studio rent for one week, wear of breeches on part of artist, statistics of Christie sales, tips of the market as they may have a bearing upon this particular picture, and so forth. A strong advertising note might be employed by some experts. "*If* you are a small man with a small purse, *these* are the pictures for you. They are *not* much to look at granted! But then neither are you. Yet who knows, some day you may occupy an honoured place in the Empire. And this poor bedraggled ugly brown little mud-pie, which is in reality *a picture* and a very good one at that, may likewise some day find itself hanging side by side with Grecos, Gainsboroughs and Cranachs. Buy! Buy! Buy! You will never regret it. You may live to bless this day. Plank down the dough and this elegant picture is yours, conveyed to your private address, at the end of the exhibition, in our plain vans."

I, with all due respect, suggest that painters exhibit their pictures with notes, if the dealers require them, on the intellectual motives of the particular adventure they are engaged on; but that they eschew the methods of the boot firm or cigar importer, as it is not likely to help them particularly.

Tyronic Dialogue: X and F

Scene: A Studio.

[*Two forms in dark tweed coats are seen gesticulating against a large blank canvas on which the sun's breakfast light is glowing. As the dialogue advances the canvas is noticed to be gradually darkening and to be becoming a picture.*]

X.: Remember, my dear F., that you are for every man you meet a little picture of himself. A badly drawn and irritating picture of himself. Therefore, never show that you notice—if a painter, writer or musician—the existence of another artist's work. Above all, never be so uncircumspect as to praise it. For the man so treated will say: " F., I was told, has said something nice about my work. The dirty rotter! I suppose he means people to think that my work is so contemptible that he can afford to praise it. Or is his game to suggest that I am a follower of his? Or does he intend to sell that drawing of mine that he gave me £5 for, and is he stimulating the market? Or does he just wish to strut down the street posing as Mr. Magnanimous? In any case he wishes to belittle me. Either it's by giving himself a cheap extra two inches: or else by chipping an inch or two off me. He thinks he'll make me appear *inoffensive.* Any way, the *dirty* dog, I'll pay him, I will! "

F.: But what are you to say if a man shows you a painting that you consider admirable?

X.: My dear F—Fool! *And* that so rarely happens!

F.: But should it happen, what is to be done?

X.: To remain on good terms with your fellow artists you must explode with derisive invective. You must sneer a little or whatever is expected of you. That will be reported to them and they will feel that all is well: that you appreciate them.

F.: But what is then left for you to do when you are shown *bad* paintings?

X.: Oh, you always say that *they* are good! Charming. jolly, or good.

F.: But does that apply to your dealings with the really good artist?

X.: If you cling to your pathetic belief in the existence of such a thing, yes: for he would never believe that you understood the world so little as not to see the damaging effect your geniality regarding him would have.

Scene: Same.

F.: B. is a troublesome fellow—or don't you find him so? I am having some trouble with B. He lies freely about me. He intrigues. He——

X.: Hush!

F.: What do you mean, dear X.?

X.: That you must never allow such things to pass

your lips. With me, of course, you may. But even indulged in with your closest friend only, it might induce in you the habit of such *naïvetés*. That is, of course, the great danger, for you, of intercourse with such a loyal old friend as I am. You might form the habit of talking nonsense.

F.: But what I have said of B. is *true*. Furthermore I can substantiate it.

X.: I can see that I shall have to instruct you once more, upon this very simple matter. Suppose, then, for instance, you utter to anyone else (a member of your little world, our "circle") what you have just said to me. What will happen? They will be embarrassed, vexed and shocked if they are well-disposed. They will say: "What a *suspicious* cuss you are, aren't you? " rather as they would speak to a dog.

F.: Suspicious! I have good reason to be.

X.: Hush, hush! "Suspicious," you understand, is the word the world has found to apply to those liable, through lack of self-control, to cause a scandal. It is a word that bears with it an element of reproach. It is contrived by society as a punishment. It is not so severe as the label "bore" (which is administered for the crime of discussing things that people are too lazy or too stupid to be attracted by), but still one that carries with it a social stigma.

F.: How true that is! I say, that's good!

X.: Yes, I thought you would think that true. I expect you are often a bore!

F.: Really X.!

X.: But that is a compliment. You were not listening. But to return to your " suspiciousness." You are supposed to take it for granted, you see, that everyone does you any slight damage they *can*. If they are competing with you they will, of course, damage you to the full extent of their ability. You are supposed, naturally, to be engaged in similar activities on your side. There are a multitude of more or less intense cross-currents as well: others battering subterraneously at you, and at each other. Your blow may arrive at the same moment in the bosom of some opponent as another blow posted from a source quite unknown to you, weeks before your own missive sped on its way. He may stagger in consequence more than you expected. Under these circumstances, suddenly to announce, as you have to me, that someone is paying you undesirable attentions of the usual malignant type is equivalent to hitting a man in the eye in a drawing room, or assaulting a lady in public who would be delighted to accommodate you in the usual way less publicly.

You see now more or less what you are doing, F.? Every civilized *milieu* is, and always has been, engaged perpetually in a sort of subconscious, sub-visible lawyer's brawl has it not? It is the devouring jungle driven underground. The instinct of bloody combat is restricted to forensic weapons.

It is a nightmare, staged in a menagerie. The psychoanalysts with their jungle of the unconscious, and monsters tipsy with libido, have made a kind of Barnum and Bailey for the educated. But people do not *apply* this sensational picture. They could do so with advantage.

Our social life is so automatic that the actors are often totally unaware of their participation in the combat about which we are talking. The world is in the strictest sense asleep, with rare intervals and spots of awareness. It is almost the sleep of the insect or animal world. No one would in the least mind, of course, being a *tiger* like Clemenceau. But what makes him or her highly indignant is to be unmasked as a *rat* or a *cat*! It is as though you burst in upon a fashionable Beauty early in the day.

Everyone outwardly and for the world is a charming fellow or woman, incapable of behaviour that is not generous and kind (always KIND, this is a key-word, F. you cannot use it too often). Everyone knows that in reality everybody is a bug, as much as he or she *dare* be. The reticences, the powers of hypocrisy, of our English race enhance this situation.

So, if you find yourself injured all of a sudden— a particularly vicious pinch administered: examine the finger-print or abrasion—retaliate at the earliest opportunity. Twenty years hence, if you cannot before. But *never* declare yourself as you have declared yourself to me. Such candour smacks of impotence. Above all, it implies, with a boring directness, the Truth that you need be no sage to know. Every kitchen-maid knows that all the people by whom she is surrounded are bugs; that if it is to their interest or if they can, they will let her down, injure or rob her.

F.: You exaggerate the viciousness——

X.: And am *suspicious*! But I only exaggerate with *you.* I am never guilty of exaggeration at any other time. You must not give me away!

Scene: Same.

X.: Ha, ha! my dear F., I am "having some trouble" with Q.

F.: Hush!

X.: I know, but observe the way in which I deal with this matter. It will be a nice little object lesson for you!

F.: I am glad to find, all the same, that you are sufficiently human to have trouble with our fellow-animals at all.

X. (*sighing*)*:* It is as an animal that I resent "trouble." However, here is the letter I have written to the cadaverous Q.:

Dear Q.—Would you, as a proof of the friendship you profess, share a secret of yours with me?

(I may be asking the impossible, for you may not know your own secret.)

O puzzling Q., you have made great speeches; you entertain with a benevolent haste all those approaches by societies and particulars, the entertaining of which would tend to make, as you see it, your importance grow. When the K society's support, even, is in question, for Yorkshire, Cambridge, or the South Pole, with an unblushing speed you interpose yourself, and replying for others, speak as though, instead of

366

being Q., as you really are, you all the while were X.

Now what I have asked myself is (you will forgive me) if you are *really* so immature as to believe that such practices are worth while? Or, if you only pretend to be (compelled in some sense to throw out ballast by the shallowness of the *milieu*). All the time you know that they are not worth so much trouble. You are affecting to be living, in short, at a point of development that you have some time passed?

Having asked my question, I will give you *my* answer first. I do not believe that the above is the answer. I believe that in fact you are only half conscious of what you do; just as the forger or murderer in most cases forges or murders as it were in his sleep. I believe in these little matters you are an automaton: that the acts of the automaton have not the full consent of your mind. That is why, my dear Q., I continue to frequent you (only keeping an eye open, the while, for the slim, but rather harmless, rascality that is in hiding), and why I remain (has it ever occurred to you how this epistolary form implies " still am, in spite of everything ")

Your obedient and humble servant,

X.

F.: But, my dear X., you must be mistaken about Q. He is a most charming fellow. He is incapable of chicanery.

X.: You have taken our last conversation to heart!

F.: Of course I have. But I mean what I say about Q.

X.: So do I.

Scene: Same.

X.: What, you, here again so soon? My dear old boy, you must be in love with your silhouette against that canvas! Or you must be trying to form a habit, or break yourself of one about which you haven't told me. Which is it?

F.: Our conversations, excellent X., attack all my habits. But since these do not disintegrate quickly enough, I return repeatedly to quicken the process.

X.: Well, what habit is it requires garroting this morning?

F.: I find that the habits you have scared away, have merely passed into their opposites; availing themselves of your reasoning, and stereotyping it. I am now going about seeing black where formerly I saw white, or *vice-versa.* Perhaps a satisfactory migration of your thought cannot be effected into me? What do you think about it?

X.: Ah, the reason for what you tell me may lie in the fact that I have been a little too brutal. Have I stamped things in too much, and buried them? Let us see if we can disinter them.

I wish you had been with me yesterday. I saw many of our friends: and I can truly say that I found them all asleep, just as I had been describing them to you at our former meeting.

368

The Objective of Art in Our Time

F.: Who did you meet, X.? I wish I had been there.

X.: Oh I met P. and P.D.R. That was in the street. They literally seem to have grown into each other. P., the smaller, sharper one, seems to do the *carrying*. P.D.R. has the appearance of hanging, rather unreally, like a Signorelli figure in the picture of the damned, on his life's partner, with the superannuated languish of an old maid. I went to see Z. and C. They discharged a lot of putrid gossip into my ear; or, since you have to grin while this is going on, into my mouth. For my contribution, I handed them a few of their own yarns back, which will be dished up at once as mine. In the evening I met Z.D.G. and D.T. in the restaurant. D.T. was already blind. So *he* was an unmixed automaton. The others were eating, making a few remarks they had made many times before, and preparing to go to a party they had been to many times already. But I need not enumerate my experiences: they are in a measure also yours. On account of the hard times, no doubt, everyone has been driven into any automaton Nirvana they can find. No more adventures, risks or efforts can be afforded. People, also, for this programme, are thrown outwards upon each other more and more. They are driven out of themselves; for in themselves imagination or effort awaits them.

That this has always characterized people, and especially civilized people, that it is, in fact, the normal thing, is indisputable. But I should be inclined to assert that our time excels in automatism.

F.: You make me uncomfortable, X. I feel that my

Wyndham Lewis the Artist

words, as I utter them, are issuing from a machine. I appear to myself under the figure of a machine, whose destiny it is to ask questions.

X.: The only difference is that I am a machine that is constructed to provide you with answers.

F.: Ha, ha! That is uncommonly good!

X.: I am alive, however. But I am beholden for life to machines that are asleep.

THE REJECTED PORTRAIT
OF T. S. ELIOT

The Rejected Portrait of T. S. Eliot

Three letters published in *The Times* on May 2, 4, and 7, 1938, respectively, are here reprinted. The sub-title of this book is *From 'Blast' to Burlington House*: but, of course, *Blast* never got *inside* Burlington House. In the person of Mr. T. S. Eliot (as painted by me) it merely essayed to break in. It was promptly repulsed, as might have been expected. So perhaps the sub-title should have read, " From *Blast to the portals* of Burlington House."

The rejection of my portrait of Mr. T. S. Eliot by the Royal Academy, and the accompanying resignation of Mr. Augustus John from the R.A. as a protest at that rejection, received such great publicity at the time that it is unnecessary to recapitulate the circumstances. Some day I will assemble the material necessary for a full account of it. These three letters to *The Times*, however, were my main contribution to the affray, and can be used as a conclusion to this polemical book.

There is only one observation I have to make. The Royal Academy is the snobbish commercial symbol of British indifference to the arts of painting, sculpture, architecture and design. It is how our particular plutocracy expresses its patronizing contempt for the things of the mind, when those things take a visual form. So long as that crushing and discouraging symbol of malignant

and arrogant mediocrity is there, a good artist in England
will be an outcast—a " rebel " as it is called. Romantic
is it not? But how much time it wastes—time that should
be spent in painting pictures, not in writing essays and
letters in defence of whatever one can get done.

I believed, before I, as it were, personally encountered
the R.A., that there was an outside chance that, seeing
how down on its luck it was, this institution might be in a
mood to "reform" itself a little, and admit a few canvases by outsiders, in order to attract the more serious
public to its exhibition. And of course it would be all
one to me where pictures of mine hung—Burlington
House, nightmare of fatuous vulgarity as it is, could not
be worse than the more intellectually pretentious small
galleries to be found immediately in its rear.

But there you are. These are the terms on which pictures have to be painted in this country and will be till
the cows come home. In the course of these pages, in
essay after essay, I have made clear what these terms
are. And the three letters from *The Times* below, with
which I close, are merely the latest shots in a desultory
engagement that has been in progress for a hundred years.

*   *   *   *   *

To the Editor of " The Times "

Sir,—Upon page thirteen of your Saturday's issue I
would venture to point out that your Art Critic and your
leading article are at variance. Your "expert" thinks one

374

The Rejected Portrait of T. S. Eliot

thing and the editorial mind another. The former opens his review of this year's Royal Academy in the following words—words which the Royal Academy will not take to heart however often they may be repeated:

"More and more it becomes evident that the Royal Academy is unable or unwilling to accommodate its institutional character to the claims of contemporary art."

Upon the same page, in a leading article, you choose to be facetious at the expense of artists like Mr. Sickert or Mr. John, who retired from the Royal Academy owing precisely to this "inability or unwillingness" on its part to pursue anything but a jealous and a sectarian policy—which, as your Art Critic very acutely points out, is actually a non-traditional (and so a "fashionable") policy.

One of the delusions of the layman is that tradition has its home, or rather shrine, in Burlington House. Nothing could be farther from the truth. At this moment there is no Royal Academician so merely academically accomplished as Mr. Augustus John and Mr. Richard Sickert, both of whom have resigned, not, as is generally supposed, because they are all for rebellion and desire chaos to come again, but because they are for the true tradition as against the false—for the living order against the dead order.

Let me illustrate this from the present Royal Academy Exhibition. The great tradition of English art is best represented there by the painting of Mr. Wilson Steer—who has never sent a picture to the Royal Academy in his life, and has been duly, and to my mind most appropriately, rewarded for this with the Order of Merit, a distinction which, significantly, has not been conferred upon any R.A.

If you turn from this triumph of exquisite scholarship by an outsider (who is only there because the Academy have bought his picture under the terms of the Chantry Bequest) to the photographic frigidity of the official pieces—either portrait or ceremonial set-piece—you are not turning from a rebel to a reactionary but from something human to something inhuman; from something that takes count of all the historic past of the art of painting to something that is ignorant of all but the barbaric present, whose "tradition" dates no farther than the camera obscura. You are in the presence, with such photographic puppetry, not of the noblest tradition of a great human art, but the ignoblest mechanical travesty of nature. For nature is not a photograph—odd as this may sound to a public who thinks of nature at second hand, in terms of movie or Press photography. Nature is only converted into a photograph by the medium of men's machines. And it is because the standards of the Academy are mechanical—not because they are academic —that all artists worth the name detest it. And if in their gallant efforts to loosen the stranglehold of this dead hand (not the "dead hand of tradition" but of the nineteenth-century robot) they are thrown into attitudes reminiscent of Laocoon—more and more "heroic" and "noble," to quote your leading article—it is in spite of themselves: it is merely because the sense of their impotence to effect a change, combined with their ever more outraged sense of the necessity of that change, leads them into " something very like direct action." These people are, after all, *painters*. That seems to be forgotten in some quarters.

I am, &c.,

WYNDHAM LEWIS

May 1, 1938.

*   *   *   *   *

To the Editor of " The Times "

Sir,—The " controversy " regarding the Royal Academy has been decorously interred—that is, the idea—by oratory at a public banquet. But before the echoes of Mr. Winston Churchill's passionate advocacy of platitude have quite died away may I make one or two remarks by way of reply?

Even the most resounding denunciations poured forth by mere artists, however famous, will just roll like water off the proverbial duck, so long as next minute an eminent ex-Minister of State can be found to turn on the " hydrants " (to use Mr. Churchill's phrase) of romantic Parliamentary rhetoric, to be broadcast by the B.B.C. upon all and sundry who publicly disagree with the pot-boiling orthodoxy at Burlington House.

If you will allow me, in my turn, to " express my opinion . . . with all that freedom which distinguishes artistic circles," I would like to point out that " authority and respect for authority " is all very well; but even in the

377

political sphere—in the terms of which Mr. Churchill thinks and perorates — a small oligarchy, which is notoriously feeble and superannuated, has never for long succeeded in holding down by force a restless population: and if to-day a plebiscite were taken of all the artists in Great Britain you would get a ninety per cent. majority for the abolition of the Royal Academy of Arts.

"The arts are essential to any complete national life," says Mr. Churchill. Indeed that is the case. You must have art, else you are not "civilized"! Therefore (as Mr. Churchill sees it) let us establish a concentration camp, for this queer but obligatory activity, in the centre of our capital, put the Royal Arms over its gates, and let the fashionable world resort there once a year for a "private view," and, this duty performed, for the rest of the year art can be forgotten about; as for the rest of the week, having gone to church on Sunday, the Sermon on the Mount can be left behind in the pew till the next Sabbath comes round.

The Royal Academy is "an institution of wealth and power for the purpose of encouraging the arts. . . . It would be disastrous if the control of this machine fell into the hands of any particular school of artistic thought which . . . would exclude all others."

But it is precisely because it has quite obviously fallen into the hands of just such a "school of artistic thought," which is exclusive in the narrowest commercial sense, that it is regarded by most artists as a "disaster." And in order to continue to prop it up and keep it intact, in the teeth of the opposition of the entire artistic world of

378

The Rejected Portrait of T. S. Eliot

England, it is found necessary, whenever a distinguished artist falls foul of it or rushes out of it, to vilify him, or at least to attempt to discredit him by clothing him with the imagery of a passionate horse, bolting from an official procession, or with the empty heroics of the Tale of the Cid. For it cannot be that Burlington House is in the wrong. To admit that would be tantamount to confessing that George III had erred when he conferred his ill-omened charter. Also the Royal Academy was probably Mr. Churchill's first love, there is always that.

I am, &c.,
WYNDHAM LEWIS

May 3, 1938.

*   *   *   *   *

To the Editor of " The Times "

Sir,—Sir William Nicholson's solicitude regarding my O.M. does him great credit. But I did what I did with my eyes open, fully aware that it might be held up against me at some future date, and that the stigma attaching to my picture, merely because of its passage (however hurried) through those galleries, would react inevitably upon its author when his O.M. came up for consideration. To the great " nobility " of my character alone this sacrifice must be set down. For somebody had to stop the

Academy from eternally protesting that all the good artists were outside because they never sent in! As for Mr. Lamb's letter, most of your readers are probably unaware that the two O.M.'s mentioned by him, Watts and Tadema, are dead. It was, of course, the living who were under discussion.

Yours, &c.,

WYNDHAM LEWIS

May 5, 1938.